BOOK LOVERS' LONDON

by
Lesley Reader

D1211193

Book Lovers' London

Written by Lesley Reader
Cover photograph
by Colin Hawkins
Photography by Andrew Kershman
Edited by Ally Ireson
Design by Metro Publications

All rights reserved. No part of this
publication may be reproduced, stored
in a retrieval system or transmitted in
any form or by any means electronic,
mechanical, photocopying, recording or
otherwise without the prior consent of
the publishers and copyright owners.
Every effort has been made to ensure the
accuracy of this book; however, due to
the nature of the subject the publishers
cannot accept responsibility for any
errors which occur, or their
consequences.

Published in 1999 by
Metro Publications
PO Box 6336
London
N1 6PY

Printed in Great Britain by
The Burlington Press
Foxton
Cambridge
CB2 6SW

© 1999 Lesley Reader

British Library Cataloguing in
Publication Data.
A catalogue record for this book is
available from the British Library.
ISBN 0 9522914 4 4

Acknowledgments

Many thanks to Andrew Kershman and Susi Koch who believed there were enough book lovers out there to warrant the book I've always wanted to write and who did all the tedious bits while I loafed around in bookshops – my favourite places in the world. My editor, Ally Ireson, deserves a special mention here for her painstaking editorial work and attention to detail. Thanks also to Edmund Daley for deathly details, the always patient and helpful staff of Lewisham Reference Library, Yau Sang Man who never minded a bookshop detour and, as always, Barbara Unger, for everything.

Contents

Introduction

My aim in writing this book was a simple one: to give anybody interested in books a guide to all things literary in London; I wanted it to be practical, comprehensive, and above all, up to date. I wouldn't have embarked on this project at all if it hadn't been for the enquiry of a German friend who had heard about London's bookfairs and asked me to find out more before she came to visit. It sounded like a simple request, but I couldn't find a book which contained the relevant information. This started me thinking and eventually, led me to decide to produce a book which did. I wanted my guide to satisfy the needs of people who like my friend, were interested in London's overall literary facilities. This meant spending months on research, and on public transport, ricocheting between places as far apart as Ealing and Enfield; and I couldn't just stick to places which sold books. Having reviewed over six hundred bookshops and other outlets, I then started a second block of research covering libraries, museums, sights of literary interest, literary walks, literary venues, courses and bookbinders; in addition, I reviewed relevant sites on the internet, so this book also includes listings for readers looking for literary information on-line.

Being a huge and cosmopolitan city, London is full of opportunities to indulge a love of the written word, and for those with the time or taste for it, to make searches for reading matter trips through wonderful little enclaves of retail idiosyncrasy. Any dedicated book lover knows that the best stuff isn't always found on well-ordered shelves but often half-way down the stairs to a basement in Camberwell, a branch library in Greenwich or an unpromising pile of airport novels on a pavement in NW1. Sources of memorable reads are dotted all over the city but sometimes it can be hard to know where to start; to exploit all the wonderful things London's specialist outlets have to offer, you have to find them first. This is where a copy of Book Lover's London should be particularly useful. Whatever you're looking for, whether it's a fresh-off-the-press novel, a directory of Motown B-sides, a photographic record of Mexican border towns, a copy of the 1972 census, or a rare nineteenth-century picture book, I hope this guide can at the very least point you in the right direction, or inspire a tube or bus trip to a new foraging ground.

I've always thought that looking for a new book to read is one of the best ways of spending time, but from experience I know it can also be pretty tiring. London always feels that much bigger and more frustrating when you're not sure where a shop a friend "sort of knows about" actually is amongst a tangle of unfamiliar streets. I hope the months I spent researching this guide can save people who read it a few of these fruitless searches and direct them to the right place (or at least somewhere that's a good bet!) that much quicker. Ideally, having found the best West End book chain, back street antiquarian bookdealer, market, auction or book fair, you can then clock up more of those delicious minutes of indecision all book lovers enjoy when faced with row upon row of books which might turn out to contain that all-time favourite read. London's a wonderful city, and a wonderful place to look for books. I hope you enjoy using this guide to find some of its literary highspots as much as I've enjoyed researching and writing it.

Lesley Reader

Borders

NEW BOOKSHOPS

A

E & R Abbott

135 George Lane
South Woodford
E18 1BA
Tel: 0181 989 6164
Fax: 0181 989 1830
Mon-Fri 9am-5.30pm, Sat 9am-5pm
Tube: South Woodford

A short walk from South Woodford tube station, this shop is mainly a stationers and art suppliers but also stocks some general fiction, as well as reference, educational, children's, and guide books and maps.

Addison's

137-139 Balham High Road
SW12 9AU
Tel: 0181 675 1143
Mon-Sat 8.30am-6pm
Tube & Rail: Balham

A small shop in the main Balham shopping area stocking new books in all general subject areas (both hardback and paperback), and with a children's section. There are also greetings cards, stationery and some discounted books on offer.

Africa Book Centre

33 King Street
WC2E 8JT
Tel: 0171 240 6649
Fax: 0171 496 0309
E-mail: africabooks@dial.pipex.com
Mon-Wed, Fri & Sat 10am-6pm,
Thurs 10am-7pm
Tube: Covent Garden

On the first floor above the African Craft Centre (well worth a browse, there's some very attractive stuff in here), the book centre is small but jam packed with pretty much anything to do with the continent's history, politics, literature and development, much of it unavailable elsewhere in London. There's a large section on women's issues, plenty of guide books, a selection of magazines, CDs and tapes and the 'Book Review' (£2.50), a regular publication for anyone interested in keeping up with what is being published in the African Studies field.

Al Hoda

76-78 Charing Cross Road
WC2H 0BB
Tel: 0171 240 8381
Mon-Sat 10am-6pm
Tube: Leicester Square

A specialist in new books on Middle Eastern Studies, Islam and the Muslim world. The shop offers language courses, books in Arabic and Farsi, some out of print titles and, for the more general reader, a very attractive selection of books on Islamic Arts.

Ian Allan

45-46 Lower Marsh
SE1 7SG
Tel: 0171 401 2100
Mon-Fri 9am-5.30pm, Sat 9am-5pm
Tube/Rail: Waterloo

Located just behind Waterloo Station, this is a specialist shop (they also have branches in Birmingham and Manchester) for transport books, magazines, videos and models. Ian Allan stocks its own range of transport books as well as a large range from other specialist and general publishers with comprehensive sections on aviation, trams and buses, railways and sea transportation. Mail order is available.

J A Allen (The Horseman's Bookshop)

1 & 4 Lower Grosvenor Place
SW1V 0EL
Main bookshop: 0171 834 5606
Antiquarian bookshop: 0171 630 7686
Fax for both: 0171 233 8001
Mon-Fri 9am-5.30pm, Sat 10am-2pm
Tube: Victoria

The shop at No.1 sells mostly art and gift items with the books concentrated at No.4: new at the front and second-hand and antiquarian at the back. Allen's is just outside the grounds of Buckingham Palace and they have a royal appointment as Equine and Equestrian Booksellers to the Queen and Duke of Edinburgh. The range of books is enormous with everything about horses covered; including riding techniques, training, therapies, management, racing, as well as fiction and humour. Mail order is available, the catalogue of new books is free and the antiquarian one issued quarterly and available for a £6 annual subscription.

Al-Noor Bookshop

82 Park Road
NW1 4SH
Tel/Fax: 0171 723 5414
Daily 10am-8pm
Tube: Baker Street, St John's Wood
A good range of books on sacred and secular Islam in both English and Arabic, with a range of subjects covered including sections on women in Islam, and Sufism.

Al Saqi Books

26 Westbourne Grove
W2 5RH
Tel: 0171 229 8543
Mon-Sat 10am-6pm
Tube: Bayswater
Specialist new, second-hand and antiquarian bookseller with old books in English about the Middle East and Islam and new books in English and Arabic on the same topics.

J Alsenthal

11 Ashbourne Parade
Temple Fortune, Finchley Road
NW11 0AD
Tel: 0181 455 0501
Mon-Thurs 9am-6pm, Fri 9am-4pm
(earlier in winter), Sat closed, Sun 9.30am-2pm
Tube: Golders Green (then bus)
This is predominantly a Jewish religious goods store but they carry a range of prayer books, books in Hebrew and books on Jewish scripture, philosophy and life.

Angel Bookshop

102 Islington High Street
N1 8EG
Tel: 0171 226 2904
Mon-Sun 9.30am-6pm
Tube: Angel
In an excellent location at the southern end of Camden passage with plenty of people passing the door, this is a small general shop – often featuring the work of local writers – which has an especially good selection of titles on antiques and collecting.

The Arcade Bookshop

3 & 4 The Arcade
Eltham High Street
SE9 1BE
Tel: 0181 850 7803
Fax: 0181 850 4950
Mon-Sat 9am-5.15pm
Rail: Eltham
Located in an arcade on the other side of the road from Woolworth's, this is one of the very few specialist children's bookshops in South-East London. The bulk of their stock is new but some titles are remaindered or discounted; cards and stationery are also on sale.

Argent's Printed Music

20 Denmark Street
WC2H 8NE
Tel: 0171 379 3384
Mon-Fri 9am-6pm, Sat 10am-6pm
Tube: Tottenham Court Road
Three floors packed with a huge range of printed music of all types and levels as well as a selection of books about music.

Army & Navy

101 Victoria Street
SW1E 6QX
Tel: 0171 834 1234
Fax: 0171 630 8822
Mon-Sat 9.30am-6pm, Sun 11am-5pm
Tube: Victoria

This good-sized department on the second floor has a dated feel to it but a good general stock of both paperback and hardback fiction and non-fiction; there are especially good sections for Oxford Dictionaries, Dorling Kindersley books, and cookery, gardening, children's and glossy picture books. They also offer 25% discount on their top ten hardback and paperback titles.

Astrology Shop
78 Neal Street
WC2H 9PA
Tel: 0171 497 1001
Fax: 0171 497 0344
Mon-Wed, Fri 9am-7pm , Thurs 9am-8pm
Sat & Sun & Bank Holidays 11am-7pm
Tube: Covent Garden
A specialist shop dealing with all aspects of astrology including a good selection of books, periodicals and magazines alongside cards, puzzles and gifts. You can get your personal horoscope prepared here as well.

Atlantis Bookshop
49A Museum Street
WC1A 1LY
Tel: 0171 405 2120
Mon-Sat 11am-6pm
Tube: Holborn or Tottenham Court Road
This small shop carries a large range of books on astrology, witchcraft, magic, myth, mind power and associated topics as well as a range of greetings cards and a huge selection of tarot cards. Browsing here is fascinating and there is plenty to interest most readers – certainly enough to convince some sceptics that this sort of thing isn't so wacky after all.

At The Sign of the Dragon
131 & 133 Sheen Lane
SW14 8AE
Tel: 0181 876 3855
Fax: 0181 876 1167
Mon & Tues, Thurs-Sat 10am-6pm,
Wed & Sun closed
Rail: Mortlake

Just a few doors from Paul Foster's, this shop has new stock supplemented by a few remaindered books. They specialise in crime, mystery, science fiction, fantasy and children's books, but also have a general stock.

The Australia Shop
26 Henrietta Street
Covent Garden
WC2E 8NA
Tel: 0171 836 2292
Fax: 0171 385 7253
Mon-Fri 11am-6pm, Sat & Sun 11am-5pm
Tube: Covent Garden
Amongst the stuffed kangeroos, didgeridoos, ice trays producing Australia-shaped ice cubes and jars of Vegimite there is a selection of guide books, some attractive coffee table volumes and a range of books on Aboriginal art.

Avalon Comics
143 Lavender Hill
SW11 5QJ
Tel: 0171 924 3609
Mon-Thurs 10am-5.45pm
Fri 10am-6.30pm
Sat 9.30am-5.30pm, Sun 11am-3.30pm
Rail: Clapham Junction
Specialist comic dealer.

The Aviation Bookshop
656 Holloway Road
N19 3PD
Tel: 0171 272 3630
Mon-Sat 9.30am-5.30pm
Tube: Archway
This is an aircraft bookshop par excellence, stocking new and second-hand books and magazines from across the globe on every aspect of aviation. The selection is stunning, covering flight worldwide from its beginnings to the present time. There are huge selections on history, technical developments, civilian and military aspects and the personal stories of individual aviators. Information is available in the shop on events

of interest to enthusiasts, as is a catalogue of new books, published every six months; a worldwide mail order service is also available.

B

Banana Bookshop

10 The Market
Covent Garden
WC2E 8RA
Tel: 0171 379 7475
Mon-Sat 10am-8pm, Sun 11am-6pm
Tube: Covent Garden

Inside the main market area this small shop stocks some full price and plenty of discounted books covering a variety of general subjects in a small upstairs area and larger but still cramped basement. Despite the squash there are some very good bargains to be had, and room for a selection of tapes and stationery.

The Barbican Music Shop

Cromwell Tower
Silk Street
Barbican
EC2Y 8DD
Tel: 0171 588 9242
Fax: 0171 628 1080
Mon-Fri 9am-5.30pm, Sat 8.45am-4pm
Tube: Barbican

Just a hundred metres from the Silk Street entrance to the Barbican Centre and close to the Guildhall School of Music and Drama. This shop stocks musical scores for all instruments and all levels through exams and beyond, plus CDs, books on music and a few gifts. The emphasis is mostly on classical music but there are a few books of more popular songs. A noticeboard carries advertisements for musical tuition across a range of instruments.

The Bargain Bookshop

135 Station Road
North Chingford
E4 6AG
Tel/Fax: 0181 524 9002
Mon-Sat 9.30am-5.30pm, Sun 11am-4pm
Rail: Chingford

Just a few metres from Chingford Station, with a mixture of discounted and full price new books, greetings cards and videos.

BBC Shop

Broadcasting House
Portland Place
W1A 1AA
Tel: 0171 765 0025
Mon-Fri 9.30am-6pm,
Sat & Sun 9.30am-6.30pm
Tube: Oxford Circus

On the left side of Broadcasting House as you head north from Oxford Circus, this gleaming modern shop stocks mostly videos, audio tapes and assorted paraphernalia linked to BBC television and radio programmes. However, there is room for a good range of cookery and gardening books plus some general titles and language courses.

BBC World Service Shop

Bush House
The Strand
WC2B 4PH
Tel: 0171 557 2576
Mon & Tues, Thurs & Fri 9.30-6pm
Wed 10am-6pm, Sat 10am-5.30pm
Tube: Aldwych

Full of BBC merchandise (particularly videos and tapes), but with a good selection of books linked to specific radio and television programmes, as well as magazines and language courses. There are also related books on media, politics, current affairs and anything with a radio or television programme tie-in. Short wave radios are sold, and leaflets on BBC World Service reception.

Beaumonts

60 Church Road
SW13 0DQ
Tel: 0181 741 0786
Mon-Sat 9.30am-5.30pm
Rail: Barnes Common

A general shop selling new books in all subject areas as well as audiobooks and some stationery and greetings cards.

Beckett's

6 Bellevue Road
Wandsworth Common
SW17 7EG
Tel: 0181 672 4413
Fax: 0181 672 1561
Mon-Sat 9.30am-6pm
Tube: Balham

Located in a row of shops overlooking Wandsworth Common: fabulous in the summer but bleak in the winter, which is when the shop lights its open fire. It's hard to imagine a more welcoming atmosphere than the one you encounter on entering this small but excellently-stocked shop on a blustery day. Although it's narrow it goes back a long way, the children's section at the rear has little chairs for small browsers and the wide-ranging selection of books is well-displayed and supplemented by a good range of greetings cards. (For gourmets, Chez Bruce – the upmarket restaurant – is next door).

Chris Beetles

8 & 10 Ryder Street
St James's
SW1Y 6QB
Tel: 0171 839 7551
Fax: 0171 839 1603
Mon-Sat 10am-5.30pm
Tube: Piccadilly Circus

Modern security concerns mean you have to ring the bell to get in but don't worry, this gallery doesn't have the snobbish, stand-offish attitude of many galleries so you need not fear going in. They specialise in Victorian painting and watercolours, book illustration (including cartoons and modern British ceramics), and stage an annual 'Illustrators' show featuring examples from around 1800, as well as a range of other exhibitions through the year. They publish and sell their show catalogues – fascinating and almost works of art in their own right – and now have around fifty on the backlist at prices from £5 to £50. Featured artists include Thelwell, William Heath Robinson, Mervyn Peake and Quentin Blake among many others. Whilst you can wander in just to look at the books it is also worth having a look at the art: the largest stock of British watercolours in the country, ranging in price from £50 to £70,000 – much of it stored in huge boxes downstairs.

Bestsellers

46 High Road
East Finchley
N2 9PJ
Tel: 0181 883 5354
Fax: 0181 883 7686
Mon-Wed, Fri & Sat 8am-6.30pm,
Thurs 8am-8pm

The stock here is very small and consists almost entirely of the latest bestseller lists, hardback and paperback, fiction and non-fiction. Titles are typically offered at 25% discount and other books can be ordered, usually at a discounted price.

Bibliophile

5 Thomas Road
E14 7BN
Tel: 0171 515 9222
Fax: 0171 538 4115
Mon-Fri 8.30am-5pm
DLR: Westferry
Tube: Mile End (then bus)

This shop deals exclusively in discounted titles. Bibliophile also runs its own discount book club with thousands of titles at below the list price and a regular detailed book club magazine for members.

Blackwell's

Originating from the world famous academic Blackwell's booksellers in Oxford (all book lovers should pay that flagship store a visit – don't miss the Norrington Room downstairs), the chain retains a serious academic emphasis with a good coverage of heavyweight literature, and less emphasis on more popular genres.
Blackwell's on-line bookshop is at http://bookshop.blackwell.co.uk

Blackwell's

100 Charing Cross Road
WC2H 0JG
Tel: 0171 292 5100
Fax: 0171 240 9665
Mon-Sat 9.30am-8.30pm, Sun 12noon-6pm
Tube: Leicester Square or Tottenham Court Road
The flagship store in London's bookshop heartland has both general and academic stock in all subject areas and a knowledgeable and helpful staff. With over sixty thousand titles in stock the shop is large, sprawling and often confusing to navigate, but it's still well worth getting to grips with.

Blackwell's Business and Law

243-244 High Holborn
WC1V 7DZ
Tel: 0171 831 9501
Fax: 0171 405 9412
Mon & Tues, Thurs & Fri 9am-7pm
Wed 10am-7pm, Sat 10am-4pm
Tube: Holborn
Specialising in law and all aspects of business including accountancy, management, banking, tax, investment, human resources management and computing.

Blackwell's City Bookshop

11 Copthall Avenue
EC2R 7DJ
Tel: 0171 638 1991
Fax: 0171 638 1594
Mon-Fri 9am-5.30pm
Tube: Bank

Located in the headquarters of the Institute of Chartered Accountants, this shop has a specialist stock on all topics relevant to work in the City, including accounting, banking, finance, investment, insolvency, law, pensions, insurance and taxation.

Blackwell's College Bookshop

Holborn College of Law
200 Greyhound Road
W14 9RY
Tel: 0171 381 3731
Mon & Wed closed, Tues 9am-5pm
Thurs & Fri 11am-6pm, Sat 9am-4pm
Tube: Barons Court
Specialising in law books with a few on business, the bookshop really only serves the needs of students at the college.

Blackwell's Medical Bookshop

King's College School of Medicine and Dentistry
Bessemer Road
SE5 9PJ
Tel/Fax: 0171 346 4074
Mon-Fri 10am-3pm and 3.30pm-5pm
Tube: Brixton
(then a bus towards Camberwell and Peckham)
A room in the old medical school building next to the main hospital catering for medical students and doctors studying for higher exams.

Blackwell's Medical Bookshop

Royal Free Hospital School of Medicine
Rowland Hill Street
NW3 2PF
Tel/Fax: 0171 830 2180
Mon-Fri 10am-12noon and 12.30pm-3pm
Tube: Belsize Park
Situated within the hospital library this is a small shop selling undergraduate medical and nursing textbooks plus some general fiction and stationery.

Blackwell's University Bookshop
158 Holloway Road
N7 8DD
Tel: 0171 700 4786
Fax: 0171 700 7687
Mon, Wed-Fri 9am-5.30pm
Tues 9.30am-5.30pm, Sat 10am-5pm
Tube: Holloway Road
Near the University of North London, a couple of minutes walk from Holloway Road tube station, the shop sells mainly books related to courses at the university, plus some general fiction and reference titles.

Blackwell's University Bookshop
119-122 London Road
SE1 6LF
Tel: 0171 928 5378
Fax: 0171 261 9536
e-mail: 100627.2554@compuserve.com
Mon, Wed-Fri 9am-6pm
Tues 9.30am-6pm, Sat 10am-5pm
Tube: Elephant & Castle
Ten minutes walk north of Elephant & Castle shopping centre, just next to South Bank University. The shop concentrates on books related to the university's courses with sections on law, business, management, marketing, education, psychology, research and health and an especially extensive range of computing books.

Blackwell's University Bookshop
University of North London
Ladbrooke House
62-66 Highbury Grove
N5 2AD
Tel: 0171 753 5087 ext.5193
Mon-Fri 10am-2pm and 3pm-4pm
Tube: Highbury & Islington
A small branch on the first floor, stocking books on law, social work, health care and cultural studies, the emphasis being towards courses in the university.

Blackwell's University Bookshop
South Bank University
Faculty of the Built Environment
Wandsworth Road
SW8 2JZ
Tel/Fax: 0171 815 8302
Mon- Fri 9.30am-2pm and 3pm-5.30pm
Tube: Vauxhall
Specialist shop meeting the needs of students of architecture, building, housing, law and management.

Bloomsbury Workshop
12 Galen Place, off Bury Place
WC1A 2JR
Tel: 0171 405 0632
Mon-Fri 10am-5.30pm
Tube: Holborn
This is a gallery and bookshop specialising in the art and literature of the Bloomsbury Group, who lived in the area at the turn of the century. There are rare first editions plus new books and pamphlets for anyone with an interest in the era. 'The Bloomsbury Group in London Walking Guide' is £1 and a good introduction to places of interest in the area, whilst the Bloomsbury Heritage Series of booklets published by Cecil Woolf describes aspects of the group in more depth. Works by Virginia Woolf, E M Forster, Leonard Woolf, Roger Fry, Vanessa Bell, Maynard Keynes and Lytton Strachey (among others), are on offer.

Blue Silver Comics
32 Northfield Avenue
West Ealing
W13 9RL
Tel: 0181 840 9446
Web: www.bluesilver.com
Mon & Tues, Thurs-Sun 10am-6pm
Wed 10am-2pm
Tube: Northfields
Specialist comic shop.

Bolingbroke Bookshop
147 Northcote Road
Battersea
SW11 6QB
Tel: 0171 223 9344
Mon-Sat 9.30am-6pm, Sun 11am-4pm
Rail: Clapham Junction
This is a small, well-stocked general shop, part of the reliable Pipeline group.

Bookcase
This is an excellent London-based chain of discount bookshops with convenient, centrally located branches. They are reliably good on large, glossy coffee table books on art, design, photography, cookery and architecture but also have good choices of fiction in both hardback and paperback, plus attractive stationery and cards.

Bookcase
26 Ludgate Hill
EC4M 7DR
Tel: 0171 236 5982
Mon-Fri 9am-5.45pm
Tube: Blackfriars, St Paul's
A small branch within sight and sound of St Paul's Cathedral. They offer the usual excellent range of large format picture books on art, architecture, film, military and photography with good gardening and fiction sections plus a few titles on business and computers. There are plenty of bargains under £2, so it's always worth popping in.

Bookcase 2
158 Waterloo Road
SE1 8SB
Tel: 0171 401 8528
Mon-Fri 9am-7.15pm, Sun 10am-6pm
Tube: Waterloo
This branch has an emphasis on art, architecture, music, politics, history, military subjects and transport as well as some academic material and hardback and paperback fiction. There is also a good CD selection and plenty of graphic novels. It's a

good place for bargains with discounted videos and an excellent value 99p table outside.

Bookcase 3
268 Chiswick High Road
W4 4PD
Tel: 0181 742 3919
Mon-Sat 9.30am-7pm, Sun 11am-5pm
Tube: Turnham Green

Bookcase 4
150 Putney High Street
SW15 1RR
Tel: 0181 780 1805
Mon-Sat 9am-6pm
Tube: Putney Bridge
This branch has the usual stock with an emphasis on art, architecture, cookery, gardening, children's, cinema, history, transport and military titles but with fiction, CDs, videos and stationery also available.

Bookcase 6
80 Victoria Street
SW1E 5JL
Tel: 0171 233 5763
Mon-Fri 8.30am-7pm, Sat 10am-7pm
Tube: Victoria
Well located for Victoria's lunchtime shoppers, this branch is small but has a fair selection of books.

Bookcase 7
138-140 Charing Cross Road
WC2H 0LB
Tel: 0171 836 8391
Mon-Sat 10am-8pm, Sun 12noon-6pm
Tube: Tottenham Court Road
A smaller and less well-stocked branch than its sister shop a couple of doors away, but this one has the convenience of being all on one floor. There are good bargains to be found and the staff choose an 'Obscure Title of the Week' for display at the desk – you haven't really understood the meaning of obscure until you've seen some of these!

Bookcase 9
148 Charing Cross Road
WC2 0LB
Tel: 0171 836 1391
Mon-Sat 10am-7.50pm, Sun 12noon-5.50pm
Tube: Tottenham Court Road
This is the branch of the chain closest to the tube station – it looks small upstairs but is packed solid with bargains, the real buys are located downstairs, with an excellent choice of fiction and a 99p section.

Bookcase 10
97-99 King Street
Hammersmith
W6 9JG
Tel: 0181 741 8801
Mon-Sat 9am-7pm, Sun 11am-5pm
Tube: Hammersmith
One of the largest, best-stocked branches. As always they have an extensive selection of illustrated art, architecture, cookery, gardening and interior design books but also a large range of health, graphic and fiction books. It's worth looking here if you are aiming to buy one of the latest bestsellers, as they may well have it at a reduced price.

Bookends
With a head office in the book village of Hay-on-Wye in Herefordshire and branches throughout England, there are several London branches of this chain. They specialise in all types of new books at bargain prices (both hardback and paperback), also offering literary and genre fiction and a range of non-fiction subjects. The book stock is made up of damaged, discounted and remaindered books from publishers, so their large stock always has a fairly rapid turnover. Branches at:

108 Charing Cross Road
WC2H 5PB
Tel: 0171 836 3457
Mon-Sat 10am-8pm, Sun 1pm-7pm
Tube: Leicester Square

In the heart of the Charing Cross Road bookselling community this is a small branch but packed with bargains. It's always worth calling in here when you're in the area.

19 New Broadway
Ealing
W5 5AN
Tel: 0181 579 2990
Mon-Sat 10am-6pm, Thurs 10am-7pm
Sun 11am-5pm
Tube: Ealing Broadway

Book Ends
1-3 Exhibition Road
SW7 2HE
Tel: 0171 589 2285
Mon-Fri 9am-6.30pm, Sat 10am-6.30pm
Sun 2pm-6pm
Tube: South Kensington
An unusual and enticing shop, about five minutes walk from South Kensington tube station with a brilliant range of books and materials for all papercrafts including origami, modelling, stencilling, decoupage, paper dolls plus a good range of art and design source books and children's books on all subjects. The highlight is the astounding range of model books which allow you to cut out and make your own human skeleton, Millennium Falcon, model aircraft or any number of famous buildings. This is a brilliant place to look for unusual gift ideas.

Bookhouse
14 Greenwich Church Street
SE10 9BJ
Tel: 0181 305 1975
Mon, Wed-Fri 10am-6pm, Tues closed
Sat & Sun 10.30am-6.30pm
Rail: Greenwich
Selling discounted new books in all subject areas, as well as cards and stationery items. They are especially good for glossy coffee table books on art and design, craft, cookery and gardening, but also worth a browse for fiction, travel and history. Other branches at:

24 Torrington Place
WC1E 7HJ
Tel: 0171 631 4383
Mon-Sat 10am-6.30pm
Sun 12noon-6pm
Tube: Goodge Street
Located between Goodge Street tube station
and Dillons (see later), it is definitely worth
calling in to browse the stock of discounted
new books with an emphasis on glossy art
and design, cookery and gardening books,
but with respectable selections of fiction
(hardback and paperback), literary criticism,
travel and children's books and plenty of
cards and gift stationery.

21-27 Upper Street
N1 0PQ
Tel: 0171 354 2637
Mon-Sat 9.30am-6.30pm, Sun 11am-5pm
Tube: Angel
A large branch with a very mix of fiction, art,
history, design and architecture and with
some academic as well as popular titles.
There is also a range of gift stationery on sale.
Pop next door to the gift shop Diva for the
best range of greetings cards in the area.

14 Villiers Street
WC2N 6NN
Tel: 0171 839 8424
Mon-Sat 9am-9pm, Sun 11am-9pm
Tube: Charing Cross
This branch is good on glossy hardbacks on a
variety of general subjects including art and
design, crafts, cookery, gardening, health and
travel, but there is also a good range of
hardback and paperback literary fiction.
Other pluses are a good selection of cards and
stationery and a relaxed atmosphere.

Booking Hall
7 Charlotte Place
W1P 1AQ
Tel: 0171 255 2123
Mon-Fri 11am-3pm and 4pm-7pm,
Sat 11am-5pm
Tube: Goodge Street
As the name suggests this shop stocks railway
books, magazines and videos, as well as
second-hand model railways.

Bookmarks
1 Bloomsbury Street
WC1B 3QE
Tel: 0171 637 1848
Fax 0171 637 3416
Mon 12noon-8pm, Tues-Fri 10am-8pm
Sat 10am-6pm, Sun 12noon-6pm
Tube: Tottenham Court Road
A Socialist bookshop with mostly new but
also a few remaindered and second-hand
books on general subjects as well as politics,
Socialist thinkers and philosophy, history and
labour issues. They also stock a good
selection of Labour Research Department
booklets. There is an excellent international
section, a good range of magazines and
periodicals, and children's books.

Books etc
Books etc is now owned by Borders, who are
set to turn the flagship Books etc on Charing
Cross Road into a Borders store in Spring
1999. The chain currently has stores in
Central London and six airport shops, but is
gradually expanding outside the area.
A free magazine, 'etcetera' is published every
two months and acts as a publicity vehicle for
new books and usually includes a competition
or two. The more substantial free offering,
'fiction etc' features extracts from new books,
printed alongside some discount coupons; this
format is supplemented by special editions
featuring the works of one author or covering
a single theme. The Books etc shops are
bright, airy, well laid out and many now have
in-store coffee bars. Branches at:

30 Broadgate Circle
EC2M 2QS
Tel: 0171 628 8944
Fax: 0171 256 8590
Mon-Fri 8am-8pm, Sat & Sun closed
Tube: Liverpool Street
This is a small shop with a reasonable general stock but also plenty of titles on finance, business and computers to browse. The shop has an excellent location overlooking the small ice skating rink in the centre of Broadgate Circus – lively and bustling at lunchtimes, especially in the summer.

26 Broadway Shopping Centre
W6 9YY
Tel: 0181 746 3912
Fax: 0181 746 3676
Mon-Thurs 8am-8pm, Fri 8am-9pm
Sat 9am-7pm, Sun 11am-5.30pm
Tube: Hammersmith
This is a small branch of the chain but, as usual, they manage to pack a huge selection into a small space which is especially well stocked with computer, fiction and travel books but also has books in all general areas, plus some greetings cards.

Cabot Place East
Canary Wharf
E14 4QT
Tel: 0171 513 0060
Fax: 0171 513 0156
Mon-Fri 8.30am-7pm, Sat 10am-6pm
DLR: Canary Wharf
In the section of Canary Wharf shops and bars furthest away from the DLR station up on the third floor, this is a medium-sized branch. Although there's no coffee shop in-store the immediate area is awash places to get a drink, and the shop itself offers the usual good general stock.

120 Charing Cross Road
WC2H 0JR
Tel: 0171 379 6838
Fax 0171 379 1569
Mon 9.30am-8pm, Tues 10am-8pm
Wed-Sat 9.30am-8pm, Sun 12noon-6pm
Tube: Tottenham Court Road
One of the first and still one of the best branches of this excellent London-based chain. The shop is due to be transformed into a branch of the parent company, Borders in Spring 1999 – hopefully it won't change too much. The atmosphere is busy, the smell of coffee from the coffee bar wafts enticingly through the large store and there's an impressive stock. There are also plenty of special deals, cards and magazines to supplement the books.

70-72 Cheapside
EC2V 6EN
Te: 0171 236 0398
Mon-Fri 8.30am-6.30pm
Tube: St Paul's, Bank
Smaller than the major London Wall branch but still occupying two floors, with a good general stock, plenty of space for displays and excellent greetings cards. It's about ten minutes west of Bank tube station.

60 Fenchurch Street
EC3M 4AQ
Tel: 0171 481 4425
Fax: 0171 702 2639
Mon, Wed-Fri 8.30am-6.30pm
Tues 8.30am-6pm, Sat & Sun closed
Tube: Fenchurch Street
Without a coffee shop but with two storeys of extremely well-stocked shelves including a large computer, business and finance section downstairs. There's plenty of spoken word stuff upstairs, as well as occasional signings to cater to the lunch-time crowd.

176 Fleet Street
EC4A 2AB
Tel: 0171 353 5939
Fax: 0171 583 5648
Mon-Fri 8.30am-6.30pm
Tube: Chancery Lane
At the corner of Fleet Street and Fetter Lane, the upstairs is fairly cramped but there is a surprisingly large basement carrying the usual large Books etc stock. There are sections on business, travel and computing, as well as plenty of talking books and greetings cards.

243 High Holborn
WC1V 7EE
Tel: 0171 404 0261
Fax: 0171 404 5187
Mon-Fri 9am-7pm
Tube: Holborn
This branch has the usual good stock, well displayed and with some special offers.

26 James Street
Covent Garden
WC2E 8PA
Tel: 0171 379 6947
Mon-Sat 10am-10pm, Sun 12noon-6pm
Tube: Covent Garden
A two storey branch with the usual excellent selection. It gets pretty packed although they still have space for some displays, cards and gifts. This branch has excellent opening hours and occasional readings and book signings.

54 London Wall
EC2M 5TR
Tel: 0171 628 9708
Fax: 0171 628 9643
Mon-Wed, Fri 8.30am-6.30pm
Thurs 8.30am-6pm, Sat & Sun closed
Tube: Moorgate
This is probably the biggest City branch of this chain, with two floors and a mezzanine balcony around part of the cavernous basement. It carries a huge stock of titles across all the subjects plus plenty of cards, spoken word tapes and gift ideas.

O2 Centre
Finchley Road
NW3 6LU
Tel: 0171 794 9390
Fax: 0171 433 3299
Mon, Wed-Sat 10am-10pm
Tues 10.30am-10pm, Sun noon-6pm
This shop opened in November 1998 and is one of the largest of the Books etc branches – comparable in size to the Whiteleys of Bayswater store. The shop ranges over one floor with an extensive range of books on all subject areas. It has a large Jewish and local history section and a particularly good children's area with plenty of kid's chairs. There are also lots of chairs and sofas for the grown-ups allowing you to browse at leisure and there's a café if you fancy refreshment.

421 Oxford Street
W1R 1FJ
Tel: 0171 495 5850
Fax: 0171 495 5851
Mon-Wed, Sat 9.30am-8pm, Thurs & Fri 9.30am-8.30pm, Sun 12noon-6pm
Tube: Marble Arch
At the Marble Arch end of Oxford Street opposite Selfridges, this is one of the larger branches. It's spacious, has excellent stock, a café and sofas to sit and read on, or just rest your feet when the shopping has got too much. They often host readings and signings.

23-26 Piccadilly
W1V 9PF
Tel: 0171 437 7399
Fax: 0171 437 7299
Mon-Wed 9.30am-8pm, Thurs & Fri 9.30am-8.30pm, Sat 9.30am-8pm, Sun 12noon-6pm
Tube: Piccadilly
A spacious branch next to Le Meridian Hotel. There is a café bar upstairs with stools overlooking the bustling street below, a selection of international newspapers to read including the International Herald Tribune, and a few sofas if you want to sit down in comfort and read.

Royal Festival Hall
Level 2, Southbank Centre
Belvedere Road
SE1 8XX
Tel: 0171 620 0403
Fax: 0171 620 0426
Daily 11am-10pm
Tube: Charing Cross, Waterloo
On the main entrance level of the Royal
Festival Hall this is a small shop with an
emphasis on music and the arts, but it also
offers the usual excellent general selection in
all other subject areas including children's
books and greetings cards. It's amazing just
how much they manage to get into a small
space – but be warned that it does get very
crowded around concert times.

Victoria Station
The Plaza
SW1E 5ND
Tel: 0171 630 6244
Mon-Sat 8am-8pm, Sun 11am-5pm
Tube: Victoria
Rather smaller than the other branches, this
one is in the high level shopping centre that
leads from the station concourse towards the
coach station. They carry a small general
stock but can easily order books in for you.

66-74 Victoria Street
SW1A 5LB
Tel: 0171 931 0677
Fax: 0171 233 5579
Mon & Tues, Fri 8.30am-6.30pm
Wed & Thurs 8.30am-7pm, Sat 9am-6pm
Tube: Victoria
This is a good-sized branch, extremely well
stocked and always busy with local office
workers at lunch-time. No coffee bar.

Whiteleys of Bayswater
W2 4YQ
Tel: 0171 229 3865
Fax: 0171 221 2393
Mon-Sat 10am-10pm, Sun 12noon-6.30pm
Tube: Queensway

If this is the future of bookshops then I can't
wait for it to arrive. This shop has a great
atmosphere and a staff with real enthusiasm
for books that is really refreshing and which
makes this as much a place just to hang out as
to actually spend money. Located on the first
floor of the shopping centre, the branch is all
on one floor but large and extensively
stocked. However the real plus is the large
number of sofas, easy chairs and tables for
browsing, the branch of Seattle Coffee
Company that forms a central part of the
store, the branch of Paperchase attached at
the back and the children's area which
consists largely of a flight of huge wooden
steps where kids are welcome to linger and
read.

Books of Blackheath
11 Tranquil Vale
SE3 0BU
Tel: 0181 852 8185
Mon-Fri 9.30am-5.30pm, Sat 9.30am-5pm
Rail: Blackheath
A local, general bookseller in the heart of the
village close to the station, other shops and
the pleasant eateries which abound in
Blackheath. In good weather take a picnic up
onto the heath itself which is nearby (if you
then fancy a long walk, from there it's a
couple of miles walk across the park to get
down to the riverside, book-buying and
weekend market joys of Greenwich).

Bookseller Crow on the Hill
50 Westow Street
Crystal Palace
SE19 3AF
Tel/Fax: 0181 771 8831
E-mail: bkscrow@aol.com
Mon-Fri 9am-7.30pm, Sat 9am-6.30pm
Sun 11am-5pm
Rail: Crystal Palace
Just up the road from the large Safeway
supermarket, this is an excellent local
bookstore which although small still has
room for a quality well-selected stock which

is displayed on both tables and shelves. They play good music, have a garden bench for browsers and a small attractive area for children. There are books in all general subject areas with an especially good choice of fiction, children's, travel, Black interest, interior design, textiles and art titles. The shop is about fifteen minutes walk from Crystal Palace Parade which is well supplied with buses and about twenty minutes from Crystal Palace Station – combine a visit here with one to the second-hand bookstores on the adjoining Church Road.

Books For Children

97 Wandsworth Bridge Road
SW6 2TD
Tel: 0171 384 1821
Fax: 0171 736 0916
Mon 10am-6pm, Tues-Fri 9.30am-6pm
Sat 9.30am-5.30pm
Tube: Fulham Broadway
This bookshop has recently doubled in size and has a huge range of books for children of all ages in every type of non-fiction and fiction area; they also supply a lot of schools and stock textbooks.

Books For Cooks

4 Blenheim Crescent
W11 1NN
Tel: 0171 221 1992
Fax: 0171 221 1517
E-mail: info@ booksforcooks.com
Web: www.booksforcooks.com
Mon-Sat 9.30am-6pm
Tube: Ladbroke Grove
Probably the most famous of the trio of excellent specialist bookshops (unrelated to each other) that make a trip to this part of London a real pilgrimage. Opened in 1982, the shop was the first to arrive in the street and has now become the most famous dedicated cookery bookshop in the world. It has eight thousand books on the shelves, has won numerous awards, is reviewed regularly in the press and shoppers come from all over

the world to visit. They sell books on all aspects of food: from specialised professional manuals to family cook books. There is a delightful tiny cafe/restaurant leading off the bookshop where a rota of cooks work in the tiny kitchen to produce divine meals (they have published their own recipe books), but with only five tables, booking is recommended. A demonstration kitchen upstairs runs regular classes and workshops and for those who need more help, there's a party-organising service. Send an SAE for the latest Books For Cooks Newsletter and Workshop List. This really is a brilliant place but very small and terribly packed at weekends – go early in the day during the week for really relaxed browsing.

Books For Life

Bethnal Green Mission Church
305 Cambridge Heath Road
E2 9LH
Tel/Fax: 0171 729 4286
Mon-Wed, Fri 9.30am-5.30pm
Thurs 10am-5.30pm, Sat 9.30am-12.30pm
Tube: Bethnal Green
Located off the foyer of the church the shop is small but well stocked with magazines, books, tapes, software, videos and stationery. There's a good selection of children's books alongside titles on pretty much every aspect of Christian life and worship. (The church is just opposite the Museum of Childhood).

Bookshop in the Crypt

St Martin's in the Fields
Duncannon Street
WC2N 4JJ
Tel: 0171 839 8362
Mon-Sat 10am-7.30pm, Sun 12noon-6pm
Tube: Charing Cross
This central London church in Trafalgar Square has regular services but also stages concerts and has a brass-rubbing centre in its crypt with an attached restaurant and bookshop. Notable mostly for its excellent range of both secular and religious greetings

cards. The shop also has a range of souvenirs with religious and Celtic themes and a small choice of books on the same topics.

The Bookshop Dulwich Village
1d Calton Avenue
SE21 7DE
Tel: 0181 693 2808
Mon-Sat 9am-5.30pm
Rail: North Dulwich
Located in the heart of Dulwich Village (the Dulwich Picture Gallery – sadly closed for renovations in 1999 – is ten minutes walk away and the excellent Crown and Greyhound pub is just around the corner), this small two-storey shop is a reliable local bookseller. The stock is well selected and displayed, there are plenty of children's books amongst a good general selection, some attractive greetings cards, an interesting array of audio books, and plenty of adverts for local events and groups.

Books Nippon
64-66 St Paul's Churchyard
EC4M 8AA
Tel: 0171 248 4956
Fax: 0171 489 1171
Mon-Fri 10.30am-7pm, Sat 10.30am-6pm
Tube: St Paul's
Located on the north side of St Paul's Cathedral, this shop specialises in books, newspapers, magazines, greetings cards and comics in Japanese and English language translations of Japanese fiction. It has a good selection of books about Japanese art, textiles, bonsai, ikebana (flower-arranging), business, sociology, sport, cookery and origami. There are also plenty of Japanese language course books, guides to Japan and information leaflets about Japanese language classes and translation services.

Bookstop
375 Upper Richmond Road West
East Sheen
SW14 7NX
Tel/Fax: 0181 876 1717
Mon-Sat 9.30am-6pm
Rail: Mortlake
New, general stock plus some greetings cards and audiobooks.

Booktree
Merton Abbey Mills
Merantum Way
SW19 2RD
Tel: 0181 540 2694
Daily 10am-5pm
Tube: Colliers Wood
This is an excellent craft shop which stocks materials for all types of craft (including a huge stock of rubber stamps), and organises workshops and demonstrations in things such as silk painting, glass painting, stencilling and using rubber stamps. There is also a good selection of craft and design source books including titles on needlecrafts and all sorts of papercrafts, including calligraphy.

Book Warehouse
Another excellent London discount chain. They have centrally-located shops, long opening hours, plenty of choice across all subject areas (both fiction and non-fiction), and a rapid turnover of stock. Branches at:

56 Haymarket
SW1Y 4RM
Tel: 0171 930 0512
Mon-Sat 10am-11.30pm
Sun 11am-11pm
Tube: Piccadilly
Conveniently located for Piccadilly Circus this bright, modern shop sells a range of heavily discounted books and music and has long enough hours to call in during a night out in town.

72-74 Notting Hill Gate
W11 3HT
Tel: 0171 727 4149
Mon-Sat 9am-10pm, Sun 9am-10am
Tube: Notting Hill Gate
Just outside Notting Hill tube station, this shop offers a reliable general stock of discounted new books with especially good sections of art and children's books and lots of choice in travel, fiction and reference. There are also CDs, cards and attractive stationery.

120 Southampton Row
WC1B 5AA
Tel: 0171 242 1119
Fax: 0171 404 5636
Mon-Fri 8.30am-10pm, Sat 9am-10pm
Sun 10am-10pm
Tube: Holborn
This is the Head Office with, as usual, plenty of illustrated titles in cookery, art, design and photography, large general non-fiction sections as well as plenty of fiction titles and lots of children's books. Current paperback fiction bestsellers are reduced by at least 50p and there are also posters, greetings cards and stationery. The shop is about ten minutes north of Holborn tube station.

110 Strand
WC2
Tel: 0171 379 3510
Every day 9am-10pm
Tube: Charing Cross, Covent Garden or Temple
Another branch of the chain, centrally located and convenient to browse if you are shopping in the Covent Garden area.

Bookworld

12 Ealing Broadway Centre
W5 2NU
Tel: 0181 840 7355
Fax: 0181 840 5769
Mon-Fri 9am -8.30pm, Sat 9am-7.30pm
Sun 10am-5.30pm
Tube: Ealing Broadway

Located in the shopping centre a few minutes walk from the tube station, and with a mixed stock of full-priced and discounted new books, both fiction and non-fiction.

Bookworm Ltd

1177 Finchley Road
NW11 0AA
Tel: 0181 201 9811
Fax: 0181 201 9311
Mon-Fri 9am-5.30pm
Sun 10am-1.30pm
Tube: Golders Green (then bus)
A small shop specialising in books for children and young adults, packed with an extensive and interesting stock. A regular newsletter advertises the events held in the shop such as parties involving favourite characters and visits by authors. Membership of The Bookworm Kids Club is free with benefits including gifts, a newsletter, competitions and prize draws.

Boosey and Hawkes Music Shop

295 Regent Street
W1R 8JH
Tel: 0171 580 2060
Mon-Fri 9am-6pm, Sat 10am-4pm
Tube: Oxford Circus
Sheet music specialists catering for all instruments, levels and tastes. They also stock a small selection of theory and reference books, as well as various musical gifts, cabinets, stands and metronomes.

Borders

203-207 Oxford Street
W1R 1AH
Tel: 0171 292 1600
Fax: 0171 292 1616
Mon-Sat 8am-11pm, Sun 12noon-6pm
Tube: Oxford Circus
Although the company already owns Books etc, this is the first UK branch of this hugely successful American book chain (there are over two hundred stores in the USA), although another is planned in Charing

Cross Road as well as stores in Brighton, Leeds and Glasgow. Claiming to stock over two hundred thousand books, CDs, videos, magazines and newspapers, the range and depth of the stock over the shop's four storeys is very impressive – and the atmosphere busy, busy, busy! There's a branch of Paperchase on the ground floor selling their usual array of stylish stationery items and a first-floor Café Espresso overlooks Oxford Street and serves light meals and snacks (getting a seat can be a pain at busy times). The queues at the tills and information counters can be annoying and there aren't really enough seats for browsing outside the cafe, but if you like your bookshops with buzz and excitement this is certainly the place to go. For a more peaceful experience visit either early or late. Borders also has a packed programme of book signings, readings, music and children's events.

Borders

The Britain Visitor Centre

1 Regent Street
SW1Y 4NS
Mon-Fri 9am-6.30pm
October-May: Sat & Sun 10am-4pm and
June-September: Sat 9am-5pm
Tube: Piccadilly Circus
The bookshop here sells an excellent range of guidebooks and general books on London and other areas of Britain.

British Chess Magazine Ltd

69 Masbro Road
Kensington
W14 0LS
Tel: 0171 603 2877
Fax: 0171 371 1477
Mon-Sat 9.30am-6pm
Tube: Shepherds Bush, Hammersmith or
Olympia
Specialist shop selling everything to do with chess: sets, clocks, computers and a stock of thousands of new and second-hand books covering every aspect of the subject.

The British Library Bookshop

96 Euston Road
NW1 2DB
Tel: 0171 412 7735
Fax: 0171 412 7172
Mon, Wed-Fri 9.30am-6pm, Tues 9.30am-
8pm, Sat 9.30am-5pm, Sun 11am-5pm
Tube: Kings Cross, Euston
This bookshop attached to the British Library has a brilliant range of around five thousand titles about books and subjects related to the library. In addition to guides and catalogues on the collections there are good selections on bookbinding and bookcrafts, calligraphy and scripts, music, history, religion and Oriental culture. There is also a large stock of gift items, particularly stationery, and plenty of greetings and postcards. The bookshop stages regular events such as book signings and you can add your name to a free mailing list for details of these and the mail order service. In

addition to the reading rooms in the library itself there are three main exhibition galleries – the real gem is The John Ritblat Gallery which houses the treasures of the British Library such as the Magna Carta, the Lindisfarne Gospels, Shakespeare's First Folio and a multitude of other awesome exhibits. The cafe/restaurant is located next to a glass tower, several storeys high, in which the King's Library (collected by King George III) is displayed: leatherbound volumes soar skywards as you drink your cup of coffee – splendid.

British Medical Journal Bookshop
Burton Street
WC1H 9JR
Tel: 0171 383 6244
Fax: 0171 383 6455
Mon-Fri 9.30am-5pm
Tube: Euston, Russell Square
Located in a building at the back of the British Medical Association, this shop stocks around six thousand medical titles and offers a free mail order service throughout the UK.

The British Museum Bookshop
Great Russell Street
WC1B 3DG
Museum switchboard: 0171 636 1555
Bookshop: 0171 323 8587
Fax: 0171 580 8699
Web: www.british-museum.ac.uk
Mon-Sat 10am-5pm, Sun 12noon-6pm
Tube: Russell Square
The bookshop here is absurdly small and crowded for a large museum serving a huge number of visitors. The stock is both general and specialist, but concentrates on the topics of most relevance to the museum's collections: ancient cultures both European and Oriental. Hopefully included in the rebuilding programme for the museum there are plans to enlarge the bookshop space.

Britten Music
136 George Lane
E18 1AY
Tel: 0181 530 6432
Mon-Fri 9am-5.30pm, Sat 9am-4.30pm
Tube: South Woodford
Excellent local music store with plenty of instruments to buy and rent, good quality advice, a brimming-over local noticeboard advertising lessons, courses and events. There is also a very good selection of sheet music for all instruments and levels both classical and popular.

Building Bookshop
The Building Centre
26 Store Street
WC1E 7BT
Tel: 0171 692 4040
Fax: 0171 636 3628
E-mail: bookshop@buildingbookshop.co.uk
Web: www.buildingbookshop.co.uk
Mon-Fri 9.30-5.15pm, Sat 10am-1pm
Tube: Gower Street
This shop specialises in technical and academic books relevant to the building industry: surveying, architecture, construction, property law and management. There are also books of general interest on interior design, woodwork and electrical installation, although they are probably more relevant for the enthusiastic amateur than the general reader.

Bush Books
113 Shepherds Bush Centre
W12 8PP
Tel/Fax: 0181 749 7652
Mon-Fri 10am-6pm, Sat 10am-5.30pm
Sun 12noon-4pm
Tube: Shepherds Bush
General bookshop selling new books plus some CDs, tapes, audiobooks, greetings cards and stationery.

C

Camden Arts Centre

Arkwright Road
NW3 6DG
Tel: 0171 435 2643
Fax: 0171 794 3371
Mon closed, Tues-Thurs 11am-7pm
Fri-Sun 11am-5.30pm
Tube: Finchley Road
This is a small bookshop surrounding the reception area, but they do stock a reasonable range of books on art and art criticism as well as a good selection of postcards.

Camden Lock Bookshop

77 Camden Lock Place
NW1 8AF
Tel: 0171 267 3824
Mon-Fri 11.30am-4.30pm,
Sat & Sun 10am-5.30pm
Tube: Camden Town
Located in the West Yard of the main market, reach it via the tow path and bridge across the canal. The stock is largely discounted new books but there is a small second-hand stock which consists mainly of material from the 1960's.

The Catholic Truth Society

25 Ashley Place
SW1P 1LT
Tel: 0171 834 1363
Fax: 0171 821 7398
Mon-Fri 9.30am-5.30pm, Sat 10am-2pm
Tube: Victoria
Small shop close to Westminster Cathedral with a good range of books on all aspects of Catholic spiritual and family life, religious biographies, books on liturgy and plenty of Bibles, prayer books and children's books.

CCBI Bookroom

Inter-Church House, 35-41 Lower Marsh
SE1 7RL
Tel: n/a
Mon-Fri 9am-4pm
Tube: Waterloo
This shop specialises in new ecumenical Christian literature and also has a few videos and tapes.

Centerprise

136-138 Kingsland High Street
E8 2NS
Tel: 0171 254 9632 ext.207
Fax: 0171 923 1951
Mon-Fri 9.30am-6pm, Sat 10am-5.30pm
Rail: Dalston Kingsland
Centerprise is an advice and legal centre, cafe, gallery, publishing, youth and reading centre a couple of minutes walk north of Dalston Kingsland Station. The bookshop is a brilliant local resource, stocking plenty of books and magazines of interest to the community, including big sections on Black fiction and non-fiction, women's and gay and lesbian issues, health, history, politics, travel, welfare rights, and local interest. There is a good children's section including plenty of education books and a variety of political and art magazines and journals. Regular readings and events are also put on through out the year.

Chamber Bookshop

The London Chamber of Commerce
33 Queen Street
EC4R 1AP
Tel: 0171 203 1840
Fax: 0171 489 0391
Mon-Fri 9am-5pm
Tube: Mansion House
Specialist bookshop dealing in all business subject areas; produces in-house publications and stocks the Membership Directory of the Chamber.

Chappells

50 New Bond Street
W1Y 9HA
Tel: 0171 491 2777
Fax: 0171 491 0133
Mon-Fri 9.30am-6pm, Sat 9.30am-5pm
Tube: Piccadilly
The entrance is unpromising, sandwiched amongst the frontages of the street's high fashion houses, but in this basement shop, alongside a brilliant range of musical instruments you'll find a monster range of scores for music ancient and modern, by composers both famous and obscure. There are also adverts for tuition in every kind of instrument, as well sheet music for all levels of musical competence.

Chapter Two

199 Plumstead Common Road
SE18 3AF
Tel: 0181 316 4972
Fax: 0181 854 5963
Mon& Tue, Thu & Fri 9.30am-1pm and 2.30pm-5.30pm, Wed closed
Rail: Woolwich Arsenal
Specialist on the Plymouth Brethren and Dispensational Christianity, stocking both new and second-hand books and Christian literature in foreign editions.

Chener Books

14-16 Lordship Lane
SE22 8HN
Tel: 0181 299 0771
Mon-Sat 10am-6pm
Rail: East Dulwich
A small local bookshop with a good general selection (mostly in paperback), plenty of display space to encourage shoppers to browse and some low display boxes that make the children's books inside accessible to junior readers. There is also a good selection of local notices.

Chess & Bridge

369 Euston Road
NW1 3AR
Tel: 0171 388 2404
Fax: 0171 388 2407
E-mail: chesscentre@easynet.co.uk
Web: www.chess.co.uk and
www.bridgemagazine.co.uk
Mon-Sat 10.30am-6pm
Tube: Euston
Two minutes east of Great Portland Street tube station, this is a specialist shop with a huge range of books as well as other items focussing on chess and bridge. The books section has titles on all aspects of both games, whilst there are also magazines, software, videos, equipment and gift items. There are separate catalogues for each of the subjects, as well a fine selection of chess sets.

Children's Book Centre

237 Kensington High Street
W8 6SA
Tel: 0171 937 7497
Fax: 0171 938 4968
Mon-Wed, Fri & Sat 9.30am-6.30pm
Thurs 9.30am-7pm
Sun 12noon-6pm
Tube: High Street Kensington
A two storey shop bursting at the seams with an excellent range of children's fiction and non-fiction books for all age ranges. There are lots of picture books and a lovely little selection of plastic, cardboard and novelty books (with squeezy toy attached) for the youngest readers. In addition to the excellent book choice there are toys and multimedia software.

Children's Bookshop

29 Fortis Green Road
Muswell Hill
N10 3HP
Tel: 0181 444 5500
Fax: 0181 883 8632
Mon-Sat 9.15am-5.45pm
Tube: Highgate (then bus)

Situated just opposite the Muswell Hill Bookshop, this vibrant specialist shop has a huge stock of books of interest to youngsters from first books through to junior-adult stage. They publish a newsletter four times a year and there are also lists of books on various topics. The staff really know their stuff, there's an excellent noticeboard for items of local interest and lots of teddy bears to cuddle.

Children's Early Learning Centres

This chain stock mostly educational pre-school toys but have a small range of books (including their own publications): cloth books, squeaky and lift-the-flap books and plastic ones to take into the bath.

Chimes Music Shop

44 Marylebone High Street
W1M 3AD
Tel: 0171 935 1587
Fax: 0171 935 0457
Mon-Fri 9am-5.30pm, Sat 9am-4.30pm
Tube: Bond Street

The shop stocks the same instruments, accessories and large array of sheet music as the other stores in the group (Barbican and Kensington). In addition it also offers a selection of books about music, predominantly classical and opera, most at full price but some also discounted.

Christian City Books

76 Bolton Crescent
SE5 0SE
Tel: 0171 582 1299
Mon-Wed, Fri 10am-6pm,
Thurs 10am-7pm, Sat 11am-3pm
Tube: Oval (then bus)

Specialist Christian stockist; all books are new.

Church House Bookshop

31 Great Smith Street
SW1P 3BN
Tel: 0171 898 1300
Fax: 0171 898 1305
E-mail: info@chp.u-net.com
Web: www.herald.co.uk/clients/c/Church-House/chb.html
Mon-Wed, Fri 9am-5pm, Thurs 9.30am-6pm
Tube: Westminster or St James's Park

Christian shop selling a range of material from Church House Publishers and other specialist publishing houses. Stock includes books for children and on youth work, and there's a range of Anglican music on CD and tape.

CIB Bookshop

90 Bishopsgate
EC2N 4AS
Tel: 0171 444 7118
Fax: 0171 444 7116
E-mail: smaguire@cib.uk
Web: www.cib.org.uk
Mon, Wed & Fri 9am-5pm
Tues & Thurs 9am-6pm
Tube: Liverpool Street

At the corner of Bishopsgate and Camomile Street, this is the highly specialist bookshop attached to the Chartered Institute of Bankers. It sells books covering all branches of banking and finance; the Library and Information service is just behind the shop.

The Cinema Bookshop

13-14 Great Russell Street
WC1B 3NH
Tel: 0171 637 0206
Fax: 0171 436 9979
Mon-Sat 10.30am-5.30pm
Tube: Tottenham Court Road

This shop is an Aladin's cave of new, rare and out-of-print books on the cinema and is also chock full of still photographs, posters, scripts and other ephemera.

The Cinema Store

4b Orion House
Upper St Martins Lane
WC2H 9EJ
Tel: 0171 379 7838
Fax: 0171 240 7689
E-mail: cinemastor@aol.com
Mon-Wed, Sat 10am-6pm
Thurs & Fri 10am-7pm, Sun 12noon-6pm
Tube: Leicester Square

Two shops selling a huge range of books, videos, laser discs, photographs, posters, postcards, T-shirts and other paraphernalia associated with vintage and modern cinema. Most of the books are new but there is a large stock of older magazines.

The City Bookstop

75 Aldgate High Street
EC3N 1BD
Mon-Fri 9am-6pm, Sat 10am-3pm
Tube: Aldgate

Just opposite Aldgate tube station, this discount bookseller is packed full of books with tables and floor piled high and shelves literally buckling under the weight. There are tables of £3.99, £5 and £7 bargains (many of these are very good quality reference and computer titles) but most books aren't marked – you have to ask the prices; discounts are around one-third off.

The City Lit Bookshop

16 Stukeley Street
WC2B 5LJ
Tel: 0171 405 3110
Mon-Fri 12noon-7.30pm, Sat 12noon-3pm
Tube: Holborn, Covent Garden

The City Literary Institute is a famous London establishment offering a vast range of part-time courses for adult learners covering the arts, social sciences, history, performance and creative arts and languages. Its small bookshop has course books and associated reading material, as well as a small general stock.

Classic Collection

Galen Place, off Bury Place
WC1A 2JR
Tel: 0171 831 6000
Fax 0171 831 5424
Web: www.classiccollection.com
Tube: Holborn

As well as vintage cameras there is a large range of photographic books.

CLC Bookshop
(Christian Literature Crusade)

26-30 Holborn Viaduct
EC1A 2AQ
Tel: 0171 583 4835
Fax: 0171 583 6059
Mon-Wed 10am-5.30pm
Thurs 10am-6pm, Fri closed, Sat 10am-5pm
Tube: Farringdon

This is the only London branch of a worldwide chain. CLC is a missionary society dedicated to using its bookshops to establish a Christian presence across the globe. The shop is huge with large sections of books on every aspect of Christianity and Christian living including foreign language and children's books alongside Bibles, commentaries, prayerbooks and books on theology, evangelism, preaching, biography and prophecy.

The Comic Shack

720 High Road
Leytonstone
E11 3AJ
Tel: 0181 539 7260 or 0181 555 9303
Mon-Fri 9.30am-5.30pm,
Sat 9.30am-6.30pm, Sun 11am-5pm
Tube: Leytonstone

This is a mecca for real comics fans, selling only new imports and second-hand American comics. The stock is huge ranging from 50p titles up to very rare 'Fantastic Four' and 'Daredevil' comics selling at a couple of hundred pounds per issue.

Comic Showcase

76 Neal Street
WC2H 9PA
Tel: 0171 240 3664
Thurs-Sat 10am-7pm, Sun-Wed 10am-6pm
Tube: Covent Garden
Located in the heart of Covent Garden this
shop has a good range of new and old
comics. They specialise in American titles,
including 'Marvel' and 'DC' but also stock an
extensive range of magazines (including 'Star
Trek' and 'The X-Files'), graphic novels,
memorabilia and more mainstream cartoon
books including 'Calvin and Hobbs', 'The
Simpsons' and 'Dilbert'.

Compendium Books

234 Camden High Street
NW1 8QS
Tel: 0171 485 8944
Mon-Sat 10am-6pm, Sun 12noon-6pm
Tube: Camden Town
The narrow front of this well-established
shop conceals a two-floor goldmine of
volumes with plenty of general stock but
specialising in New Age, philosophy, poetry,
politics, social studies, women's studies,
alternative medicine, religion and music plus
plenty of related magazines.

Cornerstone

638 High Road
North Finchley
N12 0NL
Tel: 0181 446 3056
Mon-Thurs, Sat 9.30am-5.30om
Fri 9.30am-6.30pm
Tube: West Finchley
Right near Tally Ho Corner or fifteen
minutes walk from West Finchley tube
station, this shop specialises in Christian books.
Currently all books are new but they hope to
reinstate the second-hand section soon.

Cornerstone Bookshop

299 Lavender Hill
SW11 1LN
Tel: 0171 924 2413
Rail: Clapham Junction
Mon, Tues & Thurs 9.30am-5.30pm
Wed 9.30am-1pm, Fri 9.30am-7pm
Sat 9.30am-5pm
Specialist shop selling Christian books
including a children's section as well as
music on CD and tape, plus greetings cards
and videos.

Countryside Bookshop

39 Goodge Street
W1P 1FD
Tel: 0171 636 3156
Fax: 0171 323 6879
Mon-Fri 10am-6pm
Sat 11am-5pm (Sats in August closed)
Small two storey shop that in addition to the
expected countryside subjects of natural
history, gardening, walking, fishing, crafts,
food, drink, biographies and memoirs,
guidebooks and maps, also stocks a range of
poetry and current bestsellers. There are
plenty of chairs for browsing and the
downstairs travel section is especially
welcoming with lots of sitting space.

County Bookshop

Savacentre Unit 1
Southend Lane
SE26 4PU
Tel: 0181 659 8467
Mon-Wed 8am-9pm, Thurs & Fri 8am-10pm
Sat 8am-8pm, Sun 11am-5pm
Rail: Lower Sydenham
Discount bookseller in the Savacentre
complex with a big range of general titles.
Stock includes both fiction and non-fiction,
paperback and hardback and with plenty of
travel, children's, food and cookery,
reference and gift titles.

Courtauld Gallery Bookshop

Somerset House
The Strand
WC2 0RN
Tel: 0171 848 2526
Mon-Sat 10am-6pm
Sun & Bank Holidays 12noon-6pm
Tube: Covent Garden, Holborn or Temple
This is one of the nicest little galleries in
London with a great collection of art (most
notably Impressionist and Post-Impressionist
works), extremely well displayed and on a
manageable scale when compared to the
monster galleries elsewhere in London
(Admission is £4, but free Monday 10am-
2pm; an annual season ticket is £10). The
bookshop has an excellent selection of titles
on art history and lots of monographs on
particular artists as well as some architecture
titles and a good range of postcards, prints
and assorted souvenirs featuring art from the
gallery.

Crime in Store

14 Bedford Street
Covent Garden
WC2 9HE
Tel: 0171 379 3795
Fax: 0171 379 8988
E-mail: crimebus@aol.com
Mon-Sat 10.30am-6.30pm, Sun 12noon-5pm
Tube: Covent Garden
This is a specialist shop featuring mostly full
price new hardback and paperback crime
and thriller titles but with a small sale and
second-hand section. It is everything a
bookshop should be: well organised,
brilliantly stocked, with a sofa for browsing,
related magazines to read as well as buy, a
noticeboard announcing future readings, a
reading group meeting every six weeks and
a relaxed and welcoming atmosphere aided
by good music. The capital could do with
far more bookshops like this.

Crime in Store

D

Dance Books

15 Cecil Court, Charing Cross Road
WC2N 4EZ
Tel: 0171 836 2314
Fax: 0171 497 0473
Mon-Sat 11am-7pm
Tube: Leicester Square
New and second-hand books on all aspects of
the theory and practice of dance ancient and
modern, British and foreign with videos,
tapes and CDs also on sale.

Dar Al-Taqwa

7A Melcombe Street
NW1 6AE
Tel: 0171 935 6385
Fax: 0171 224 3894
Mon-Sat 9am-6pm
Tube: Baker Street
General bookshop with a new stock covering
all standard subject areas including children's
books, philosophy, psychology, social, Arabic
and women's studies and Islam.

Daunt Books

193 Haverstock Hill
NW3 4QG
Tel: 0171 794 4006
Fax: 0171 431 2732
Mon-Sat 10am-9pm, Sun 11am-7pm
Tube: Belsize Park

Outpost in northern London of the fabulous central London shop (see below). As well as carrying a small general stock they specialise in travel books and are a cut above the rest as they seem to get books others don't. Titles are arranged by geographical location so you'll find guide books, travelogues, history and fiction about and by authors from that area altogether on the shelves – it makes browsing wonderful. This small branch isn't as absorbing or as comfortable as the main shop but if you're in the area, do drop in.

Daunt Books for Travellers

83 Marylebone High Street
W1M 3DE
Tel: 0171 224 2295
Fax: 0171 224 6893
Mon-Sat 9am-7pm
Tube: Baker Street

There is absolutely nothing to compare to this stunning shop anywhere else in London (although they do have a small branch in the north of the city see above). Located about fifteen minutes walk from Baker Street (and also accessible from Bond Street tube station) the shop's entrance is unremarkable, but conceals a very large and beautifully designed interior. It is in the back of the shop that the best is hidden: upstairs there is a balconied rear room and below, a stunning basement lined floor to ceiling with books. The really original feature of the place is that the books are arranged by country, and include guides, maps, travel accounts, history, sociology, art, craft and literature (both ancient and modern). It's a simple, effective idea brought off splendidly. Anyone with an interest in a place overseas will find something here and

quite likely something they haven't come across elsewhere. There are comfortable chairs downstairs for browsing.

Davenports

5,6 & 7 Charing Cross Tube Arcade
The Strand
WC2N 4HZ
Tel: 0171 836 0408
Fax: 0171 379 8828
Mon-Fri 9.30am-5.30pm
Sat 10.15am-4.30pm

Having sold magic equipment and published magic books for over a hundred years, the store is stocked with a huge array of magic equipment for the beginner and expert (how about the 'Demon Arm Chopper'?), together with a wide range of videos and new and second-hand magic books including plenty from overseas. Mail order is available with a catalogue at £7.

Daybreak Books

68 Baring Road
SE12 0PS
Tel: 0181 857 1188
Tues-Fri 9am-1pm and 2pm-5.30pm
Sat 9am-5.30pm
Rail: Lee (or a bus ride from Lewisham)

Christian bookshop also selling gift items, stationery, cards and music.

Design Museum Bookshop

Butler's Wharf
Shad Thames
SE1 2YD
Tel: 0171 403 6933
Mon-Sun 11.30am-5.45pm
Tube: London Bridge, Tower Hill

Located conveniently near the coffee shop on the ground floor of this museum devoted entirely to design. The shop, although not enormous, sells a broad range of books as well as gifts related to subjects covered by the museum, including exhibition catalogues and also general material on design

Dillons

The Dillons chain (now owned by the HMV Group who also own Waterstone's), has almost a schizophrenic personality, with some academic and specialist shops and then main and shopping centre stores which seem to emphasise more popular titles. But regardless of which type of branch you visit, there are often pretty good offers to be had and the free magazine 'Dillons Book Review' (available in all stores), is a good way of finding out the latest 'hot' thing in the world of books. Branches at:

82 Gower Street
WC1E 6EQ
Tel: 0171 636 1577
Fax: 0171 580 7680
Mon-Fri 9am-7pm, Sat 9.30am-6pm,
Sun 12noon-6pm
Tube: Goodge Street
This is the original and now flagship Dillon's store – just around the corner from London University, it's probably the best academic bookshop in London. It stocks tens if not hundreds of thousands of titles ranged over five floors and staff know both what they have and where it should be, as well as enough information to give advice on titles in their specialist fields. In addition, if a book is in print and the store doesn't have it, staff can also place an order and give you a reasonable idea of how long it'll take to arrive. The second-hand section on the first floor is fairly extensive, well-organised and encompasses the full range of academic subjects. They also stock new discounted titles, so drop in here before you buy in the other departments.

782 High Street
North Finchley, N12 8JY
Tel 0181 446 9669
Fax: 0181 446 3663
Mon-Fri 9am-5.30pm
Sat 9am-6pm, Sun 11am-4pm
Tube: Woodside Park

10-12 James Street
W1M 5HN
Tel: 0171 629 8206
Fax: 0171 495 2049
Mon, Wed-Fri 9.30am-8pm, Tues 10am-8pm
Sat 10am-7.30pm, Sun 12noon-6pm
Tube: Oxford Circus
Conveniently close to Oxford Street (about fifty yards) not far from Selfridges, this is a pleasant branch of the chain, nowhere near as extensive as the larger Oxford Street branch or the Gower Street flagship, but convenient and well stocked.

Unit S9 Wood Street
The Bentall Centre
Kingston, Surrey
KT1 1PH
Rail: Kingston

28 Margaret Street
W1N 7LB
Tel: 0171 580 2812
Fax: 0171 637 1790
E-mail: lonmarg@dillons.eunet.co.uk
Mon-Wed, Fri 9am-6pm
Thurs 9am-7pm, Sat 9.30am-6pm
Tube: Oxford Circus
Located in the building that was previously Mowbray's religious booksellers (established in 1894), there is still an extensive religious books section in the basement selling mostly Christian theology, philosophy and material on world religion plus candles, devotional objects and crucifixes. The rest of the shop is a standard Dillon's store with the usual excellent range well set out and displayed, and with plenty of chairs in which to browse and relax.

19-23 Oxford Street
W1R 1RF
Tel: 0171 434 9759
Fax: 0171 434 3154
Mon-Fri 9.30am-10pm
Sat 9.30am-8pm, Sun 12noon-6pm
Tube: Tottenham Court Road

This branch is not as big or as well-stocked as the Gower Street branche (see p.28) but it is convenient for Oxford Street shoppers or those browsing in nearby Charing Cross Road. It also has in its favour a busy, bustling atmosphere, good general stock and plenty of staff to help with queries.

213 Piccadilly
W1V 0LE
Tel: 0171 434 9617
Fax: 0171 734 0681
Mon-Wed, Thu & Fri 9.30am-10pm
Tues 10am-10pm, Sat 9.30am-8pm
Sun 12noon-6pm
Tube: Piccadilly Circus
This shop has a narrow frontage but is fairly extensive inside, although without the stock of the larger branches nearby.

Queen Mary and Westfield College
329 Mile End Road
E1 4NT
Tel: 0171 775 3144
Fax: 0181 981 6774
Tube: Whitechapel

Thames Valley University
St Mary's Road
W5 5RF
Tel: 0181 840 6205
Fax: 0181 840 6729
Tube: South Ealing

Dillons Arts

8 Long Acre
WC2H 9LH
Tel: 0171 836 1359
Fax: 0171 240 1267
E mail: longacre@dillons.eunet.co.uk
Mon, Wed-Sat 9.30am-10pm, Tues 10am-10pm, Sun 12noon-7pm
Tube: Covent Garden
An excellent range of books and magazines spread over two floors that fall into the broad area of arts, design and media. The glossy, illustrated books are on the ground floor,

with film, TV, music, poetry, magazines, theatre and scripts (plus a somewhat incongruous computer section) in the basement. The shop is sadly due to close at some point in 1999 so please phone before making a special trip.

Dillons Business Bookshop

72 Park Road
NW1 4SH
Tel: 0171 723 3902
Fax: 0171 706 1127
Mon-Fri 9.30am-6.30pm, Sat 10am-1pm
Tube: Baker Street
Located next to the London Business School.

Dillons City Business Bookshop

9 Moorfields
EC2Y 9AE
Tel: 0171 628 7479
Fax: 0171 628 7871
E-mail: loncbus@dillons.eunet.co.uk
Mon, Wed-Fri 9am-6pm, Tues 9.30am-6pm
Tube: Moorgate
This shop specialises in all aspects of business and finance with hefty sections on financial markets, personal finance, investment, accounting, business management and economics. The only general stock is made up of current bestsellers – go elsewhere if you're after anything else.

Dorling Kindersley

10-13 King Street
WC2E 8HN
Tel: 0171 836 5411
Fax: 0171 240 1466
Mon-Fri 10.30am-6.30pm, Sat 10.30am-6pm
Sun 12noon-6pm
Tube: Covent Garden
Stocking only the fabulously-illustrated adult, children's and reference books and multimedia materials from the innovative publishers, this shop is a brilliant place to browse and enjoy the artistry of the titles on offer.

The Dover Bookshop

18 Earlham Street
WC2H 9LN
Tel: 0171 836 2111
Fax: 0171 836 1603
E-mail: images@thedoverbookshop.com
Web: www.thedoverbookshop.com
Mon-Wed 10am-6pm, Thurs-Sat 10am-7pm
Tube: Leicester Square
Dover are American publishers of craft and design books, titles which feature a huge range of copyright-free images (making them excellent project resources). As well as standard design books, the range includes postcard and stencil books, punch-out masks and model and paper doll books (from Shirley Temple to Pope John Paul II). Some material is now available on CD-Rom and the shop has its own mail order catalogue.

Dress Circle

57/59 Monmouth Street
WC2H 9DG
Tel: 0171 240 2227
Fax: 0171 379 8540
E-mail: online@dresscircle.co.uk
Web: www.dresscircle/co.uk
Mon-Sat 10am-7pm
Tube: Leicester Square, Covent Garden
Billing themselves as 'The Greatest Showbiz Shop in the World' this store has a huge stock of musical scores, soundtracks (on CD and tape), videos, magazines, posters and merchandise associated with current West End shows, plus a small selection of new books about stars of stage and screen both current and past. A brilliant place for browsing if glamour is your bag, and close to both Covent Garden and Theatreland. Send an A5 SAE for their catalogue.

Dulwich Books

6 Croxted Road
SE21 8SW
Tel: 0181 670 1920
Mon-Sat 9.30am-5.30pm
Rail: West Dulwich
Excellent local bookstore, part of the Pipeline group, with a good general stock, well displayed and organised. The shop offers all the general subject areas you'd expect but is especially good in art and design with lots of volumes that would make brilliant gifts, as well as having extensive travel and fiction sections. There are Open University set books on sale and the children's section in the corner has tiny chairs for small browsers. There's also a good selection of greetings cards and audiobooks. Café Rouge is a short walk away for a post-browse coffee.

Dulwich Music Shop

2 Croxted Road
SE21 8SW
Tel: 0181 766 0202
Mon-Sat 9.30am-5.30pm
Rail: West Dulwich
Although small this shop is well stocked with sheet music for every instrument and level, every voice or combination of voices and every style of music. You can't see from outside but there must be literally thousands of scores on the shelves at the back. This stash is brilliant enough but the real bonus is the atmosphere: what better place to look through violin music than with a row of violins suspended from the ceiling, or to wonder about jazz music with the gleaming saxophones in the cabinet an inch away? There's a good selection of CDs, videos, greetings cards, mugs, T-shirts and many other gift items for music lovers and a visit here can be combined with one to The Dulwich Bookshop a couple of doors away.

Daunt Books for Travellers

E

Eastside Bookshop
178 Whitechapel Road
E1 1BJ
Tel: 0171 247 0216
Fax: 0171 247 2882
Mon-Fri 10am-5.30pm, Sat 10am-5pm
Tube: Whitechapel
Eastside is Whitechapel's centre for the written and spoken word and acts as a base for writers and artists groups, publishing, video-making and street theatre. It also hosts events, sponsors competitions and bursaries (including 'Eastside Stories', a bursary for first-time novelists in Tower Hamlets, Hackney and Newham) and produces a quarterly newsletter. The centre started as a small bookshop in 1977 and remains an excellent outlet for general stock including local issues, Black and Asian fiction, politics, race, gay and lesbian sections, health, political magazines and children's books. There is also a wide range of dual language books, including titles in Arabic, Bengali, Chinese, Somali and Tamil.

Economist Bookstore
Clare Market
Portugal Street
WC2A 2AB
Tel: 0171 405 5531
Fax: 0171 430 1584
Mon & Tue, Thu & Fri 9am-7pm
Wed 9am-9.30am, Sat 9.30am-6pm
Tube: Aldwych
Located very close to the London School of Economics, the stock includes a wide range of academic and professional titles that can broadly come under the heading of economics, but which extends into related areas.

The Economist Shop
15 Regent Street
W1Y 4LR
Tel: 0171 839 1937
Fax: 0171 839 1921
Web:www.economist.com
Mon-Fri 9am-6pm, Sat 10am-5pm
Tube: Piccadilly
The range of books published by The Economist and reports by The Economist Intelligence Unit are prominently displayed but the shop also has an excellent range of titles in the areas of global and national economics, investment, trade, finance, management, marketing and human resources. There are some comfortable chairs for browsing at the back.

Elgin Books
6 Elgin Crescent
W11 2HX
Tel: 0171 229 2186
Fax: 0171 792 1457
Tues-Sat 10am-6pm
Tube: Ladbroke Grove
Small shop on two floors with a literary air and a good range of highbrow fiction, biography, history, travel and a large children's section in the basement. Noticeboards advertise local services and display current book reviews.

ENO Shop
31-32 St Martin's Lane
WC2N 4ER
Tel: 0171 240 0270
Mon 10am-6pm, Tues-Sat 10am-7.30pm
Tube: Leicester Square
Part of the MDC group that has classical music stores throughout London, this store specialises in opera and is the only branch which sells books: a small selection on classical music and opera. The 'MDC Classic Express' is a free monthly newspaper for classical music enthusiasts featuring mail order forms. MDC has a web site at www.mdcmusic.co.uk

Esperanto Bookshop

140 Holland Park Avenue
W11 4UF
Tel: 0171 727 7821
Fax: 0171 229 5784
E-mail: eab@esperanto.demon.co.uk
Web: esperanto.demon.co.uk
Mon-Fri 9.30am-6pm
Tube: Holland Park
Created in the nineteenth century, Esperanto is a language which aims at operating as a neutral second language which people worldwide can learn with relative ease. This highly specialised shop stocks relevant learning materials, including audio tapes and videos, and imported literature in Esperanto.

Eurocentre

21 Meadowcourt Road
SE3 9EU
Tel: 0181 318 5633
Fax: 0181 318 9057
Mon-Fri 1pm-2.10pm
Rail: Blackheath, Lee
Located in an English language school the specialism here is English course materials and texts for learners. The shop is open to the public but only during the school lunch-hour.

European Bookshop Ltd

5 Warwick Street
W1R 6BH
Tel: 0171 734 5259
Mon-Sat 9.30am-6pm
Tube: Piccadilly Circus
A range of books, audio materials and videos to help the learning of the main European languages. There are also texts on teaching English as a foreign language and fiction and non-fiction books.

Exchange Books

792 Holloway Road
N19 3JH
Tel: 0171 281 7382
Mon-Sat 11am-9pm
Tube: Archway
General shop with a selection of new and second-hand books.

Extra Cover

101 Boundary Road
St John's Wood
NW8 0RG
Tel: 0171 625 1191
Tues-Sat 10am-5.30pm, Sun-10am-2pm
Tube: South Hampstead
A specialist shop in the same district as Lords Cricket ground, stocking new and second-hand books – including Wisden's – on cricket, plus a few football titles. They also have some prints.

F

Faith House Bookshop

7 Tufton Street
SW1P 3QN
Tel: 0171 222 6952
Fax: 0171 976 7180
Mon-Wed, Fri 9.30am-5pm, Thurs 10am-5pm
Tube: Victoria
Bookseller of new Christian books located a very short walk away from Westminster Abbey with a supplementary range of stationery, cards, videos and music.

Fielders

54 Wimbledon Hill Road
SW19 7PA
Tel: 0181 946 5044
Fax: 0181 944 1320
Mon-Fri 9am-5.30pm, Sat 9.30am-6pm
Tube: Wimbledon
Selling books in Wimbledon for over seventy years, the downstairs of the shop is a brilliantly-stocked stationery and art store (the shop organises art classes for all levels –

ask for the leaflet), whilst the upstairs book department is a good general store with a particularly large and welcoming children's section. There are plenty of cut-price offers, reviews of the latest books are on display alongside the books (an excellent idea for browsers), and there's a customer comment book.

The Finchley Bookshop
(Faculty Books)
98 Ballards Lane
N3 2DN
Tel: 0181 346 7761
Fax: 0181 343 3659
Mon-Sat 9.30-5.30pm
Tube: Finchley Central

This is a welcoming and attractively laid out bookshop with soothing music in the background and a particularly large children's section offering picture books right through to a young adult range with plenty of non-fiction as well as fiction. Adults are also well catered for with a comprehensive selection across all subject areas, but with especially good sections on travel, computers and reference. The shop also stocks audiobooks and cards.

For Books
58 Cowcross Street
EC1M 6BP
Tel: 0171 336 6533
Mon-Fri 8am-8pm, Sat 9am-5pm
Tube: Farringdon

Opposite the entrance to Farringdon tube station, this shop is packed full of new and second-hand books, all at bargain prices. The range of subjects and books is excellent, encompassing general and more serious titles in fiction, history, travel, philosophy and the social sciences. There's plenty of paperback fiction for around £3 but whatever your area of interest it's well worth a look.

Forbidden Planet
71-75 New Oxford Street
WC1A 1DG
Tel: 0171 836 4179
Mon-Wed, Sat 10am-6pm,
Thurs & Fri 10am-7pm
Tube: Tottenham Court Road

Plenty of book signings, notices about events and bookmarts and quantities of merchandise supplement the huge stock of books (horror, sci-fi, fantasy, graphics and non-fiction) and comics (new and second-hand) spread over two floors. Justifiably a mecca for comic and sci-fi enthusiasts.

Four Provinces Bookshop
244 Gray's Inn Road
WC1X 8JR
Tel: 0171 833 3022
Tues-Sat 11am-4pm
Tube: Chancery Lane, Kings Cross

An Irish bookshop with a small but interesting range of books on all things Irish including history and politics, biography, literature and music and with several courses and aids to learning Irish. There are also plenty of leaflets available advertising events with an Irish flavour.

W & G Foyle Ltd
113-119 Charing Cross Road
WC2H 0EB
Tel: 0171 437 5660
Fax: 0171 434 1580
Mon-Wed, Fri & Sat 9am-6pm
Thurs 9am-6pm
Tube: Tottenham Court Road

Foyles is the largest independent bookshop in London with a massive stock covering all subject areas. It remains an idiosyncratic place to shop, with a rambling lay-out and an unusual payment system as well as a mix of stairs, lifts and escalators to the various floors. Still, in an age of sterile book supermarkets, Foyles remains a wonderful anachronism cherished by many, including Tim Waterstone, whose favourite shop it is.

R D Franks

Kent House
Market Place
Oxford Circus
W1N 8EJ
Tel: 0171 636 1244
Fax: 0171 436 4904
Mon-Fri 9am-5pm
Tube: Oxford Circus
Located in one of London's major garment-manufacturing areas, this shop stocks a huge range of fashion magazines from across the globe and an excellent range of books on every aspect of fashion including design, textiles, technique, cutting and pattern-making. The shop also sells workshop equipment, produces a catalogue and offers a mail order service. Staff will try to get special orders for you on request.

Free Association Books

57 Warren Street
W1P 5PA
Tel: 0171 388 3182
Fax: 0171 388 3187
E-mail: fab@melmouth.demon.co
Tube: Warren Street
This is a specialist publisher dealing primarily in psychoanalysis and psychotherapy but with some additional titles concerning organisational, child and adolescent, cultural and social studies. They produce an annual catalogue and offer a mail order service.

Freedom Press Bookshop

Angel Alley
84b Whitechapel High Street
E1 7QX
Tel: 0171 247 9249
Fax: 0171 377 9526
Mon-Fri 10.30am-6pm, Sat 11am-5pm
Tube: Whitechapel
This anarchist publisher's bookshop is located two doors down from the Whitechapel Art Gallery, in an alleyway off the main road. It has a huge stock of history, sociology, politics and ecology books and magazines but the specialisation is anarchism and there are many titles here that you won't find elsewhere.

The French Bookshop

28 Bute Street
SW7 3EX
Tel: 0171 584 2840
Mon-Fri 8.30am-6pm, Sat 10am-7pm
Tube: South Kensington
Close to the Institute Français this is the place for books in French on pretty much any subject, including dictionaries, language courses and children's books. There are also selections of French newspapers (supplied on the day of publication), magazines (including the French version of the London listings magazine, Time Out) and even French versions of Monopoly and Trivial Pursuit. Bute Street is awash with lovely little patisserie and coffee shops.

French's Theatre Bookshop

52 Fitzroy Street
W1P 6JR
Tel: 0171 255 4300 (sales)
0171 387 9373 (switchboard)
Fax: 0171 387 2161
E-mail: theatre@samuelfrench-london.co.uk
Web: www.samuelfrench-london.co.uk
Mon-Fri 9.30am-5.30pm, Sat 11am-5pm
Tube: Warren Street

This large, well laid out and welcoming shop
(there's plenty of seats for browsing) stocks
scripts (including musicals) and books on
every aspect of theatre and performance art.
The selection encompasses everything from
writing through auditions and improvisation
to performance itself, including guides to
acting, lighting, make-up, costume and stage
management as well as books on the great
figures of the theatre; they also stock CDs of
sound effects. Join the free mailing list for the
twice-yearly 'Parades', a supplement to 'The
Guide to Selecting Plays' (published by
French's), which lists over two thousand
plays for amateur production. French's are
also publishers of play scripts and Samuel
French Ltd (details as above) issue licenses for
public performance of copyrighted plays.
Mail order is available.

French Travel Centre Bookshop

178 Piccadilly
W1V 0AL
Tel: 0171 491 9995
Fax: 0171 491 0600
Mon-Fri 10am-6pm, Sat 10am-5pm
Tube: Piccadilly

A good selection of guidebooks and maps
about France plus cookery, culture, history,
language books, children's titles, videos and
CDs. Conveniently located on the first floor
of the travel centre, a visit here is easily
combined with making reservations or
getting holiday information.

Friends Book Centre

Friends House, Euston Road
NW1 2BJ
Tel: 0171 663 1030
Fax: 0171 663 1001
Tues-Fri 10am-5pm
Tube: Euston

Bookshop operated by the Society of Friends
(Quakers) specialising in books on religion
and theology, pacifism and peace education
(both new and second-hand). The shop also
offers greetings card, and a mail order service.

G

Garden Books

11 Blenheim Crescent
W11 2EE
Tel: 0171 792 0777
Fax: 0171 792 1991
Mon-Sat 9am-6pm
Tube: Ladbroke Grove

Very close to Portobello Road market, selling
new and second-hand books on all aspects of
growing things: garden design, flowers,
flower arranging and pretty much anything
associated with the topic, both here and
abroad. For more general readers there's a
small, quality selection on interior design and
some unusual greetings and post cards. There
is a twice-yearly catalogue, mail order service
and staff are both knowledgeable and helpful.

Gay's the Word

66 Marchmont Street
WC1N 1AB
Tel: 0171 278 7654
Mon-Sat 10am-6.30pm, Sun 2pm-6pm
Tube: Russell Square

A good range of (both fiction and non-
fiction) books of gay and lesbian interest and
some feminist material. Most books are new
but there are some second-hand ones and
good music, cards and posters. There is a
mailing list to keep up to date with the latest
publications and book lists are occasionally
published.

Geographer's A–Z Map Company

44 Gray's Inn Road
WC1X 8HX
Tel: 0171 440 9500
Fax: 0171 440 9501
Mon-Fri 9am-5pm
Tube: Chancery Lane
The London showroom and shop of this
specialised firm famous for town maps, atlases
and plans of parts of Britain and above all
London. There are a few OS maps and plans
by other companies but this is predominantly
an A–Z outlet – the latest offering is the A–Z
of London on CD-Rom.

Stanley Gibbons

399 Strand
WC2R 0LX
Tel: 0171 836 8444
Fax: 0171 836 7342
E-mail: shop@stangiblondon.demon.co.uk
Mon-Fri 8.30am-6pm, Sat 9.30am-5.30pm
Tube: Aldwych, Covent Garden
This famous stamp dealer (the biggest stamp
shop in the world) has a large book section
devoted to the history of postage stamps and
postal systems worldwide, catalogues of
stamps and a selection of books on other
collectable items such as toys, coins,
banknotes and postcards. Mail order is
available and there is an annual reading list of
available titles

George Godber Bookshop (King's Fund)

11-13 Cavendish Square
W1M 0AN
Tel: 0171 307 2591
Fax: 0171 307 2801
Web: www.kingsfund.org.uk
Mon-Fri 9.30am-1pm and 2pm-5pm
Tube: Oxford Circus
The King's Fund is a charity focussing on
health and social care and a specialist
publisher in the same field, with over one
hundred and fifty titles, and a bookshop at
their premises about five minutes walk from

Oxford Street (come out of the back door of
John Lewis and go straight across Cavendish
Square, the shop is rather hidden away down
an alleyway). Health care is the major
emphasis, with a wide range of titles, and not
only those published by the King's Fund.

Golden Square Books

16 The Village
Golden Square
W1R 3AG
Tel: 0171 434 3338 and
0171 434 3337 (mail order)
Fax: 0171 434 3835
E-mail: 100574.3056@compuserve.com
Mon-Fri 10.30am-7pm, Sat 10.30am-6pm
Tube:Piccadilly Circus
This must be the most browser-friendly
bookshop in London with table and chairs, a
coffee and tea machine to buy refreshments
and public toilets on the premises. The shop
specialises in mostly new books (although
there is a second-hand section), on
philosophy, psychology, theology, personal
development and related areas. There are
regular meditation sessions and evening
courses, weekly lectures on a range of
spiritual movements and the related arts and
regular book signings and talks. There are
also plenty of leaflets advertising other
courses and talks of interest in the subject
areas covered by the book stock. Just a short
walk from Regent Street and Piccadilly
Circus, this is a welcome haven from retail
lunacy.

The Golden Treasury

27 Replingham Road
SW18 5LT
Tel: 0181 333 0167
Mon-Fri 10am-6pm, Sat 9.30am-5.30pm
Tube: Southfields
Specialist shop selling new books for children
of all ages from the youngest up to teenage
level in fiction and non-fiction and with a
rang of audiobooks, games and multimedia
material.

Good News Christian
50 Churchfield Road
W3 6DL
Tel/Fax: 0181 992 7123
Mon-Wed, Fri &Sat 9am-5.30pm,
Thurs 9am-7pm
Tube: Acton Town
Christian bookshop covering all aspects of the faith plus a small selection of music on tape and CD.

Good News Shop
654 High Road
Leyton
E10 6RN
Tel: 0181 539 2906
Mon-Sat 9am-6.30pm
Rail: Leyton Midland Road
A shop specialising in Christian literature, music and greetings cards.

Gosh Comics
39 Great Russell Street
WC1B 3PH
Tel: 0171 636 1011
Fax: 0171 436 5053
E-mail: gosh-com@easynet.co.uk
Mon-Wed, Sat & Sun 10am-6pm
Thurs & Fri 10am-7pm
Tube: Tottenham Court Road, Holborn
The ground floor features a huge range of comics (both old and new) in good condition and clearly filed and labelled. Downstairs houses a range of comic books, but a look down here really confirms that there's really no alternative to the magazines themselves.

Grant and Cutler
55-57 Great Marlborough Street
W1V 2AY
Tel: 0171 734 2012
Fax: 0171 734 9272
E-mail: postmaster@grant-c.demon.co.uk
Web: www.grant-c.demon.co.uk
Mon-Wed, Fri & Sat 9am-5.30pm
Thurs 9am-7pm
Tube: Oxford Circus

This is the UK's largest foreign language bookseller: fancy something in Albanian, Setswana, Faroese, Azerbaijani or Korean? – they should have it. With over one hundred and fifty languages covered, from every corner of the globe, you'll have to come up with something pretty obscure to confound the people here. Language courses, dictionaries, foreign language books and some audio materials together make up an impressive stock. A huge variety of catalogues are available free on request and on the shop's web site, and worldwide mail order is available (with postage charged extra). Around fifteen minutes walk from Oxford Circus tube station, just opposite the back door of Marks and Spencer's Oxford Street store.

Grays of Westminster
40 Churton Street
Pimlico
SW1 2LP
Tel: 0171 828 4925
Fax: 0171 976 5783
Mon-Fri 9.30am-5.30pm
Tube: Pimlico
Specialist dealer in new and second-hand Nikon cameras with a small stock of mostly new books about the cameras, their use and their history.

Green Ink Books – The Irish Bookshop
8 Archway Mall
Junction Road
N19 5RJ
Tel: 0171 263 4748
Tues-Sat 10am-6pm
Tube: Archway
In a totally depressing location up a windy, concrete alleyway immediately behind Archway tube station, this shop specialises in books about Ireland and the Irish. It has large selections on literature, history, politics and travel and both English and Irish language books. There are plenty of notices about Irish events and music on tape and CD.

Greens

17 Marylebone High Street
W1M 3PD
Tel: 0171 935 7227
Mon-Fri 9am-6pm
Tube: Baker Street, Bond Street
Despite the unpromising entrance, in this shop beneath a newsagents there is a good selection of general book titles. Most are full price but there are some bargain shelves, as well as a particularly good range of fiction.

Greenwich Book Time

277 Greenwich High Road
SE10 8NB
Tel: 0181 293 0096
and
44 Greenwich Church Street
SE10 9BL
Tel: 0181 293 3902
Daily 10am-7.30pm
Rail: Greenwich
These shops sell a small range of discounted new books, and whilst the range isn't brilliant with everything at just £1, they are always well worth a browse.

Guanghwa

7 Newport Place
WC2H 7JR
Tel: 0171 437 3737
Mon-Sat 10.30am-7pm
Sun 11am-7pm
Tube: Leicester Square
The main floor sells a big range of books in Chinese plus dictionaries and some books in English on popular oriental subjects such as Tai Chi and Feng Shui. Downstairs is a specialist art department with a great range of Chinese art books and all the papers, brushes and inks necessary for Chinese painting.

Guildhall Library Bookshop

Aldermanbury
EC2P 2EJ
Tel: 0171 332 1858
Fax: 0171 600 3384
Mon-Fri 9.30am-4.45pm
Tube: Moorgate
Specialists in new books to do with London.

Highgate Bookshop

H

Hammicks

259 High Street
Walthamstow
E17 7BH
Tel: 0181 521 3669
E-mail: walthamstow@hammicks.co.uk
Mon-Fri 9am-5.30pm, Sat 9am-6pm
Rail: Walthamstow Central

In the midst of the daily Walthamstow market (Thurs, Fri and Sat are the best days), this is a small general shop with plenty of fiction titles but also well-stocked New Age, local history, Black writers, travel, children's and gay and lesbian sections, and lots of greetings cards. Senior citizens are eligible for a 5% discount card.

Other branches at:

Hammicks Legal Bookshop

191-192 Fleet Street
EC4A 2AH
Tel: 0171 405 5711
Fax: 0171 831 9849
E-mail: Fleetstreet@hammicks.co.uk
Mon, Wed & Fri 9am-6pm, Tues 9am-6.30pm
Thurs 9am-7pm, Sat 10am-5pm
Tube: Aldwych

Very close to the Royal Courts of Justice and near the Inns of Court, this specialist bookshop boasts deep pile carpeting, lots of wood panelling and shelves full of fake leatherbound bookcovers. All this combines to create a learned and opulent atmosphere around books which cover every aspect of the law and jurisprudence – there is also a good section on computing. In addition, the shop offers a range of journals and an interesting section of literature which features the law, plus a few cards, prints and gifts suitable for those in the legal profession.

Harrods Children's Book Department

87 Brompton Road
SW1X 7XL
Tel: 0171 225 5721
Fax: 0171 225 5611
Mon, Tues & Sat 10am-6pm
Wed-Fri 10am-7pm, Sun closed
Tube: Knightsbridge

Located on the fourth floor (the main bookshop, Waterstone's is on the second – see p.84), the stock here is vast with all ages catered for with first books up to young adult age supplemented by tapes, videos and stationery. However, this is very clearly a bookshop in which adults buy books for children: shelves are set very high, there are no toys, no small tables or chairs (or big ones for that matter), no area where adults and children can relax and read together and generally very little to induce browsing or to entice junior readers to come in or stay. Sadly, the message seems to be leave the children at home.

Hatchards

187 Piccadilly
W1V 0LE
Tel: 0171 439 9921
Fax: 0171 494 1313
E-mail: 187picc@hatchards.co.uk
Mon, Wed-Sat 9am-6pm
Tues 9.30am-6pm, Sun 12noon-6pm
Tube: Piccadilly Circus

Now taken over by Dillons, this shop, founded by John Hatchard in 1797 – his portrait is on the staircase – retains much of the elderly charm and character that gained it Royal Warrants as booksellers to the Queen, Duke of Edinburgh and Prince of Wales. The shop is full of dark wood, plush carpet and comfortable chairs but is still enviably well stocked, hiding the paperback fiction section away in the basement. Next door is Fortnum and Mason, the high class food emporium that is definitely worth a mouth-watering browse in its own right.

Hayward Gallery Bookshop

South Bank
Belvedere Road
SE1 8XZ
Tel: 0171 960 5210
Gallery: Mon, Thurs-Sun 10am-6pm, Tues &
Wed 10am-8pm – the bookshop closes ten
minutes before the gallery each day
Tube: Waterloo
Featuring an excellent range of modern art
and photography books plus gifts, posters,
cards and stationary in addition to the large
choice of merchandise that accompanies each
current show. Hayward Membership (£20
for under 25's and concessions, £40 for
everyone else) gets you unlimited access to
the gallery. There's also the Aroma café and
reading area – it isn't especially comfortable
but there's always a good range of current art
books available for browsing.

Hebrew Book and Gift Centre

18 Cazenove Road
N16 6BD
Tel: 0171 254 3963
Mon-Thurs 10am-6pm, Fri closed
Sat 10am-2pm
Rail: Stoke Newington
This shop specialises in Hebrew books.

The Hellenic Bookservice

91 Fortress Road
NW5 1AG
Tel: 0171 267 9499
Fax: 0171 267 9498
Mon-Fri 9.30am-6pm, Sat 10am-5pm
Tube: Tufnell Park
This shop specialises in new books related to
Greece: from prehistoric, through classical to
modern times including titles on art,
literature, language and travel. There is also a
large second-hand department.

Helter Skelter

4 Denmark Street
WC2H 8LL
Tel: 0171 836 1151
Fax: 0171 240 9880
Mon-Wed, Fri 10am-7pm
Thurs 10am-8pm, Sat 10am-6pm
Tube: Tottenham Court Road
Well stocked shop featuring a huge range of
books on all genres of modern music, music
journalism and the music business plus some
more general books, and a large variety of
magazines, videos and postcards.

Thomas Heneage Art Books

42 Duke Street
SW1Y 6DJ
Tel: 0171 930 9223
Fax: 0171 839 9223
E-mail: artbooks@heneage.com
Mon-Fri 9.30am-6pm
Tube: Green Park
Top class shop selling a mixture of new and
used books on all aspects of art including
particular painters and all applied arts
worldwide. The stock is huge, with many
items that are unavailable elsewhere.

G Heywood Hill

10 Curzon Street
W1Y 7FJ
Tel: 0171 629 0647
Fax: 0171 408 0286
Mon-Fri 9am-5.30pm , Sat 9am-12.30pm
Tube: Green Park
Located just at the rear of Shepherd Market
off Piccadilly, this is a new, second-hand and
antiquarian bookshop combined. The books
are stacked on tables, reach from floor to
ceiling and spill over every surface – there's a
general stock but with the best coverage in
literature, history, biography, travel and
children's books (the last form a large
department in the basement). This shop was
established in 1936 and retains an old-
fashioned, refined air that makes a visit feel
like a step back in time.

The Highgate Bookshop

9 Highgate High Street
N6 5JR
Tel: 0181 348 8202
Mon-Sat 10am-6pm, Sun 12noon-5pm
Tube: Highgate
On the corner of Bisham Gardens (Waterlow Park is nearby for a pleasant summer walk, and the many charity shops in the High Street are definitely worth a browse), this is a local shop serving a fairly literary part of London. The stock is general but extensive and well laid out and there is plenty of shelf space devoted to the latest titles to keep readers up to date with what is on the market. (This shop is part of the Pipeline Group.)

Hobgoblin

24 Rathbone Place
W1P 1DG
Tel: 0171 323 9040
Mon-Sat 10am-6pm
Tube: Tottenham Court Road
Specialist folk music shop with instruments, tapes, CDs and a big range of printed music including English, Irish and Scottish, plus adverts for instrument tuition.

Holland and Holland

31-33 Bruton Street
W1 8JS
Tel: 0171 499 4411
Fax: 0171 499 4544
Mon-Fri 9.30am-6pm, Sat 10am-5pm
Tube: Bond Street, Piccadilly Circus
Rather hidden away in the basement of a specialist gunsmith and supplier of shooting accessories and country clothing , the bookshop (mostly new books but with some second-hand stock) has a large selection of both guides and fabulous picture books on Africa. There are also sections on hunting and individual accounts of safaris, fishing, guns, wildlife and field sport;. as well as a range of game conservancy publications. Plenty of comfortable chairs are dotted about to accommodate browsers.

Holloway Stationer and Booksellers

357 Holloway Road
N7 0RN
Tel: 0171 607 3972
Mon-Sat 9am-6pm
Tube: Holloway Road
In the main Holloway Road shopping area, this is primarily a stationers but has a small selection of popular fiction and non-fiction mostly in paperback, as well a few reference, dictionary and cookery titles.

Housemans & Porcupine

5 Caledonian Road
Kings Cross
N1 9DX
Tel: 0171 837 4473
Fax: 0171 278 0444
Housemans: Mon-Sat 10am-6.30pm
Porcupine: Mon-Sat 11am-6pm
Tube: Kings Cross
Located in one of the seediest parts of central London, upstairs Housemans has books, stationery and cards with a good selection on politics, current affairs, gay issues, ecology, pacifism and labour. Downstairs, Porcupine has large sections on Trotskyism, Marxism, labour history, fiction, art and media, politics, sociology, psychoanalysis and ethnicity and gender issues.

I

The Imperial War Museum Shop

Lambeth Road
SE1 6HZ
Tel: 0171 416 5000
Fax: 0171 416 5374
Daily 10am-6pm.
Tube: Lambeth North
The shop is inside the museum, for which you have to pay (entry is free after 4.30pm), but if you just want to go to the shop you can tell the clerk in the ticket office who'll admit you without charge. The shop stocks posters, postcards and gifts that relate to the museum's focus on modern warfare.

However, the shop's main emphasis is on learned texts (some of them Imperial War Museum publications) and general interest books that include titles on both world wars, more recent major conflicts, warfare on land, in the sea and air, and poetry, autobiography and fiction that relates to war. The museum is especially engaging in its explanation of the way war impinges on ordinary people and the shop reflects the theme, stocking books on wartime life, fashion and food in Britain.

Index Bookcentre
10-12 Atlantic Road, SW9 8HY
Tel: 0171 274 8342
Mon-Sat 10am-6pm
Tube: Brixton
This is the only remaining Index Bookshop in London now that the Charlotte Street branch has shut down. The shop has a good general stock but specialises in politics and current affairs and has large sections on Black, women's and Green issues as well as gay and lesbian interest. There are also magazines and periodicals and a children's section.

In Focus
8-10 Royal Opera Arcade
Pall Mall, SW1Y 4UY
Tel: 0171 839 1881
Fax: 0171 839 8118
Mon-Fri 10am-5.45pm, Sat 10am-4pm
Tube: Piccadilly Circus
Specialising in binoculars and telescopes, this shop also stocks a comprehensive range of birdwatching books.

Institute of Contemporary Arts Bookshop
Nash House, The Mall
SW1Y 5AH
Tel: 0171 925 2434
Fax: 0171 873 0051
E-mail: info@ica.org.uk
Web: www.ica.org.uk
Mon-Sat 12noon-9pm, Sun 12noon-8pm
Tube: Piccadilly Circus

Founded in 1947 the ICA, is at the cutting edge of contemporary arts in London. The bookshop is small but has an extensive stock on art theory, design, individual artists, film studies, live arts, critical and cultural theory and new technologies together with magazines, periodicals, cards and videos.

Intermediate Technology Bookshop
103-105 Southampton Row
WC1B 4HH
Tel: 0171 436 9761
Fax: 0171 436 2013
E-mail:itpubs@itpubs.org.uk
Web: www.oneworld.org/itdg/publications.html
Mon-Fri 9.30am-6pm, Sat 11am-6pm
Tube:Russell Square
Specialising in intermediate technology, the bookshop sells a huge range of specialist titles on development and related issues, enterprise development, the environment, agriculture and pretty much anything of interest to those wanting to know about environmental issues worldwide and what can be done to help. They also sell cards, magazines and gift items. Catalogues and mail order are available.

International Islamic Dawah Centre
57 Park Road
NW1 6XU
Tel: 0171 724 8099
Fax: 0171 724 7370
Daily 9am-8pm
Tube: Baker Street
Slightly larger than the Al-Noor bookshop opposite (see p.4) and with a huge stock of books about Islam in both Arabic and English. There are also plenty of videos, CDs, tapes and religious and gift items.

NEW BOOKSHOPS

The Islington Green Bookshop
76 Upper Street
N1 0NU
Tel: 0171 359 4699
Fax: 0171 354 9855
Mon-Sat 10am-10pm, Sun 12noon-6pm
Tube: Angel
Just a few doors away from the Screen on the Green cinema, this is a great place to browse before or after a movie and is an example of all that is best in independent bookselling: their stock is selective and well displayed and the staff both knowledgeable and helpful. The shop is especially strong on fiction but also has good history, travel, gender and psychology sections.

Italian Bookshop by Messaggerie
7 Cecil Court
WC2 4EZ
Tel: 0171 240 1634
Tues-Sat 10.30am-6.30pm
Tube: Leicester Square
An excellent stock of books in a wide variety of subjects in Italian but also in English about everything to do with Italy, with a range of dictionaries, language courses, Italian film videos, magazines and children's books.

It is Well
19 Balaam Street
E13 8EB
Tel: 0171 473 2333
Mon-Sat 10am-5pm
Tube: Plaistow
Bookshop stocking titles on all aspects of Christian life plus Christian music and greetings cards.

J

Jambala
247 Globe Road
E2 0JD
Tel: 0181 981 4037
Mon, Thurs-Sat 10.30am-5.30pm
Tues & Wed 10.30am-7pm
Tube: Bethnal Green
Just around the corner from the London Buddhist Centre the books in this fine little bookshop have a serious slant with plenty on Buddhism (there is an excellent selection of magazines), men's and women's studies, self development, mind and body alongside recent bestsellers and a well-selected choice of fiction – overseas fiction is particularly good. Most books are full price but there are a couple of bargain shelves. Don't think of visiting this shop without calling in at The Cherry Orchard vegetarian restaurant next door. If you're from outside the area it's well worth a trip across London just to visit these two spots.

Japan Centre Bookshop
212 Piccadilly
W1V 9LD
Tel: 0171 439 8035
Fax: 0171 287 1082
Mon-Sat 10am-7.30pm, Sun 10am-6pm
Tube: Piccadilly Circus
This shop has books on both the ground and first floor (there's a Japanese food hall in the basement), with an excellent stock of Japanese language titles, magazines and newspapers but also an extensive selection of books in English about Japan covering martial arts, history, Japanese society, business, religion, travel, art and design, as well as Japanese literature in translation. There is an extensive range of Japanese language courses, textbooks and dictionaries as well Japanese CD's and videos.

Jewish Memorial Council Bookshop

25-26 Enford Street
W1H 2DD
Tel: 0171 724 7778
Fax: 0171 706 1710
Mon-Thurs 9.30am-5.30pm, Fri 9.30am until
4pm in summer, 1pm in winter
Tube: Marylebone, Baker Street
New books on every aspect of Jewish
history, religion and culture.

John Jones Art Shop

4 Morris Place
Stroud Green Road, Finsbury Park
N4 3JG
Tel: 0171 281 5439
Mon-Fri 8am-6pm, Sat & Sun 10am-5pm
Tube: Finsbury Park
This is a large complex with a gallery,
framing centre and restoration and
conservation workshop, as well as an art
materials shop. Amidst all this art
equipment, are three bookcases devoted to
techniques in all media including
calligraphy, papercraft and drawing.

John Lewis

278 Oxford Street, W1A 1EX
Tel: 0171 629 7711
Fax: 0171 629 7712
Mon-Wed & Fri 9.30am-6pm
Thurs 10am-8pm, Sat 9am-6pm
Tube: Oxford Circus
Situated on the fifth floor, the book
department's stock is respectable with all
general non-fiction areas covered, plenty of
computer books and a good children's
selection, plus a wide choice of fiction.
However, there isn't a single chair or stool
for browsers, the modern atmosphere of
relaxed bookbuying has unfortunately not
impinged here and the result is a sterile,
unexciting spot in an otherwise brilliant
department store (especially sad as they sell
some of the best sofas in London – a pity
they don't move a few up here).

Joseph's Bookstore

2 Ashbourne Parade
Finchley Road
NW11 0AD
Tel/Fax: 0181 731 7575
Mon-Fri 9.30am-6pm
Sat & Sun 10am-5pm
Tube: Golders Green
(then a bus along Finchley Road)
Ashbourne Parade is on Finchley Road at
the corner of Ashbourne Avenue. The shop
has a good general stock, pleasant
atmosphere, a selection of magazines,
audiobooks and classical music for sale and a
broad range of books of Jewish interest.
There is also a local noticeboard and the
store has recently moved into publishing,
having published their first title at the
beginning of 1998.

Junction Books

Unit 6
The Junction Centre
St John's Hill
SW11 1RU
Tel: 0171 738 9551
Mon-Fri 8.30am-8.15pm
Sat 9.30am-7.15pm, Sun 11.30am-6pm
Rail: Clapham Junction
In the shopping centre attached to Clapham
Junction Station, selling a great range of cards
but also a reasonable selection of new books
with plenty of paperback fiction, history,
politics, philosophy, film, music, sport and
children's titles – mostly full price but with a
few discount bargains as well. The shop is
located a few metres from the station ticket
office, so it's the ideal place to pick up that
last minute read.

K

Karnac Books
118 Finchley Road
NW3 5HT
Tel: 0171 431 1075
Tube: Golders Green
and
58 Gloucester Road
SW7 4QY
Tel: 0171 584 3303
Fax: 0171 823 7743
E-mail: books@karnacbooks.com
Web: www.karnacbooks.com
Mon-Sat 9am-6pm
Tube: Gloucester Road
A largely academic stock concentrating on psychology, psychotherapy, psychoanalysis, gender studies, philosophy and related fields – the company also publishes books and translations in these fields, for which it has an international reputation. A worldwide mail order service is available. Visit whichever shop is most convenient as the stock is similar in both shops.

KDK Gallery
324 Portobello Road
W10 5RU
Tel: 0181 960 4355
Fax: 0181 964 1615
Tube: Ladbroke Grove
A new gallery dedicated to the art of photography and books associated with 1960's pop stars and their music. There are permanent displays of photos, prints and books, plus changing exhibitions.

Keltic Bookshop
25 Chepstow Corner
Chepstow Place
W2 4XE
Tel: 0171 229 8560
Fax: 0171 221 7955
Mon-Fri 10an-5.30pm, Sat 10am-5pm
Tube: Notting Hill Gate
Specialist shop stocking a large range of materials for teaching and learning English including course texts, workbooks, dictionaries, grammar books, tapes and multimedia material for both students and teachers.

Kensington Music Shop
9 Harrington Road
SW7 3ES
Tel: 0171 589 9054
Fax: 0171 225 2662
Mon-Fri 9am-5.30pm,
Sat 9am-4pm
Tube: South Kensington
A small shop (related to Chimes and Barbican) but jammed full of music scores for every instrument, covering every period and style. The shop also stocks books on the history, theory and study of classical music.

Kensington Temple Bookshop
Kensington Temple
Kensington Park Road
Notting Hill Gate
W11 3BY
Tel: 0171 727 4877
Fax: 0171 229 7343
Mon-Fri 10am-6pm, Sat 10am-7pm
Tube: Notting Hill Gate
A large bookshop with books and magazines on all aspects of Christianity.

KICC Bookshop
411A Brixton Road, SW9 7DG
Tel: 0171 733 8333
Mon-Sat 9.30am-6pm
Tube: Brixton
and
1-3 Darnley Road
Off Mare Street, E9 6QH
Tel: 0181 533 0003
Fax: 0181 525 0002
Mon-Sat 9.30am-6pm
Rail: London Fields
Christian bookshops selling a wide range of music, videos and books plus other gift items.

Kilburn Bookshop

8 Kilburn Bridge
Kilburn High Road
NW6 6HT
Tel: 0171 328 7071
Fax: 0171 372 6474
Mon-Sat 10am-6pm
Tube: Kilburn

This excellent local bookshop makes good use of limited space with books attractively displayed and especially good selections of travel guides, fiction and general interest books plus a few literary magazines and cards.

Kirkdale Bookshop

272 Kirkdale
SE26 4RS
Tel: 0181 778 4701
Mon-Sat 9am-5.30pm
Rail: Sydenham

The stock is pretty evenly split between new, second-hand and out of print books with a good selection of modern first editions and antique books with illustrated covers. Second-hand prices are very good, and there is a large 20p bargain selection outside. This is an excellent little local bookshop, which also stocks some audiobooks and cards.

Kiwi Fruits

7 Royal Opera Arcade
Pall Mall, SW1Y 4UY
Tel: 0171 930 4587
Fax: 0171 839 0592
Mon-Fri 9am-5.30pm
Sat 10am-4pm
Tube: Piccadilly Circus

This small shop is full of gifts and souvenirs from New Zealand but also has an excellent range of books. They have plenty of glossy picture books, detailed guidebooks that you won't find anywhere else in London, books about immigration, books of Maori interest and on Maori language and lots of New Zealand literature and children's titles. They also have a good stock of current New Zealand magazines.

Krypton Comics

252 High Road
Tottenham
N15 4AJ
Tel: 0181 801 5378
Fax: 0181 376 3174
Mon-Wed 10am-6pm
Thurs & Fri 9.30am-7pm, Sat 9am-6pm
Tube: Seven Sisters Road

Situated next to Tesco's, this is a specialist comic shop with the usual range of imports and back numbers of major titles.

L

Lambs Legal and Medical Bookshop

21 Store Street
WC1E 7DH
Tel: 0171 580 7632
Fax: 0171 580 8970
E-mail: lambs@globalnet.co.uk
Mon-Fri 9am-6pm, Sat 10am-4pm
Tube: Goodge Street

As the name suggests, this is a specialist shop for medical and legal texts although there is also a stock of books on library science. Books are all new and there are regular catalogues.

LCL International Booksellers

102-104 Judd Street
WC1H 9NF
Tel: 0171 837 0486
Fax: 0171 833 9452
Mon-Fri 9.30am-5.30pm
Sat 10am-2pm
Tube: King's Cross, Russell Square

A specialist language shop with books, dictionaries, language courses and literature in over a hundred languages. The shop also stocks a range of tapes and videos.

Liberty
214-220 Regent Street
W1R 6AH
Tel: 0171 734 1234
Fax: 0171 573 9876
Mail order phone line:
0171 573 9445 (Mon-Fri 9.30am-5.30pm)
Mon-Wed, Fri & Sat 10am-6.30pm
Thurs 10am-8pm, Sun (variable)
Tube: Oxford Circus
This is one of the most characterful shops in London and well worth a visit in its own right. The book department is on the second floor of the Tudor Building, sandwiched between the ABC Café at one end and the art gallery at the other. It sells only non-fiction titles on art and design (including interior design, fashion, textiles, crafts and antiques), cookery and gardening. The atmosphere is brilliant, as is the range of books – fitting for a store that has become famous for its distinctive style since it was established in 1875 as a shop specialising in goods imported from the Orient.

Librairie La Page
7 Harrington Road, SW7 3ES
Tel: 0171 589 5991
Fax: 0171 225 2662
Mon-Fri 8.20am-6pm, Sat 10am-5pm
Tube: South Kensington
Selling a fine range of French cards, books, stationery, videos and magazines, the shop has a selection of dictionaries, language courses and children's books, as well as a noticeboard with local information and adverts. Together with the shop in nearby Bute Street (see p.35), they can provide most French language books.

Lillywhites Ltd
24-36 Regent Street, SW1Y 4QF
Tel: 0171 915 4000
Fax: 0171 930 2330
Mon-Fri 10am-8pm,
Sat 10am-7pm, Sun 11am-5pm
Tube: Piccadilly Circus
This fabulously-stocked specialist sports equipment and clothing shop has a range of books and videos in the relevant departments. Major areas covered are fitness (including running, training, nutrition and body building), golf, football and racket sports.

Linguaphone Language Centre
124-126 Brompton Road
SW3 1JD
Tel: 0171 589 2422
Fax: 0171 584 7052
Mon-Sat 9.30am-5.30pm
Tube: Knightsbridge
Almost opposite Harrods, this shop specialises in the full range of Linguaphone language courses, from the economical travel packs for the major European langauges to the more extensive and expensive starter, intensive, professional and advanced courses which include CD-Rom and video learning as well as the traditional audio techniques. The stock is supplemented by courses from other publishers in languages that Linguaphone does not cover, so tuition in more than fifty languages from Afrikaans to Zulu via Punjabi and Swedish is on offer. There are also children's courses, illustrated dictionaries and CD-Roms in the main European languages and a range of Linguaphone English courses for non-native speakers.

London Buddhist Centre
51 Roman Road
E2 0HU
Tel: 0181 981 1225
Mon 12noon-4.30pm
Tues & Wed 11am-6pm
Thurs & Fri 12noon-5.30pm.
Tube: Bethnal Green
If there are classes in the evening the bookshop is also open late. Run by the excellent Jambala Bookshop around the corner (see p.44), this bookshop has an extensive stock of new books on Buddhism from all traditions.

London City Mission Bookshop

175 Tower Bridge Road
SE1 2AH
Tel: 0171 407 7585
Fax: 0171 403 6711
Mon-Fri 9am-5pm
Tube: Tower Hill or London Bridge

Small selection of books on Christianity and theology plus a few music tapes produced by the mission.

London Transport Museum

39 Wellington Street
WC2 7BB
Tel: 0171 379 6344
Mon-Thurs, Sat & Sun 10am-6pm
Fri 11am-6pm
Tube: Covent Garden

As the museum shop it has plenty of posters, cards and souvenirs on offer, many of them in bold and very attractive designs. It also has a good range of bus, tram and railway books from specialist publishers such as British Bus Publishing, Capital Transport Publishing, Ian Allan and Middleton Press plus a range of fairly esoteric videos, such as 'Central Line – Driver's Eye View'.

London Yacht Centre

13 Artillery Lane
E1 7LP
Tel: 0171 247 2047
Mon-Wed & Fri 9am-5.30pm
Thurs 9am-6pm, Sat 10am-3pm
Tube: Liverpool Street

About five minutes walk from Liverpool Street station, this shop's stock offers everything a sailor needs, from toilets and pumps to compasses and anchors. The ground floor book section includes titles on the technical aspects of sailing, sailing abroad, meterology, construction and painting, racing, history, adventure voyages and literature that features sailing. There is a range of charts including Admiralty, Stanfords and Imray Yachting Charts as well as videos and sailing software.

Lovejoys

99A Charing Cross Road
W1P 9HF
Mon-Sat 10am-10.30pm, Sun 10am-8pm
Tube: Leicester Square, Tottenham Court Road

The ground floor has a good general range of new full price and discounted books in many subjects areas with some good bargains. The adult videos and books are well out of general view in the downstairs basement.

M

Maghreb Bookshop

45 Burton Street
WC1H 9AL
Tel: 0171 388 1840
Opening hours vary, call before visiting
Tube: Euston, Russell Square, King's Cross

This tiny shop specialises in new, rare and out of print books on the Maghreb countries of North Africa (Tunisia, Algeria, Libya, Morocco and Mauritania), the Arab World and Islam. Many of the books are unavailable elsewhere (the shop claims 'here you can find the unfindable'), and they offer a worldwide mail order service.

Manor House Books

80 East End Road
Finchley
N3 2SY
Tel: 0181 349 9484
Fax: 0181 346 7430
Mon-Thurs 9.30-5pm
Fri & Sat closed, Sun 9.30am-1pm
Tube: Finchley Central

Located in the Sternberg Centre, this is a specialist shop selling new books on religion, theology, Judaica and the Middle East. From the same address the proprietor, John Trotter operates a second-hand and antiquarian business specialising in the same areas, but to see these books it is best to ring and arrange an appointment.

Manna Christian Centre

147-149 Streatham High Street
SW16 6EG
Tel: 0181 769 8588
Mon-Sat 9.30am-5.30pm
Rail: Streatham
Christian material including books on
theology, prayer, scripture and the Christian
way of life plus a selection of children's titles.

The Marine Society

202 Lambeth Road
SE1 7JW
Tel: 0171 261 9535
Fax: 0171 401 2537
E-mail: amc@marinesociety.org.uk
Web: www.marinesociety.org.uk
Mon-Fri 9am-5pm
Tube: Lambeth North
This is a highly specialised bookselling service
dealing only in technical titles for seamen
working towards their professional deck and
engineering exams. Most of the business is
mail order with books supplied against
orders, so ring first before visiting.

Maritime Books

23 Nelson Road , SE10 9JB
Tel: 0181 853 1727
Daily 10am-6pm
Rail: Greenwich
A specialist shop stocking a good range of
second-hand and new discounted books on
all things maritime. They stock both British
and overseas, ancient and modern maritime
publications.

Marylebone Books

University of Westminster
Marylebone Road
NW1 5LS
Tel: 0171 911 5049
Fax: 0171 911 5046
E-mail: bookshop@westminstere.ac.uk
Mon-Thurs 9.30-6.30pm
Fri & Sat 9.30am-5.30pm
Tube: Baker Street

Located in the courtyard of the main
University of Westminster campus the shop
stocks only academic books relevant to the
university's courses. They have large sections
on management, human resources, computer
science and life science but their particular
specialities are housing and tourism. There is
also a Marylebone Books at the university's
other campus at Northwick Park in Harrow.

The Meditation Shop

St James Market, off 52 Haymarket
SW1Y 4RP
Tel/Fax: 0171 925 1777
Mon-Fri 11am-7pm, Sat 11am-5.30pm
Sun 12noon-5pm
Tube: Piccadilly Circus
Shop selling gifts, stationery and "everything
you need for a life of peace and harmony".
They stock a lot of volumes on meditation
and spiritual matters and specialise in the
writings of Sri Chinmoy.

Mega-Byte Computer Bookshop

18-19 Aldgate Barrs Shopping Centre, E1 7PJ
Tel: 0171 481 2651
Fax: 0171 481 2652
E-mail: info@megabytebooks.co.uk
Web: www.megabytebooks.co.uk
Mon-Fri 10am-6pm
Tube: Aldgate
A superbly-stocked shop in the underground
shopping complex at the junction of Mansell
Street and Whitechapel High Road. All
aspects of computing are covered, with most
titles discounted by around 10%.

Mega-City Comics

18 Inverness Street, NW1 7HJ
Tel: 0171 485 9320
Mon-Wed, Sat & Sun 10am-6pm
Thurs & Fri 10am-7pm
Tube: Camden Town
Featuring mostly comics: current and back
issues, UK and import. There is also a
selection of books on film, TV and horror.

51

Mencap Bookshop
123 Golden Lane
EC1Y ORT
Tel: 0171 696 5569
Fax: 0171 608 3254
Mon-Fri 9am-5.30pm
Tube: Barbican
A specialist shop stocking a good range of titles on the development, care and education of children and adults with special needs. Stock focusses in particular on mental handicap and includes Mencap's own information packs and leaflets.

Methodist Church Bookshop
25 Marylebone Road
NW1 5JR
Tel: 0171 486 5502
Fax: 0171 935 1507
Mon-Fri 10am-4pm
Tube: Baker Street
Christian bookshop with new books on all aspects of religion and theology plus music, stationery and greetings cards.

Metropolitan Books
64 Exmouth Market
London, EC1
Tel: 0171 278 6900
Open: Mon-Sat 10am-7pm
Tube: Farringdon
This is a wonderful little bookshop selling new books on just about any subject but largely dealing in fiction, art and design and children's titles. The great thing about this shop is the service, with knowledgeable staff and a good ordering system if the book you want isn't in stock. They also have a keenly-priced discount shelf with titles like Ian McEwan's 'Amsterdam' for £10.99 rather than the recommended price of £14.99. Exmouth Market is an up-and-coming area and there are already a lot of cappucino bars in which you can sit and get stuck into your new purchases. There are also several good second-hand bookshops on the street if you want to browse further (see p.98 and p.103).

Mighty World of Comicana 2
237 Shaftesbury Avenue
WC2H 8EH
Tel: 0171 836 5630
Fax: 0171 836 5640
Mon-Wed 10.30am-6.30pm
Thurs-Sat 10am-7pm, Sun 10am-4pm
This incarnation of Comicana (1 is now extinct) is packed full of current and back copies of pretty much any Marvel or DC comic, with prices from 40p upwards.

T Miles and Company Ltd
276 St Paul's Road
Islington
N1 2LH
Tel: 0171 226 3445
Fax: 0171 226 0230
Mon-Fri 9am-5.30pm
Tube: Highbury and Islington
This is an independent shop selling new books with a general stock including all areas of fiction and non-fiction, especially children's, food and drink, gardening and travel.

Military History Bookshop
77-81 Bell Street
NW1 6TA
Tel: 0171 723 2095
Fax: 0171 723 4665
Mon-Fri 10am-5pm, Sat 10am-2pm
Tube: Edgeware Road
Highly specialised shop dealing in new and second-hand books on military history – catalogues are issued every ten to twelve weeks and mail order makes up a large proportion of their business.

Metropolitan Books

The Modern Book Company

19-21 Praed Street
W2 1NP
Tel: 0171 402 9176
Fax: 0171 724 5736
Mon-Wed, Fri 9am-5.30pm
Thurs 9am-7pm, Sat 9am-1pm
Tube: Paddington
Large general bookseller with an extensive
general and academic stock of new books in
all subject areas; catalogues and mail order are
available.

Motor Books

33 & 36 St Martins Court, WC2N 4AL
Tel: 0171 836 6728
Fax: 0171 497 2539
E-mail: 100772.1231@compuserve.com
Mon-Fri 9.30am-6.00pm,
Sat 10.30am-5.30pm, Thurs till 7pm
Tube: Leicester Square
This shop is overflowing with new books,
magazines and videos on motoring, railways,
canals, aviation, naval and military subjects.
There is a catalogue for £1 and mail order.

Multilingual Gallery

228A St Paul's Road
N1 2LJ
Tel: 0171 359 1200
Mon-Thurs 12noon-7pm, Fri 12noon-5pm
Tube: Highbury & Islington
The Multilingual Gallery supplies teachers
for language courses throughout London. At
the centre they have a video-lending library
for their students as well as a second-hand
bookshop which specialises in foreign
language teaching materials and fiction.
French, Spanish, German and Italian are the
most well-represented languages but are by
no means the only ones on offer.

Murder One, New Worlds and Heartlines

71-73 Charing Cross Road
WC2H 0NE
Tel: 0171 734 3483
Mon-Wed 10am-7pm, Thurs-Sat 10am-8pm
Tube: Leicester Square
Specialists in new, remaindered and second-
hand paperback and hardback crime (the
largest section), romance and sci-fi. The
shop has an extensive stock, a free mailing
list, a noticeboard with reviews of books,
hosts signings and readings and also offers a
range of relevant magazines.

The Museum Bookshop

36 Great Russell Street
WC1B 3PP
Tel: 0171 580 4086
Fax: 0171 436 4364
Mon-Fri 10am-5.30pm, Sat 11am-5.30pm
Tube: Tottenham Court Road
A shop specialising in new and second-hand
books in the same subject areas as the
nearby British Museum: archaeology,
Egyptology, the Middle East and
Prehistoric, Medieval and Roman Britian –
the shelves are packed solid. Don't be put
off by the locked door – just go along the
passage to the office at the back and the
shop will be opened up for you.

The Museum of Childhood

Cambridge Heath Road
E2 9PA
Tel: 0181 980 3204
Mon-Thurs 10.30am-5.30pm
Sat 10.15am-1pm and 2pm-5.30pm
Sun 2.30pm-5.30pm
Tube: Bethnal Green Road
This shop located on the ground floor of
the museum has a small selection of new
books on toys, their history and collecting
them – there's a bigger selection in the
Victoria & Albert Museum shop (see p.80),
of which this museum is an offshoot.

The Museum of Garden History Shop

Lambeth Palace Road
SE1 7LB
Tel: 0171 261 1891
Fax: 0171 401 8869
Mon-Fri 10.30am-4pm
Sun 10.30am-5pm, Sat closed
Tube: Lambeth North
The gift shop attached to this specialist
museum features a range of new and second-
hand books on all aspects of gardening,
including 'how to' guides and design and
history titles. They also have a range of cards
and gifts related to the museum.

The Museum of London Shop

London Wall
EC2Y 5HN
Tel: 0171 600 3699
Mon-Sat & Bank Holidays 10am-5.50pm
Sun 12noon-5.50pm
Tube: St Paul's or Barbican
A range of general history books as well as
those concentrating on London from Celtic,
Roman and Viking times up to the present,
with an interesting selection of London-
based fiction and children's books. There is a
good range of old Ordnance Survey maps of
London from the nineteenth century and
some guidebooks, plus plenty of gift and
souvenir ideas for museum visitors.

The Museum of the Moving Image Bookshop

South Bank
SE1 8XT
Tel: 0171 928 3535
Daily: 10.30am-6.30pm
Tube: Waterloo
This is the bookshop and gift shop attached
to MOMI which is in the same building as
the NFT and its dedicated bookshop (see
p.55). Their book stock largely overlaps but
the MOMI shop has a greater range of gift
items, posters, cards and ephemera.
Nonetheless, both shops are worth a visit.

Muslim Bookshop

233 Seven Sisters Road
N4 2DA
Tel: 0171 272 5170
Fax: 0171 272 3214
Mon-Sat 10am-7pm, Sun 11am-6pm
Tube: Finsbury Park
This shop offers a range of halal foods,
traditional clothing and religious items as well
as a mix of books and magazines on Islam
worldwide in both Arabic and English, plus
Arabic language courses and dictionaries.

Mustard Seed

21 Kentish Town Road
NW1 8NH
Tel: 0171 267 5646
Mon-Fri 11.30am-6.30pm
Tube: Camden Town
Specialist Christian bookstore with a large
stock on the Creation and apologetics.

Muswell Hill Bookshop

72 Fortis Green Road
N10 3HN
Tel: 0181 444 7588
Fax: 0181 442 0693
Mon-Sat 9.30am-6pm, Sun 12noon-5pm
Tube: Highgate
In the main Muswell Hill shopping area and
opposite the Children's Bookshop (see p.22),
this double-fronted general shop is extremely

well stocked. It has books in all subject areas plus cards, gift stationery, posters, a community noticeboard, as well as recent book reviews and news kept in a prominent folder. The shop also hosts regular literary events. The people of Muswell Hill are lucky to have this shop on their doorstep.

Mysteries

9-11 Monmouth Street
WC2 H9DA
Tel: 0171 240 3688 or 0171 836 4679
Fax: 0171 240 4845
Mon-Sat 10am-6pm
Tube: Leicester Square
A shop specialising in anything associated with what could loosely be called 'New Age' subjects. It has an excellent range of books covering women's studies and spirituality, yoga, health, diet, Tibetan and Western Buddhism, astrology, mythology, shamanism and magic.

The Mysterious Bookshop

82 Marylebone High Street
W1M 3DE
Tel: 0171 486 8975
Mon-Sat 10.30am-6.30pm
Tube: Bond Street
Stocking a roughly equal mix of new and second-hand crime titles – fiction as well as some true crime – with a good choice of hardbacks as well as paperbacks and hundreds of second-hand books at £3 each. The shop has plenty of seats for browsers, stocks magazines on crime writing and has bags and T-shirts advertising the shop plus some shelves of rare and collectible volumes including Sherlockiana.

N

The National Army Museum Bookshop

Royal Hospital Road
SW3 4HT
Tel: 0171 730 0717
Fax: 0171 823 6573
Daily 10am-5.15pm
Tube: Sloane Square
The museum extensively covers the history of the British army and the life of the soldier from ancient through to modern times; its bookshop stocks volumes dealing with topics across the same spectrum, as well as gift items.

The National Film Theatre Shop

South Bank
Waterloo
SE1 8XT
Tel: 0171 928 3535
Daily 10am-9pm
Tube: Waterloo
For anyone with an interest in cinema this shop is a 'must see'. They stock an excellent range of books, magazines, videos and cards illustrating all aspects and eras of film and media, including technical and production stages as well as the appreciation and criticism of the finished product.

The National Gallery

Trafalgar Square
WC2N 5DN
Tel: 0171 839 3321 (switchboard)
Bookshop: 0171 747 2870
Mon & Tue, Thurs-Sat 10am-5.30pm
Wed 10am-8.30pm
Sun 12noon-5.30pm
Tube:Charing Cross

It's worth remembering that the shop shuts thirty minutes before the gallery itself so don't leave a visit to the shop too late. There are two shops in the gallery, a small one called the Room Three Shop in the older part of the building and a much larger, better-stocked one in the Sainsbury Wing. At least half of this shop is taken up with a brilliant selection of postcards, greetings cards, stationery (this is the place to get your 'The Sunflowers' notebook or ruler) and souvenirs including ties, silk scarves, ceramics and T-shirts. The range of books is also excellent, including guides to the collection, exhibition catalogues and gift books, with a large section on individual artists, art history, conservation, art theory, museum studies, architecture and sculpture.

National Map Centre

22-24 Caxton Street
SW1H 0QU
Tel: 0171 222 2466
Fax: 0171 222 2619
E-mail: info@mapsnmc.com
Mon-Fri 9am-6pm
Tube: St James's Park

Specialising in the full range of Ordnance Survey maps, plans and books, there is also a huge stock of worldwide maps and guidebooks spread over two floors. The shop is located just a few minutes from the passport office in Petty France.

The National Portrait Gallery Shop

St Martin's Place
WC2 0HE
Tel: 0171 306 0055
Mon-Sat 10am-6pm
Sun 12noon-6pm
Tube: Leicester Square

This refurbished basement bookshop has a good selection of art, history, costume, biography and photography books. Next door is a huge gift shop were you can find a great selection of post cards from the gallery's collection and some less conventional gifts.

The National Theatre Bookshop

Royal National Theatre
South Bank
SE1 9PX
Tel: 0171 452 3333
Mon-Sat 10am-10.45pm
Tube: Waterloo

At foyer level in the Royal National Theatre complex this shop concentrates on books, magazines and scripts covering all aspects of the British theatre from ancient to modern times. There is also some fiction, reference books on related subjects such as cinema and music as well as a range of cards.

J G Natural History Books

17 Streatham Vale
SW16 5SE
Tel/Fax: 0181 764 4669
E-mail: jgbooks@btinternet.com
Web: www.cyberzone.co.uk/jgbooks/jgbooks.htm
Mon & Tues, Thurs & Fri
10am-1pm and 2.30pm-6pm
Wed closed, Sat 10am-6pm
Rail: Streatham Common

This shop, situated next door to a pet shop selling reptiles and amphibians, specialises in new and second-hand books about these creatures plus some on gemmology (the study of gems). They claim to have the largest stock of reptile books in the UK and their catalogue runs to seventeen pages. It's worth noting that they do not carry a general natural history stock.

The Natural History Museum Bookshop

Cromwell Road
SW7 5BD
Tel: 0171 938 9063
Fax: 0171 938 8880
Mon-Sat 10am-5.50pm, Sun 11am-5.50pm
Tube: South Kensington

Located near but separate from the gift shop in the bowels of the museum, to get into the bookshop you sign the book at reception and get a specially-coloured sticker indicating you haven't paid to visit the rest of the displays. There are sections on all areas relevant to the museum including evolution, dinosaurs, ecology and conservation, gardening, geology and the whole of the plant and animal kingdoms, although apart from the selection of Natural History Museum publications (both academic and popular), you are unlikely to find anything here you couldn't buy elsewhere.

Neal Street East

5 Neal Street
WC2H 9PU
Tel: 0171 240 0135
Mon-Wed 11am-7pm, Thurs-Sat 10am-7pm
Sun & Bank Holidays 12noon-6pm
Tube: Covent Garden

The shop specialises in items imported from the East, and is a brilliant place to just browse amongst gorgeous things or find that unusual gift item. They also carry a large and eclectic stock of books relating to Asia, including travel guides and writing and books on Asian textiles, cookery, religions (especially Buddhism), meditation and medicine plus specialised sections on Japanese culture, origami, bonsai and ikebana (flower arranging), Feng Shui and Chinese calligraphy and brush painting (the materials are available here also). There's a great mix of specialist and more general books, plenty of them gorgeous coffee table items. Highly recommended for anyone with an interest in the East.

Neals Yard Remedies

15 Neal's Yard
Covent Garden
WC2H 9DP
Tel: 0171 379 7222
Mon 10am-6pm, Tues-Fri 10am-7pm
Sat 10am-5.30pm, Sun 11am-5pm
Tube: Covent Garden

As well as selling natural toiletries and a huge range of oils in their signature blue glass bottles, Neal's Yard also stock an excellent range of books on aromatherapy, natural and alternative remedies, flower therapy, homeopathy, diet and nutrition and women's health. It's a great place to visit for those with an interest in homeopathic treatment.

New Beacon Books

76 Stroud Green Road
N4 3EN
Tel: 0171 272 4889
Fax: 0171 281 4662
Mon-Sat 10.30am-6pm
Tube: Finsbury Park

Long-established and highly experienced specialist sellers of new books on Black Britian and Europe, Africa, the Caribbean and African America plus plenty of titles on Asia, the Middle East and South America. Both fiction and non-fiction titles are stocked and there is a great children's section reflecting the overall emphasis of the shop. The staff are highly knowledgeable, can produce specialist book lists to cater for individual interests, publish monthly lists of new books and have a worldwide mail order service. Greetings cards and magazines are also in stock.

Newham Parent Centre Bookshop

745-747 Barking Road
E13 9ER
Tel: 0181 552 9993 or 0181 472 2000
Fax: 0181 471 2589
Tues-Fri 9.30am-5pm, Sat 10am-5pm
Tube: Upton Park

Brilliant local shop next to Newham Parents Centre with an excellent general stock, including sections on history, sociology, education, business, multi-ethnic issues and politics plus a range of political, art and environmental magazines. The children's section takes up about half the shop with loads of educational books and games as well as welcoming little chairs for small visitors. This is an excellent local resource.

New Revelation Pentecostal Church

151 Deptford High Street
SE8 3NU
Tel: 0181 469 2113
Mon-Sat 10am-7pm
Rail: Deptford

Christian bookshop attached to the Pentecostal church in the heart of Deptford market, stocking a range of religious books.

Nomad Books

791 Fulham Road
SW6 5DH
Tel: 0171 736 4000
Fax: 0171 736 9454
Mon-Fri 9am-8pm, Sat 10am-6pm
Sun 11am-5pm
Tube: Parsons Green

The downstairs section of this shop specialises in travel with an excellent selection of guidebooks, maps and travel literature and a comfortable sofa on which to enjoy them. Upstairs is a more general bookshop which is especially good on art, design, gardening and cookery and has a big children's section at the rear. There is a regular reading group (phone for details).

OCS Bookshop

2 Grosvenor Parade
Uxbridge Road
W5 3NN
Tel: 0181 992 6335
Fax: 0181 993 0891
Tues-Sun 10am-6pm
Tube: Ealing Common

This shop specialises in books, magazines and newspapers in Japanese plus courses and dictionaries for Japanese language learners and books in English about Japan.

Offstage

37 Chalk Farm Road
NW1 8AJ
Tel: 0171 485 4996
Mon-Sat 10am-6pm
Tube: Chalk Farm

A specialist film and theatre bookshop with a huge range of books on all aspects of both media including, drama history and criticism, costume, design, scripts, physical theatre and dance, direction, animation and production. There is a second-hand department downstairs with a big stock of old programmes and a good selection of specialist magazines and greetings cards. There's also a notice board advertising local events, services and workshops and classes of interest.

Olive Tree

27 North Mall
Edmonton Green
N9 0EQ
Tel: 0181 807 9224
Fax: 0181 364 0221
Mon-Sat 9am-5.30pm
Rail: Edmonton Green

In the precinct opposite Edmonton Green station, specialising in Christian books and stocking cards, music, videos and stationery.

Orbis Bookshop

66 Kenway Road
Earl's Court
SW5 0RD
Tel: 0171 370 2210
Fax: 0181 742 7686
Mon-Fri 10am-5.30pm, Sat 10am-4.30pm
Tube: Earls Court

This shop is a specialist in Polish books, magazines and newspapers, and stocks dictionaries as well as books about Russia and the Former Soviet Union, Poland and Central and Eastern Europe.

Ottakar's

This nationwide chain (winners of the Chain Bookseller of the Year 1997 at the British Book Awards), has branches from Aberdeen to Yeovil but only three in London. Their hallmark is welcoming, attractive shops with lots of easy chairs, good music, excellent, well-displayed stock and usually a special offer of some sort on the go.

Branches at:

6-6a Exchange Centre
Putney
SW15 1TW
Tel: 0181 780 2401
Fax: 0181 780 0861
Mon-Wed, Fri & Sat 9am-6pm
Thurs 9am-7pm, Sun 11am-5pm
Tube: Putney Bridge

A large branch with plenty of browsing chairs, good stock well-selected and displayed and a children's area. The shopping centre itself is pleasant and attractive with places to get a coffee and a good range of shops.

61-63 St Johns Road
SW11 1QX
Tel: 0171 978 5844
fax: 0171 978 5855
Mon-Wed, Fri 9am-7pm
Thurs 9am-8pm, Sat 9am-6pm
Rail: Clapham Junction

This branch has a big children's section but also a good range of books covering history, cookery, gardening and fiction plus an attractive selection of greetings cards.

Ottakar's at the Science Museum

Exhibition Road
SW7 2DD
Tel: 0171 938 8255
Fax: 0171 581 2899
Mon-Sun 10am-6pm
Tube: Knightsbridge

Selling a range of new books (mostly full price, but with a few sale bargains) on all areas covered by the museum, with an especially large choice of Science Museum publications and books on the history and philosophy of science. About half of the shop is taken up with children's books and educational materials and there is a big selection of CD-Roms. Regular lectures at the museum by authors of current publications are organised. The shop is beyond the gift shop, which is also worth a browse for some great gifts and souvenirs for both adults and children.

Owl Bookshop

211 Kentish Town Road
NW5 2JU
Tel: 0171 485 7793
Fax: 0171 267 7765
Mon-Sat 9.30am-6pm
Tube: Camden Town, Kentish Town

This is a justifiably popular local shop selling new books. It is well stocked and there are good selections in every fiction and non-fiction area with some tempting special offers. Children's books are a particular strength, the shop is welcoming and child-friendly and there are regular readings and events.

P

Padre Pio Bookshop

264 Vauxhall Bridge Road
SW1V 1BB
Tel: 0171 834 5363
Mon-Sat 10am-5.30pm
Tube: Victoria

Catholic bookshop selling Bibles and prayer books as well as theological books and some religious gift items.

Pan Bookshop

158-162 Fulham Road
SW10 9PG
Tel: 0171 373 4997
Fax: 0171 370 0746
Mon-Fri 9.30am-9.30pm, Sat 10am-10pm
Sun 11am-9pm
Tube: South Kensington

A previous winner of The Independent Bookseller of the Year award at the National Book Awards, this shop is conveniently located just near the Virgin Fulham Road cinema and has a brilliant general stock (don't get misled by the name, they stock a lot more than just Pan books). The displays are enticing, staff are knowledgeable and it's unfair to pick out a particular subject area as all are well covered. However, the art and design sections are particularly broad whilst the children's corner is full of things to lure junior browsers into reading. There are plenty of coffee shops in the area in which to relax with your purchases – Cornerstones, 178 Fulham Road, is a few minutes west towards Fulham and has excellent coffee and a laid-back atmosphere.

Parliamentary Bookshop

12 Bridge Street
SW1A 2JA
Tel: 0171 219 3890
Mon-Thurs 9.30am-5.30pm
Fri 9am-4pm
Tube: Westminster

Right opposite the Houses of Parliament and specialising in official parliamentary publications but also stocking a range of material on current affairs and politics.

Pathfinder Bookshop

47 The Cut
SE1 8LL
Tel: 0171 401 2409
Mon 4pm-6pm Tues-Thurs 5pm-7pm,
Fri closed, Sat 10am-6pm
Tube: Waterloo

This shop is located around the corner from the Old Vic theatre and opposite the Young Vic (the café/bar in here is well worth a visit). It's a radical bookshop stocking titles that describe the revolutionary struggles of people throughout the world with large sections on liberation movements, Marx, Trotsky and Lenin. They also stock current and back copies of 'New International – A Magazine of Marxist Politics and Theory'. If you join the Pathfinders Readers Club (details from the shop) you get at least 15% discount on all Pathfinder titles.

PC Bookshop

11, 19 & 21 Sicilian Avenue
WC1A 2QH
Tel: 0171 831 0022
Fax: 0171 831 0443
E-mail: orders@pcbooks.demon.co.uk
Web: www.pcbooks.co.uk
Mon-Fri 9.30am-6pm, Sat 10.30am-4.30pm
Tube: Holborn
and
34 Royal Exchange
Threadneedle Street
EC3V 3LP
Tel: 0171 621 0888
Mon-Fri 8.30am-6pm
Tube: Bank

Specialist shop selling books on every aspect of computers including programming, graphics, databases, operating systems, desktop publishing and the Internet, both in relation to PC and Apple Mac hardware. If you are searching for the latest book on any software programme this is the shop to visit. As you might expect they also run an excellent on-line service.

Photographer's Gallery Bookshop

5 & 8 Great Newport Street
WC2H 7HY
Tel: 0171 831 1772
Fax: 0171 240 0591
Mon-Sat 11am-6pm, Sun 12noon-6pm
Tube: Leicester Square

This small shop at the back of the gallery (admission is free and there are always worthwhile exhibitions) stocks an impressive range of photographic monographs and anthologies plus plenty of technical and theory books, a range of magazines and some interesting art postcards.

The Pitshanger Bookshop

141 Pitshanger Lane
W5 1RH
Tel/Fax: 0181 991 8131
Mon-Fri 9.30am-6pm, Sat 9am-6pm
Sun 11am-2pm
Tube: Ealing Broadway (then a bus)
Located next to the public library this shop has a good range of fiction and non-fiction in hardback and paperback. They also have greetings cards and gift stationery, audiobooks and a selection of classical music.

Platinum Age Comics/
Bayswater Books

27A Craven Terrace
Lancaster Gate
W2 3EL
Tel: 0171 402 7398
Daily 11am-7pm
Tube: Lancaster Gate
Specialist comic shop with current and back issues plus a general selection of second-hand books.

Playin' Games

33 Museum Street
WC1A 1LH
Tel: 0171 323 3080
Mon-Sat 10am-6pm
Sun 12noon-4pm
Tube: Tottenham Court Road
Shop selling all the equipment for a huge range of both popular and obscure board and indoor games, and an excellent selection of related books.

PMS Bookshop

240 King Street
W6 0RF
Tel/Fax: 0181 748 5522
Mon-Thurs, Sat 10am-6pm
Fri 10am-7pm
Tube: Hammersmith
Located in the Polish Centre, the shop specialises in Polish books, tapes and CDs, videos and magazines. There are also language courses and dictionaries for those who want to learn Polish and books in English about Poland.

Politico's

8 Artillery Row
SW1P 1RZ
Tel: 0171 828 0010
Fax: 0171 828 8111
E-mail: politicos@artillery-row.demon.co.uk
Web: www.politicos.co.uk
Mon-Fri 9am-6.30pm, Sat 10am-6pm
Sun 11am-5pm
Tube: Victoria, St James's Park
Located between the Houses of Parliament and Victoria Station, this must be the only bookshop in London with two televisions broadcasting live coverage of the proceedings in Parliament. Specialising in both new and second-hand political books there is a huge stock covering every aspect of the subject, with titles ranging from the extremely serious to the more light-hearted – here you can find volumes such as 'Guide to the House of Commons', 'Be Your Own Spin Doctor' and 'A Day in the Life of Humphrey the Downing Street Cat'. In addition to books there are gift items, political photographs, autographs, postcards and ephemera and there's an excellent coffee shop on the balcony upstairs.

Pollock's Toy Museum

1 Scala Street
W1P 1LT
Tel: 0171 636 3452
Mon-Sat 10am-5pm
Tube: Goodge Street

The shop attached to this small museum is both a toy shop, with an interesting range of traditional toys, and a bookshop with titles on the history of toys and collecting, and a huge array of the toy theatres (cardboard cut-outs) for which Benjamin Pollock was famous.

Popular Book Centre

87 Rochester Row
SW1P 1LJ
Tel: 0181 541 3761
Fax: 0181 569 6293
Mon 10am-5.30pm,
Tues-Thurs 9.30am-5.30pm, Fri 9.30am-6pm
Sat 9.30am-3.45pm
Tube: Victoria

Popular, long-standing London chain with a large selection of mostly popular fiction but with some non-fiction and literary fiction titles as well. There are loads of magazines from serious titles like the 'New Yorker' and 'History Today' through popular, mainstream titles to 'girlie' mags, discreetly hidden at the back. They offer 50% credit on books returned in good condition.

Portobello Bookshop

328 Portobello Road
W10 5RU
Tel: 0181 964 3166
Mon-Thurs 11am-6pm, Fri & Sat 9am-6pm
Tube: Notting Hill Gate

Right at the far north end of Portobello Road, this shop has an excellent stock covering every subject but is especially good in art, photography, craft, design and architecture, history, Black studies and overseas topics, especially those related to China and Japan. There is a good paperback fiction area and pleasant classical music on the radio adds to the welcoming atmosphere.

Primrose Hill Books

134 Regent's Park Road
NW1 8XL
Tel: 0171 586 2022
Fax: 0171 722 9653
E-mail: primrose@netcomuk.co.uk
Mon-Sat 10am-6.30pm, Sun 11am-6pm
Tube: Chalk Farm

An excellent little gem in a quiet and very smart local shopping area. Upstairs is a huge general range of new books with a good well-displayed hardback and paperback stock; fiction, travel and biography are especially well represented. On shelves outside and in the basement, second-hand books are on sale – there's a very good quality stock across all subjects including fiction (hardback and paperback), travel, art, and architecture. A wonderful little bookshop.

Arthur Probsthain

41 Great Russell Street
WC1B 3PL
Tel/Fax: 0171 636 1096
Mon-Fri 9am-5.30pm, Sat 11am-4pm
Tube: Holborn

This specialist in books on Oriental and African subjects and relevant language courses has both new and second-hand stock. The shop issues five catalogues each year covering the different subject areas (they list both new and forthcoming books of interest and a selection of the second-hand material). They have plenty of books here that you'll find nowhere else, making this shop essential for people seriously interested in studying these parts of the world.

Prospero's Books

32 The Broadway
Crouch End
N8 9SU
Tel: 0181 348 8900
Fax: 0181 348 3604
Mon-Sat 9.30am-6.30pm,
Sun 11.30am-5.30pm
Rail: Crouch Hill
Small, but excellent general shop selling new
books, very close to the Clock Tower in the
main shopping street. It's cosy and
welcoming and despite not being very big,
manages to stock a good selection of titles.
The stock is especially strong in art and
design, travel, health, religion, psychology
and fiction.

Protestant Truth Society Bookshop

184 Fleet Street
EC4A 2HJ
Tel: 0171 405 4960
Mon-Fri 9.30am-5.30pm
Tube: Aldwych
Christian bookshop featuring a large selection
of religious books including theology, the
sermons of eminent preachers and
inspirational works. There is also a range of
children's books plus greetings cards, music
and videos.

Q

QBS Asian Bookshop

112 Whitfield Street
W1P 5RU
Tel: 0171 387 5747
Fax: 0171 388 2662
Mon- Fri 10am-6pm, Sat 11am-5pm
Tube: Warren Street
This shop specialises in books from and
about India (there are a few on other parts of
South Asia) in Hindi, Punjabi, Tamil, Marati
and Gujerati. There is also a large selection
of books in English on all aspects of the
subcontinent and a selection of language
courses, dictionaries. and tapes and CDs.

R

Rare Camera Co

18-20 Bury Place
WC1A 2JL
Tel: 0171 405 8858
Mon-Sat 9am-5.30pm
Tube: Holborn
With a very small stock of books about
particular models of camera, this isn't a place
to browse (there are no general books about
photographic technique). It is however a
good place to visit if you need a book about
a specific camera.

Rathbone Books

76 Haverstock Hill
NW3 2BE
Tel: 0171 267 2848
Fax: 0171 267 1810
E-mail: books@rathbonebooks.co.uk
Web: www.rathbonebooks.com
Mon-Fri 10am-5pm, Sat 10am-1pm
Tube: Chalk Farm, Belsize Park
This is a specialist shop for psychology,
psychoanalysis and psychotherapy books.
Currently all stock is new but there are plans
for a second-hand section. They publish
three or four catalogues each year.

RCOG

27 Sussex Place
·NW1 4RG
Tel: 0171 772 6275
Fax: 0171 724 5991
Mon-Fri 9am-5pm
Tube: Baker Street
Specialist medical bookshop for the Royal
College of Obstericians and Gynaecologists,
with an emphasis on all aspects of healthcare
for women.

Reads Books

4 George Street
W1H 4RA
Tel/Fax: 0171 486 5650
Mon-Sat 10am-6.30pm
Sun 10am-1pm
Tube: Bond Street

A small local bookseller about ten minutes walk from Oxford Street. There is a good selection in both fiction and non-fiction areas and an excellent range of good value greetings cards.

Regent Bookshop

73 Parkway, NW1 7PP
Tel: 0171 485 9822
Mon-Sat 9am-6.30pm, Sun 12noon-6pm
Tube: Camden Town

General bookstore selling new books and greetings cards which often has special offers.

RICS Bookshop

12 Great George Street
SW1P 3AD
Tel: 0171 222 7000 (ask for London bookshop)
Fax: 0171 222 9430
Web: www.rics.org.uk (e-mail addresses for RICS departments are listed on the site)
Mon-Fri 9.30am-5.30pm
Tube: Westminster

Specialist shop selling books related to the theory and practice of chartered surveying including building, architecture, business, management, engineering, surveying and law. A general catalogue is available (check the web site) as is a mail order service. The shop is located at reception level in the Royal Institute of Chartered Surveyors.

Riverside Bookshop

18/19 Hay's Galleria
Tooley Street
SE1 2HN
Tel: 0171 378 1824
Fax: 0181 314 5966
Mon-Fri 9am-6pm
Tube: London Bridge

Hay's Galleria is a large, airy shopping and restaurant complex on the bank of the River Thames. Its bookshop has a well-displayed, carefully chosen selection of books across the general subject areas and a friendly team of helpful staff.

Riverside Bookshop

49 Shad Thames
Butler's Wharf
SE1 2NJ
Tel: 0171 403 3730
Mon-Fri 9.30am-6pm, Sat 10am-6.30pm
Sun 11am-6.30pm
Tube: Tower Hill, London Bridge

Branch of the Hay's Galleria shop (see above) with a similarly broad and well-chosen stock but located in the heart of Shad Thames which is an area of London well worth exploring.

The Rocks

46-62 Tower Bridge Road
SE1 4TL
Tel: 0171 394 3442
Mon-Wed 9.30am-6pm, Thurs 9.30am-7pm
Fri & Sat 9.30am-8pm
Tube: Elephant & Castle (then a bus)

A few hundred metres north of the New Kent Road/Old Kent Road junction with a large range of Christian books, audio material and greetings cards.

Roundabout

370 Mare Street
E8 1HR
Tel: 0181 985 8148
Mon-Fri 9am-6pm, Sat 8am-7.30pm
Rail: Hackney Central

This shop is a newsagents and stationers as well as a bookseller. The range is general with plenty of popular fiction and non-fiction and some school and college texts.

The Royal Academy Shop

Royal Academy of Arts
Burlington House
W1V 0DS
Tel: 0171 300 8000
Fax: 0171 300 8001
Mon-Thurs, Sat & Sun 10am-5.45pm
Fri 10am-8.15pm
Tube: Piccadilly Circus
This small shop is at the top of the grand
staircase of the entrance hall – there is no
admission fee to this part of the building. The
shop has books on art technique and the
work of individual artists alongside catalogues
of exhibitions (look out for reductions on
previous shows) and periodicals on art.
Alongside the books there are plenty of gifts
and cards.

Ruposhi Bangla

220 Tooting High Street
SW17 0SG
Tel: 0181 672 7843
Fax: 0181 767 9214
E-mail: ruposhi.bangla@btinternet.com
Mon-Sat 10am-5.30pm
Tube: Tooting Broadway
This is a specialist shop for Bengali books
(including children's), music, posters, maps
and videos. The shop also stocks things
related to Bangladesh including artifacts
(which make lovely gifts) and Bengali
language courses. Bengali software for IBM
and Apple computers is available as are books
in Bengali on learning English and lists of
publications from both India and Bangladesh.

S

St James's Art Books

15 Piccadilly Arcade
SW1Y 6NH
Tel: 0171 495 6487
Fax: 0171 495 6490
Mon-Fri 10am-6pm, Sat 10am-5pm
Tube: Piccadilly Circus, Green Park
Located in a small arcade of shops just around
the corner from Fortnum and Mason, this
shop is occupied by two booksellers and a
dealer in modern and twentieth century
prints. One of the booksellers specialises in
Old Masters, Islamic and Oriental Art whilst
the other has mostly titles on twentieth
century art. The shop has a mixture of new,
second-hand and rare books – the selection is
floor-to-ceiling and extensive, making the
shop well worth a visit.

St Paul's Cathedral Shop

The shop is in the crypt, with the entrance
on the north side of the cathedral. Whilst this
is certainly the place to go for a guidebook
about the cathedral (in French, German and
Japanese in addition to English), the selection
of other books is very small.

St Paul Multimedia

199 Kensington High Street
W8 6BA
Tel: 0171 937 9591
Fax: 0171 937 9910
E-mail: St.Paul@dial.pipex.com
Tube: High Street Kensington
Christian bookshop with a huge range of
books, CDs, videos and tapes. The books
cover all areas of Christan theology, scripture,
liturgy and prayer as well as everyday issues
from a Christian perpsctive. There is a large
children's selection and also some books on
world religions.

St Paul's Multimedia

Morpeth Terrace
SW1P 1EP
Tel: 0171 828 5582
Fax: 0171 828 3329
E-mail:
stpaulsbywestminstercathedral@ukbusiness.com
Web: www.ukbusiness.com/
stpaulsbywestminstercathedral
Mon-Sat 9.30am-6pm
Tube: Victoria

Next door to Westminster Cathedral, the stock in this shop is vast. In what must be one of the largest religious bookshops in London, every aspect of Christianity for both the lay reader and serious student is covered. They also stock a huge range of videos, tapes, CD's, greetings cards and gift items.

Salvationist Bookshop

117-121 Judd Street
WC1H 9NN
Tel: 0171 387 1656
Fax: 0171 383 3420
Mon-Fri 8.45am-4.30pm
Sat 9am-12.30pm
Tube: Russell Square

Christian bookshop specialising in material published by and for the Salvation Army and including Bibles, prayer books and books for children including early picture books and recorded music and videos.

John Sandoe Books

10 Blacklands Terrace
SW3 2SR
Tel: 0171 589 9473
Fax: 0171 581 2084
Mon & Tue, Thurs-Sat 9.30am-5.30
Wed 9.30am-7.30pm
Tube: Sloane Square

This shop is all that is best in independent bookshops and proves outlets don't have to be huge to carry a big stock. This tiny three storey shop, just fifty metres from the Kings Road, is packed solid with a brilliant range of literature, arts, architecture, history,

biography, reference, travel, drama and children's books with plenty of unusual editions and books you're unlikely to find elsewhere. The owners are incredibly well-informed and welcoming and despite the danger of dislodging piles of books at every turn (have a look at the ingenious display system upstairs to make the most of every inch) this place is well-worth a visit.

Schotts

48 Marlborough Street
W1V 2BN
Tel: 0171 437 1246
Mon-Fri 9am-5.30pm
Tube: Oxford Circus

Music publisher with a huge range of classical sheet music for all instruments and standards. The shop also has tutor's notices and some CD's on sale.

Selfridges

400 Oxford Street
W1A 1AB
Tel: 0171 629 1234
Fax: 0171 495 8321
Mon-Wed 10am-7pm, Thurs & Fri 10am-8pm,
Sat 9.30am-7pm, Sun 12noon-6pm
Tube: Oxford Circus
Located in the basement next to the crockery, this is an extensive department with a large, well-displayed stock and a few discounted titles. All fiction and non-fiction areas are covered, the paperback fiction is especially extensive and computing and business books supplement the more general non-fiction stock. The travel section is very broad and there are plenty of attractive glossy art, design, gardening and food titles. There are also a good many chairs for comfy browsing.

Serpentine Gallery

Kensington Gardens
W2 3XA
Tel: 0171 298 1502
Fax: 0171 402 4103
E-mail: bookshop@serpentinegallery.org
Daily 10am-6pm
Tube: South Kensington, Lancaster Gate
The gallery is located in the heart of Kensington Gardens and specialises in modern and contemporary art. The bookshop compliments the gallery with books concerning modern art theory, criticism and monographs, modern philosophy, media and cultural studies and a selection of artists' books. Most North American University Press titles are in stock as well as an extensive range of art and cultural journals. The bookshop often hosts readings and events.

The Sherlock Holmes Memorabilia Company

230 Baker Street
NW1 5RT
Tel: 0171 486 1426
Fax: 0171 935 0522
E-mail: sales@shmc.demon.co.uk
Web: www.sh-memorabilia.co.uk
Mon-Fri 9.30am-5.30pm,
Sat 10am-5pm, Sun 11am-4pm
Tube: Baker Street
This shop has books by Conan Doyle and others about his creation Sherlock Holmes.

Shipley

70 Charing Cross Road
WC2H 0BB
Tel: 0171 836 4872
Fax: 0171 379 4358
E-mail: artbook@compuserve.com
Web: www.artbook.co.uk
Mon-Sat 10am-6pm
Tube: Leicester Square
A specialist art bookseller with a shop packed full of new and second-hand books on every aspect of art, design, photography and fashion plus magazines and exhibition catalogues. Offers an international mail order service.

Silver Moon Women's Bookshop

68 Charing Cross Road, WC2H 0BB
Tel: 0171 836 6848
Fax: 0171 379 1018
Mon-Wed, Fri & Sat 10am-6.30pm
Thurs 10am-8pm, Sun 12noon-6pm
Tube: Leicester Square
Europe's largest women's bookshop specialises in new books about and by women and has a good range of cards, T-shirts and other gift items. Male customers are welcome but are requested not to browse among the lesbian books which are discreetly placed downstairs (where there is also an excellent noticeboard – women's adverts only). 'Silver Moon Quarterly' is published every three months listing a selection of the books on offer and mail order details.

Sims Reed

43a Duke Street
St James's
SW1Y 6DD
Tel: 0171 493 5660
Fax: 0171 493 8468
E-mail: sims-reed@antiquarian.com
Mon-Fri 9am-6pm
Tube: Green Park

A specialist art bookseller at the very top of the quality and price range with a mixture of new, second-hand, rare and antiquarian volumes. All areas are stocked but they are particularly good on avant-garde art. The shop is located just across the road from Thomas Heneage and is a few minutes walk from the Royal Academy.

W H Smith

It's very easy to be snotty about the popular book stock of this general stationery, newspaper, magazine, music and video store but in many areas it is the only bookshop on offer. The chain sells a huge volume of books each year, many of them at cut prices (£1 or £2 off targeted paperback offers abound, with even bigger reductions on hardbacks). They offer a book-ordering service and their contemporary fiction section has a broad selection of modern, literary paperbacks as well as classics. Don't expect any special offers at their station bookshops, for these you'll need to aim for the high street stores. The W H Smith Clubcard is a way of collecting points on purchases which can then be exchanged for goods. They also operate The Internet Bookshop (see p.169). Station branches at:

Cannon Street Station
EC4N 6AP
Tel: 0171 623 8230
Mon-Fri 6am-7.30pm

Charing Cross Station
WC2N 5HS
Tel: 0171 839 4200
Mon-Sat 7am-9pm, Sun 8am-7.30pm

Just at the front exit of the station, but there's also a smaller section on the concourse that has newspapers, magazines, and a reasonable book selection.

City Thameslink
65 Ludgate Hill
EC4M 7JH
Tel: 0171 329 8828
Mon-Fri 7.30am-7.30pm

Typical station branch with a few fiction, business, computing and general non-fiction titles, but with much more of an emphasis on audio and video tapes and magazines.

Fenchurch Street Station
EC3M 4AJ
Tel: 0171 480 7295
Mon-Fri 7am-7.45pm

King's Cross Station
N1 9AP
Tel: 0171 837 5580
Fax: 0171 837 5603
Mon-Sat 6.30am-9.45pm
Sun 7am-8.45pm

Large branch at the front entrance, with a good book selection for travellers.

Liverpool Street Station
Western Mall
EC2M 7QA
Tel: 0171 628 1617
Fax: 0171 628 6057
Mon-Sat 7am-8pm

The larger of the two branches on this station, but still only useful for travellers in search of a read rather than people after specialist titles.
and

Retail Units 8-10
Station Concourse
EC2M 7QH
Tel: 0171 377 1833
Mon-Sat 8am-7pm, Sun 8.45am-7pm
A small branch on the main concourse with a
limited selection of books.

London Bridge Station
SE1 9SP
Tel: 0171 403 3288
Mon-Fri 6am-8pm
Sat 8.30am-4pm
Mostly magazines and stationery but with a
fair selection of paperback fiction and general
interest stuff at the back. The stock includes
travel guides, health, reference and cookery
with some children's and education books.

St Pancras Station
NW1 2QL
Tel: 0171 837 5703
Fax: 0171 837 5603
Mon-Wed 7am-8pm, Thurs 7am-8.30pm
Fri 7am-9pm, Sat 7am-7pm, Sun 10am-6.30pm

Victoria Station
SW1V 1JT
Tel: 0171 630 9677
Fax: 0171 976 6385
Mon-Sun 7am-9.45pm (9.15pm for first floor)
Two storey glass centrepiece to the station;
with the books and magazines on the ground
floor. This is a good place to buy a book for
your journey. The stock is general but
concentrates on fiction, travel and audiobooks.
and
Victoria Station (East)
SW1V 1JT
Tel: 0171 828 2853
Mon-Fri 7am-8.30pm
Sat 7am-8pm, Sun 10.30am-7.30pm
Carrying a much smaller book stock than the
main branch, this shop mostly offers
newspapers and magazines.

Waterloo Station
SE1 7NQ
Tel: 0171 261 1616
Fax: 0171 633 9982
Mon-Sun 6am-11pm
Located in a central island in the middle of
the station with a small selection of books
amongst the newspapers and magazines.
The other branch (Mon-Sun 7am-9pm),
located amongst the shops along the edge of
the station concourse has a larger book
selection.

Other branches at:

5 Alderman's Hill
Palmer's Green
N13 4YD
Tel: 0181 886 4743
Mon-Fri 8.30am-5.30pm, Sat 8.30am-6pm

Arndale Centre
Wandsworth
SW18 4TG
Tel: 0181 877 1979
Mon-Fri 8.30am-5.30pm, Sat 8.30am-6pm

The Aylesham Centre
Rye Lane
Peckham
SE15 5EW
Tel: 0171 358 9601
Mon-Fri 9am-5.30pm, Sat 9am-6pm
Rail: Peckham Rye
Small shop in the main shopping street, with
around half the space taken up with books; it
has the usual prominent display of popular
fiction with some good-priced special offers,
and a reasonable general stock.

21-23 The Broadway
Ealing
W5 2NH
Tel: 0181 567 1471
Mon-Wed, Fri 8.30am-6pm, Thurs 8.30am-
6.30pm, Sat 9am-6pm, Sun 11am-5pm
Tube: Ealing Broadway

64 The Broadway
West Ealing
W13 0SU
Tel: 0181 579 3461
Mon-Fri 9am-5.30pm, Sat 9am-6pm
Tube: West Ealing

29 The Broadway
Mill Hill
NW7 3DA
Tel: 0181 959 1316
Mon-Sat 9am-6pm
Rail: Mill Hill Broadway

Brent Cross Shopping Centre
Hendon
NW4 3FB
Tel: 0181 202 4226
Fax: 0181 202 8369
Mon-Fri 10am-8pm,
Sat 9am-7pm, Sun 11am-5pm
Tube: Brent Cross

370/372 Chiswick High Road
Turnham Green
W4 5TA
Tel: 0181 995 9427
Mon-Fri 8.45am-5.45pm, Sat 9am-6pm
Tube: Turnham Green

Elephant & Castle Shopping Centre
SE1 6SZ
Tel: 0171 703 8525
Mon-Sat 8.30am-5.30pm
Tube: Elephant & Castle
On the ground floor of the shopping centre
– cheerier inside than it appears from the
street – it has a small general book selection.

889 Finchley Road
Golders Green
NW11 8RR
Tel: 0181 455 0036
Mon-Sat 9am-5.30pm
Tube: Golders Green
A small branch just opposite the tube station
with a selection of general books.

Forest Hill Station
Devonshire Road, SE23 3HD
Tel: 0181 699 2789
Mon-Fri 7.30am-5.30pm
(from 8.45am for first floor books and music)
Sat 8.30am-5.30pm
Right next to rather than in the station, this
two storey branch has books and music on
the first floor. There's a small selection but
they provide a reasonable choice in fiction,
children's and education books as well as a
limited range of reference titles.

9-10 Harben Parade
Finchley Road
NW3 6JS
Tel: 0171 722 4441
Mon-Sat 9am-5.45pm, Sun 10am-4pm
Tube: Swiss Cottage
Good selection of general, popular books on
the ground floor of this fair–sized high street
branch.

766 High Road
North Finchley
N12 9QH
Tel: 0181 445 2785
Mon-Sat 9am-6pm
Tube: Woodside Park

125 High Street North
East Ham
E6 1HZ
Tel: 0181 552 4875
Mon-Sat 9am-6pm, Sun 10am-4pm
Tube: East Ham

92-94 Eltham High Street
SE9 1BW
Tel: 0181 859 3019
Mon-Sat 9am-5.30pm
Rail: Eltham
Small two storey branch in the centre of the
main Eltham shopping area.

111-115 High Street
Putney
SW15 1SS
Tel: 0181 788 2573
Mon-Fri 8.30am-5.30pm, Sat 8.30am-6pm
Sun 11am-4pm
Tube: Putney Bridge
Books are upstairs – a good range with plenty
of price offers.

180-182 Streatham High Street
SW16 1BH
Tel: 0181 677 3031
Mon-Fri 9am-5.30pm, Sat 9am-6pm
Rail: Streatham

110 High Street
Wood Green
N22 6HE
Tel: 0181 889 0221
Fax: 0181 889 9159
Mon-Wed, Fri & Sat 9am-6.30pm
Thurs 9am-7pm, Sun 11am-5pm
Tube: Wood Green

124 Holborn
Holborn Circus
EC1N 2TD
Tel: 0171 242 0535
Fax: 0171 242 3081
Mon-Fri 8am-5.30pm
Tube: Holborn

Hornton Court
132-136 Kensington High Street
W8 7RP
Tel: 0171 937 0236
Fax: 0171 376 2434
Mon-Sat 9am-6.30pm
(newspapers from 8.30am), Sun 11am-5pm
Tube: High Street Kensington
The ground floor is taken up by stationery,
magazines, music and video but the book
department downstairs has a good selection
of general titles, with plenty of special offers.

113 Kilburn High Road
NW6 6JH
Tel: 0171 328 3111
Mon-Sat 9am-5.30pm
Tube: Kilburn
A small, high street branch with the emphasis
on other goods but a small, general selection
of popular books.

King's Mall
King Street Northside
Hammersmith
W6 0PZ
Tel: 0181 748 2218
Mon-Thurs 9am-5.45pm, Fri & Sat 9am-6pm
Tube: Hammersmith
This shop is big and spacious with a very
good general book selection, plenty of
children's books and lots of special offers –
definitely one of the better London branches.

11 Kingsway
WC2B 6YA
Tel: 0171 836 5951
Mon-Fri 8.30am-5.30pm
Tube: Aldwych
There is more of an emphasis here on
magazines, videos, music and stationery, but
the shop has a small general book stock,
with a reasonable paperback fiction section.

The Lewisham Centre
SE13 7EP
Tel: 0181 318 1316
Fax: 0181 318 7478
Mon-Fri 8.30am-5.45pm
Sat 8.30am-6pm, Sun 10am-4pm
Rail: Lewisham
Large convenient branch in the main
Lewisham shopping centre with a good-
sized book selection taking up a large part of
the store.

15 Lime Street
Leadenhall Market
EC3M 7AA
Tel: 0171 283 4135
Fax: 0171 283 4165
Mon-Fri 8am-6pm
Tube: Fenchurch Street, Bank
Catering mainly as a source of diversions for office workers, there are plenty of magazines, video and audio titles in this branch but also travel, fiction and cookery books in plentiful number as well as some on special offer. Leadenhall Market has been excellently refurbished and is full of places to eat, drink, relax and enjoy book purchases – but get there outside the frantic lunch-hour for a more peaceful visit.

117 Muswell Hill Broadway
N10 3RS
Tel: 0181 883 1706
Mon-Fri 9am-5.30pm, Sat 9am-6pm
Tube: Highgate (then bus)

320 North End Road
Fulham
SW6 1NG
Tel: 0171 385 9585
Mon-Sat 9am-5.30pm
Tube: Fulham Broadway

92 Notting Hill Gate
W11 3QB
Tel: 0171 727 9261
Mon-Fri 8.30am-6.30pm
Sat 9am-6pm, Sun 11am-5pm
Tube: Notting Hill Gate

The Plaza
120 Oxford Street
W1N 9DP
Tel: 0171 436 6282
Fax: 0171 637 0918
Mon-Wed, Fri & Sat 10am-7pm
Thurs 10am-8pm, Sat 12noon-6pm
Tube: Tottenham Court Road, Oxford Circus

Located at the far end of the ground floor of the off-street shopping centre, this is a huge branch with an extensive book range. There are lots of special deals on popular titles.

68-72 Powis Street
Woolwich, SE18 6LQ
Tel: 0181 854 7108
Mon-Sat 8.30am-5.30pm
Rail: Woolwich Arsenal

36 Sloane Square
SW1W 8AP
Tel: 0171 730 0351
Fax: 0171 259 0242
Mon-Fri 8.45am-6.30pm
(newspapers and magazines from 8am)
Sat 9am-6.30pm, Sun 11am-5pm
Tube: Sloane Square
One of the biggest branches in Central London, with a very good book selection in fiction, travel, cookery, children's books and audiobooks.

The Stratford Centre
Stratford East
E15 1XE
Tel: 0181 534 5955
Mon-Sat 9am-6pm, Sun 11am-5pm
Tube: Stratford

Surrey Quays Shopping Centre,
Redriff Road, SE16 1LL
Tel: 0171 237 5235
Mon-Thu, Sat 9am-6pm, Fri 9am-8pm
Tube: Surrey Quays

22 Temple Fortune Parade
Temple Fortune, Finchley Road
NW11 0QS
Tel: 0181 455 2273
Mon-Sat 9am-6pm
Tube: Golders Green (then a bus)
General, single-floor store that has a small selection of general interest books but with an emphasis on music, stationary and other goods.

82 Walm Lane
Willesden Green
NW2 4RA
Tel: 01881 459 0455
Mon-Sat 9am-5.30pm
Tube: Willesden Green

23 Winslade Way
Catford
SE6 4JU
Tel: 0181 690 1972
Mon-Sat 9.30am-5.30pm
Rail: Catford, Catford Bridge

16 Wimbledon Bridge
SW19 7NW
Tel: 0181 543 1055
Mon-Sat 8.30am-6pm, Sun 11am-5pm
Tube: Wimbledon

Next to Waterstone's, the book section isn't much competition but can be useful for special offers on popular titles.

SoHo Original Books

12 Brewer Street
W1R 3SN
Tel: 0171 494 1615
Fax: 0171 734 6243
Mon-Sat 10am-1am, Sun 10am-11pm
Tube: Piccadilly Circus

Because it's situated at the top of Rupert Street market, in the heart of gaudy neon-lit Soho, this shop is often given a wide berth by people who are just after general books. But they're missing out on a good range (upstairs) of discounted books – especially music, photography and fiction titles. The licensed adult or sexually explicit material is well out of sight downstairs.

Soma

38 Kennington Lane
SE11 4LS
Tel: 0171 735 2101
Fax: 0171 735 3076
Mon-Fri 9.30am-5.30pm, Sat 10am-4pm
Tube: Kennington

This shop specialises in Asia, Africa and the Caribbean and in all minority and social interests; increasingly material of Irish interest is also on offer. The children's stock is wider, including books in a huge range of Asian and African languages. The shop is now extending the range by adding Spanish and French titles. As major importers of Black American titles and of books from India, (they are agents for Penguin India, amongst other publishers), this area of stock is pretty extensive, with volumes you're unlikely to find elsewhere. The children's section also includes material for children on AIDS, adoption and coping with bullying. Also on sale are crafts imported from co-operatives in India, as well as posters and cards.

Sotheby's Bookshop

34-35 New Bond Street
W1A 2AA
Tel: 0171 493 8080
Fax: 0171 293 5909
Web: www.sothebys.com
Mon-Fri 9am-5.30pm
(Also open at the weekend if there is a viewing – ring to check.)
Tube: Bond Street

In the entrance hall of the famous auction house, the bookshop stocks an excellent range of titles of interest to collectors of pretty much anything including art, photography, antiquities, glass, clocks, jewellery, carpets, textiles, porcelain and ceramics. The shop also stocks books on interiors, travel, gardens and food and drink. Sotheby's catalogues are on sale, those from past sales offered at half price. Sotheby's also produce an attractive mail order catalogue and can deliver worldwide. The café is a quiet, refined place for a coffee.

Sound and Vision

132 Lordship Lane
SE22 8HF
Tel: 0181 299 6115
Tues-Sat 10am-5.30pm
Tube: East Dulwich
A wonderfully original shop with a selection
of music CD's and vinyl records (mostly jazz
and guitar), gifts and cards, and books on
interior design, textiles, cookery, health, and
for children. There is also a noticeboard
advertising local events and services. Nearby
the Blue Mountain Café is the place to go for
a brilliant coffee.

Southgate Bookshop

62 Chase Side
N14 5PA
Tel: 0181 886 4805
Mon-Fri 11am-5.30pm, Sat 10.30am-5.30pm
Tube: Southgate
General shop selling new as well as second-
hand books plus some greetings cards.

South Kensington Bookshop

22 Thurloe Street
SW7 2LT
Tel: 0171 589 2916
Mon-Fri 10am-8pm
Sat 11am-7pm, Sun 12noon-7pm
Tube: South Kensington
Discount bookshop with a good selection of
glossy, large format art and design, cookery
and gardening books. It's also worth a look
for reference, biography, travel and
paperback fiction.

SPCK

Partnership House
157 Waterloo Road, SE1 8XA
Tel/Fax: 0171 633 9096
E-mail: partnership@spck.co.uk
Mon-Sat 9.30am-6pm
Tube: Waterloo
A small local shop selling new stock about
Christianity.

SPCK Bookshop

Holy Trinity Church
Marylebone Road, NW1 4DU
Tel: 0171 388 1659
Mail Order: 0345 626 747
Fax: 0171 388 2352
E-mail: london@spck.co.uk
Mon-Fri 9am-5pm
Tube: Great Portland Street
Titles on all aspects of Christian theology and
life. Mail order is available.

Spink and Son Ltd

5-7 King Street
St James
SW1Y 6QS
Tel: 0171 930 7888
Fax: 0171 747 6920
Mon-Fri 9am-5.30pm
Tube: Green Park or Piccadilly Circus
This specialist coin dealer has a third floor
bookshop with a large specialist new and
second-hand stock of titles covering all
aspects of numismatics.

Sportspages

Caxton Walk
94-96 Charing Cross Road
WC2H 0JG
Tel: 0171 240 9604
Fax: 0171 836 0104
Mon-Sat 9.30am-7pm
Tube: Leicester Square
Books on every sport imaginable from fishing
and American football to greyhound and
pigeon racing, with large sections on sports
psychology, training and exercise. There is a
range of sports-related magazines and football
programmes from Premier and Scottish
League clubs. The place has a relaxed
atmosphere and there is often a television
showing the latest footie match. The shop is
a favourite place for sports book signings and
Mohammed Ali is among the sports stars to
have visited here.

Spurgeon's Book Room
Spurgeon's College
189 South Norwood Hill
SE25 6DJ
Tel/Fax: 0181 653 3640
Mon-Fri 10am-4pm during term times.
(At other times ring to check opening hours).
Rail: Crystal Palace or Norwood Junction
In the grounds of the theological college which specialises in the training of Baptist ministers, this shop sells a range of Christian and theological books (not only those from a Baptist perspective). It also stocks a range of cards small gift items, posters, tapes and CD's. Most books are new but there are often some special offers and a few second-hand titles.

Sri Aurobindo Society Bookshop
171 Finchley Road,
NW3
Tube: Swiss Cottage or Finchley Road
Small shop selling Asian goods plus a selection of books on philosophy and spirituality, concentrating on the works of the Indian masters.

Stanfords
12-14 Long Acre
WC2E 9LP
Tel: 0171 836 1321
Fax: 0171 836 0189
Mon, Wed-Fri 9am-7.30pm
Tues 9.30am-7pm, Sat 10am-7.30pm,
closed on Sunday
Tube: Leicester Square
Probably the best-stocked guidebook and travel bookshop in London, Stanfords ranges over two floors, with a massive selection of worldwide maps (they are Ordnance Survey agents) and nautical charts. They also stock a comprehensive range of magazines, globes, atlases and books on walking, climbing, boats and seamanship.
There are other smaller branches at:

Stanfords at British Airways
156 Regent Street, W1R 5TA
Tel: 0171 434 4744
Fax: 0171 434 4636
Mon-Fri 9.30am-6pm, Sat 10am-4pm
Tube: Oxford Circus, Piccadilly Circus

Stanfords at Campus Travel
52 Grosvenor Gardens, SW1V 0AG
Tel: 0171 730 1314
Fax: 0171 730 1354
Mon-Wed, Fri 8.30am-6.30pm
Thurs 8.30am-8pm, Sat 10am-5pm
Tube: Victoria

The Stationery Office Bookshop
123 Kingsway, WC2B 6PQ
Tel: 0171 242 6393
Fax: 0171 831 1326
Mon-Fri 9am-5.30pm, Sat 10am-3pm
Tube: Holborn
This shop is big on government publications including those from the British Standards Institute, the Health and Safety Executive, the Ordnance Survey and the National Statistical Office. However, they also stock a wide range of business, economics, law, management, reference and transport titles from many other publishers.

Rudolf Steiner Bookshop
Rudolf Steiner House
35 Park Road
NW1 6XT
Tel: 0171 724 7699
Fax: 0171 724 4364
E-mail: rsh@cix.compulink.co.uk
Mon-Fri 10.30am-2pm and 3pm-6pm
Sat 10.30am-2pm and 3pm-5pm
Tube: Baker Street
This bookshop specialises in texts which discuss or develop the ideas of Rudolf Steiner and the Anthroposophical movement. It also has general stock including education, child development, parenting, medicine and health books. Mail order is available.

Stepping Stones

97 Trafalgar Road
SE10 9TS
Tel: 0181 853 2733
Daily 10am-6pm
Rail: Greenwich
This shop is located about fifteen minutes walk (it's worth the effort) from the centre of Greenwich, beyond the Maritime Museum. It's a brilliant little shop selling gifts, cards and 'New Age' items with a range of books on alternative medicine, self-development and improvement, religion and philosophy.

Stoke Newington Bookshop

153 Stoke Newington High Street
N16 0NY
Tel: 0171 249 2808
Fax: 0171 249 7845
Mon-Sat 9.30am-5.30pm
Rail: Stoke Newington
This large shop for new books has an enticing window display, a good selection of stock, soothing music, lots of greetings cards, special offers and leaflets about local events. They are especially well-stocked in fiction and children's books but also have a good non-fiction selection and make a strong feature of newly published books. An excellent local shop.

Henry Stokes and Co

58 Elizabeth Street
SW1W 9PB
Tel: 0171 730 7073
Fax: 0171 730 5568
Mon-Fri 9.30am-6pm, Sat 9.30am-1pm
Tube: Victoria or Sloane Square
Selling greetings cards and stationery, there is also a book department largely stocking hardback gift books in a variety of non-fiction subject areas.

Swedenborg Society Bookshop

20-21 Bloomsbury Way
WC1A 2TH
Tel: 0171 405 7986
Fax: 0171 831 5848
E-mail: swed.soc@netmatters.co.uk
Mon-Fri 9.30am-5pm
Tube: Tottenham Court Road or Holborn
This bookshop specialises in the philosophical writings of Emanual Swedenborg (in both English and the original Latin) and books about his life and works. A free catalogue is available.

T

Tactical Café, Bar & Bookshop

27 D'Arblay Street
W1V 3SJ
Tel: 0171 287 2823
Mon-Fri 9am-11pm
Sat 12noon-11pm, Sun 12noon-10.30pm
Tube: Oxford Circus, Tottenham Court Road
Located very close to Berwick Street with the street market just down the road and the glitz and shimmer of Soho all around. Tactical is both a café, a bar and a small bookshop offering a selective range of books and magazines for sale. The publications are all modern mostly with an alternative perspective. The non-fiction side is equally selective with titles on media, film and culture.

Talking Bookshop

11 Wigmore Street
W1H 9LB
Tel: 0171 491 4117
Fax: 0171 629 1966
Mon-Fri 9.30am-5.30pm, Sat 10am-5pm
Tube: Bond Street, Oxford Circus

This shop is just a short walk from Oxford Street and stocks purely spoken word tapes. The range is startling and includes bestsellers, classics, drama and poetry, radio comedy and children's books as well as some non-fiction, stress reduction, self-improvement and language courses. There's also a range of normally hard to find unabridged books – much lengthier and pricier than more common offerings, but if you want the real thing on tape, this is definitely the place to look.

The Tate Gallery Shop

The Tate Gallery
Millbank
SW1P 4RG
Tel: 0171 887 8008
Daily 10.30am-5.40pm
Tube: Pimlico

The shop stocks a huge number of books on the Tate's collections: British art from 1500 and international contemporary and modern art. Many are art essays or monographs on artists but there are also books on recent exhibitions, art history and theory. It's a good place to look for unusual gifts and stationery items as well as more expensive things and a huge array of postcards of the exhibits. In May 2000 an additional site, the Tate Gallery of Modern Art, will open in the refurbished Bankside Power Station across the Thames from St Paul's Cathedral. The exact nature of that bookshop remains to be seen, but it will undoubtedly be worth a look.

The Theosophical Society in England

50 Gloucester Place
W1H 4EA
Tel: 0171 935 9261
Fax: 0171 935 9543
Mon 5.30pm-9.30pm
Tues-Fri 2pm-7pm, Sat 11am-4pm
Tube: Marble Arch

This bookshop is in the foyer of the British headquarters of the Theosophical Society which is a centre for lectures and meditation and has a library. The bookshop has mostly new full price books concerning Theosophy but also has books about other religions, and has some discounted and second-hand titles.

John Thornton

455 Fulham Road
SW10 9UZ
Tel: 0171 352 8810
Mon-Sat 10am-5.30pm
Tube: Fulham Broadway

Although a specialist in theology books, of which there is a huge range, there is also a large stock in other areas, especially art, literarture and biography and some wonderful leatherbound volumes. The shop is about five minutes west of Stamford Bridge football ground.

The Tintin Shop

35 Floral Street
WC2E 9DJ
Tel: 0171 836 1131
Mon-Sat 10am-6pm
Tube: Covent Garden or Leicester Square

All the books in the Tintin series plus videos, gifts, household linen, posters, stationery and postcards.

Alec Tiranti

27 Warren Street
W1P 5DG
Tel: 0171 636 8565
Mon-Fri 9am-5.30pm
Sat 9.30am-1pm
Tube: Warren Street

Specialist shop stocking tools, materials and equipment for carving, sculpture and modelling with a book selection to match. The range of books includes the technical and inspirational as well as artists' source works, and is supplemented by the Tiranti technical booklets which explain how to work in a variety of materials.

Titles
113A Anerley Road
SE20 8AJ
Tel: 0181 776 7144
Fax: 0181 674 0630
Mon-Sat 9am-6pm
Rail: Anerley
and
The Blenheim Shopping Centre
High Street
Penge
SE20 8RW
Tel: 0181 676 8088
Mon-Sat 9.30am-6pm
Rail: Penge East or Penge West
The Anerley Road branch is a general shop specialising in bargain and discounted new books whilst the Penge shop also stocks some full price titles.

Trailfinders
194 Kensington High Street
W8 7RG
Tel: 0171 938 3999
Mon-Wed, Fri & Sat 9am-6pm
Thurs 9am-7pm
Tube: High Street Kensington
This well-established travel agents also has a travel clinic for immunisations and malaria advice, a travel equipment shop and bookshop. There are a couple of thousand travel titles here, almost all overseas guidebooks and maps.

The Travel Bookshop
13-15 Blenheim Crescent
W11 2EE
Tel: 0171 229 5260
Fax: 0171 243 1552
Web: www. thetravelbookshop.co.uk
Mon-Sat 10am-6pm
Tube: Ladbroke Grove
One of the few specialist travel bookshops in London, and the inspiration for the film 'Notting Hill' starring Hugh Grant and Julia Roberts. There are plenty of spots to sit and browse and an excellent range of new and second-hand books and magazines. The shop demonstrates a delightfully eclectic definition of what comprises 'travel' with guides, phrasebooks, history, anthropology, religion and philosophy all rubbing shoulders. Catalogues and mail order are available.

Triangle Bookshop
The Architectural Association
36 Bedford Square
WC1B 3EG
Tel: 0171 631 1381
Fax: 0171 436 4373
Mon-Fri 10am-6.30pm
Tube: Gower Street
The specialisation here is architecture and design with a large selection of new books and magazines from both this country and overseas.

Unsworth Booksellers
12 Bloomsbury Street
WC1B 3QA
Tel: 0171 820 7709
Fax: 0171 637 7334
Mon-Sat 10am-8pm, Sun 12noon-8pm
Tube: Tottenham Court Road
One of the largest shops in the area with an excellent stock of new, discounted and second-hand books in all subject areas but specialising in books on the arts, social sciences, history and classics. The small stock of antiquarian books are in the basement, with a catalogue published twice a year.

URC Bookshop

86 Tavistock Place
WC1H 9RT
Tel: 0171 916 2020
Fax: 0171 916 2021
Mon-Fri 9am-4.30pm
Tube: Kings Cross or Russell Square
On the corner of Tavistock Place and
Wakefield Street, a specialist shop selling
Christian and theology books and literature
on the United Reformed Church Movement.

V

Vermilion Books

10a Acton Street (off Gray's Inn Road)
WC1R 4PD
Tel: 0181 741 8375
Mon only 12noon-6pm
(other days by prior appointment)
Tube: King's Cross
Selling an excellent range of hardback and
paperback books in all subject areas, books
are discounted 30% for hardbacks and 50%
for paperbacks off the publishers price.

Vertigo

14 Grove Lane
SE5 8SY
Tel: 0171 701 5058
Fax: 0171 207 7338
Mon-Sat 10am-6pm
Rail: Denmark Hill
A small shop with a hugely eclectic stock of
full price and discounted new and
secondhand books on art, cinema,
contemporary fiction and philosophy, cultural
studies and psychoanalysis. It's a bit like an
ICA for the suburbs. There's a good bargain
tray outside, some magazines for sale and an
excellent choice of greetings cards and
postcards with attitude.

Victoria and Albert Museum Shop

Cromwell Road
South Kensington
SW7 2RL
Tel: 0171 938 8434
Fax: 0171 988 8623
Mon 12noon-5.30pm, Tues-Sun 10am-5.30pm
Tube: South Kensington
One of the best museum shops in London
with a brilliant range of cards, stationery and
gift items as well as books. The selection
covers all areas featured in the museum, and
so includes art and design history, worldwide
design, textiles, interior design, ceramics,
photography, media, fashion and costume,
architecture and gardening.

Village Books

17 Shrubbery Road
Streatham
SW16 2AS
Tel: 0181 677 2667
Mon-Sat 11.15am-5.30pm (it's a good idea to
ring before making a special journey).
Rail: Streatham or Streatham Hill
Selling new and second-hand books on all
general subjects but with a large stock of
volumes on esoteric subjects. The shop is a
short distance from Streatham High Road.

Village Games

Camden Lock
NW1 8AF
Tel/Fax: 0171 485 0653
Wed-Sun 10.30am-5.30pm
Tube: Camden Town
Just out the back of the main Camden Lock
market, this tiny shop specialises in games and
puzzles of all sorts. It has a good range of
books on subjects from the more mainstream
chess and Go through to Mah Jong and
mathematical and geometric puzzles.

Vintage Magazine Shop

39 Brewer Street
W1R 3FD
Tel: 0171 439 8525
E-mail: vintage.soho@ndirect.co.uk
Mon-Thurs 10am-8pm
Fri & Sat 10am-10pm, Sun 12noon-8pm
Tube: Piccadilly Circus
The basement is stocked to overflowing with back issues of magazines of every variety. Just as an indication of the range they have 'Eagle', 'Life', 'Vogue', 'Harpers', 'Marvel', 'GQ' and 'i-D', as well as vintage film and motoring magazines – it's a collector's paradise. The shop also specialises in movie postcards, photographs, posters and other memorabilia. Other branches at:

247 Camden High Street
NW1 7BU
Tel: 0171 482 0587
Mon-Fri 10am-6.15pm,
Sat & Sun 10am-6.45pm
Tube: Camden Town
and
55 Charing Cross Road
WC2H 0NE
Tel: 0171 494 4064
Mon-Sat 10am-10pm, Sun 12noon-8pm
Tube: Leicester Square

Volume One

Unit LSU2, Centre Court
Wimbledon, SW19 8YE
Tel: 0181 944 8879
Fax: 0181 944 8922
Mon-Wed, Fri 9.30am-7pm,
Thur 9.30am-8pm, Sat 9am-6pm
Sun 11am-5pm
Tube: Wimbledon
Part of a small national chain, the store efficiently mixes a wide general stock (especially good in popular fiction, computers and travel), with posters, cards, videos and stationery. Upstairs in the Centre Court shopping centre there are many places you can relax and buy a coffee or some food.

W

Walthamstow Music

116 Hoe Street
E17 4QR
Tel: 0181 520 2163 or 520 5448
Fax: 0181 509 3005
Mon-Fri 9am-5.30pm, Sat 9am-5pm
Train: Walthamstow Central
A brilliant local music store with an excellent range of instruments and sheet music (both classical and popular), for all instruments and levels, including exam pieces.

Waterstones

The chain was started in 1982 by Tim Waterstone with his branch on Old Brompton Road, but is now owned by the HMV Group which also owns Dillons. However, so far at least, the chain retains a distinctly literary atmosphere with an emphasis on serious rather than popular titles (although you'll find these as well), carpeted shops with plenty of chairs for reading, and soothing music. The quarterly 'W', the Waterstones Magazine, is good value at £1 with selections from the latest books – and readers can use coupons in the magazine to claim free copies of featured books. For people intending to travel outside London, Waterstones at 153-157 Sauchiehall Street in Glasgow (Tel: 0141 332 9105) might well be the best bookshop in the country. Their web site is at www.waterstones.co.uk
Branches at:

128 Camden High Street
NW1 0NB
Tel: 0171 284 4948
Fax: 0171 482 3457
Mon, Wed-Fri 9.30am-8pm,
Tues 10am-8pm, Sat 9.30am-6pm,
Sun 12noon-6pm
Tube: Camden Town

121-125 Charing Cross Road
WC2 0EA
Tel: 0171 434 4291
Fax: 0171 437 3319
Mon-Sat 9.30am-8pm, Sun 12noon-6pm
Tube: Tottenham Court Road
A bit confusingly spread over two shops that are a few metres apart, the section closest to Tottenham Court Road tube has the fiction and children's books whilst the other shop is the largest with everything else spread over five floors, including a good range of academic titles.

145-147 Cheapside
EC2V 6BJ
Tel: 0171 726 6077
Fax: 0171 726 6079
Mon-Fri 8am-6.30pm
Tube: St Paul's
Not far from the back wall of St Paul's Cathedral, this is a fairly small branch with the usual excellent Waterstones fiction selection (both paperback and hardback) and, not surprisingly given its City location, extensive sections downstairs on computing, business and finance.

City University
Northampton Square
EC1V 0HB
Tel: 0171 608 0706
Fax: 0171 251 2813
Tube: Farringdon, Angel

64 Ealing Broadway Centre
W5 5JY
Tel: 0181 840 5905
Fax: 0181 567 3246
Mon-Fri 9.30am-7pm
Sat 9.30am-6pm, Sun 11am-5pm
Tube: Ealing Broadway

266 Earls Court Road
SW5 9AS
Tel: 0171 370 1616
Fax: 0171 244 6644
Mon-Fri 9.30am-9pm, Sat 9.30am-7pm
Sun 12noon-6pm
Tube: Earl's Court
A big branch with plenty of cards, tables and chairs and well-displayed book selections, which include lots of sci-fi and fantasy. This branch is often the venue for signings and readings.

9-13 Garrick Street
WC2E 9AU
Tel: 0171 836 6757
Fax: 0171 836 4458
Mon-Sat 10am-8pm, Sun 12noon-6pm
Tube: Covent Garden
Fiction and travel are very prominent on the ground floor but there is the usual extensive Waterstones stock in the basement. If you fancy a coffee there are a good many cafés in the area.

Goldsmiths' College
University of London
New Cross
SE14 6NW
Tel: 0181 469 0262
Fax: 0181 694 2279
Mon-Fri 9am-7pm, Sat 9am-5.30pm
Tube: New Cross Gate
Located inside the college, selling academic books to accompany the college courses. The shop has a general stock including subjects such as art and design, philosophy, psychology, women's studies, economics, computing and literature.

68 & 69 Hampstead High Street
NW3 1QP
Tel: 0171 794 1098
Fax: 0171 794 7553
Mon-Fri 10am-9pm, Sat 10am-8pm
Sun 12noon-6pm
Tube: Hampstead

A large, well-stocked and bustling branch of this chain with two floors packed with every subject under the sun – but sadly only a few life-saving chairs and tables where you can relax and browse. There are often readings and signings.

London Guildhall University
Calcutta House
Old Castle Street
E1 7NT
Tel: 0171 247 0727
Fax: 0171 247 0513
Tube: Aldgate

Imperial College School of Medicine
Charing Cross Campus
Reynold's Building
St Dunstan's Road
W6 8RP
Tel: 0181 748 9768
Tube: Barons Court

Imperial College School of Medicine
Hammersmith Campus
Du Cane Road
W12 0NN
Tel: 0181 742 9600
Fax: 0181 383 2500
Tube: East Acton

Imperial College
Imperial College Road
SW7 2AZ
Tel: 0171 589 3563
Fax: 0171 591 3810
E-mail: imperialcollege@waterstones.co.uk
Tube: South Kensington

10-12 Islington Green
N1 2XH
Tel: 0171 704 2280
Fax: 0171 704 2152
Mon-Sat 9.30am-10pm
Sun 12-6pm
Tube: Angel

This branch has a decidedly literary feel, long opening hours, plenty of signings and magazines for sale as well as books. The shop overlooks Islington Green which is a reasonable spot to relax in when the weather is fine.

193 Kensington High Street
W8 6SH
Tel: 0171 937 8432
Fax: 0171 938 4970
Mon-Fri 9.30am-9pm
Sat 9.30am-7pm, Sun 12noon-6pm
Tube: High Street Kensington
A large branch with a wide selection of books over three floors, and a good deal of academic stock. There are plenty of tables displaying promoted books and large computing, accountancy and business sections as well as an especially good selection of fiction. This branch often hosts readings and signings by well known authors.

Kings College
Macadam House
Surrey St
WC2R 2LS
Tel: 0171 836 0205
Fax: 0171 240 9723
Tube: Aldwych

150-152 Kings Road
SW3 3NR
Tel: 0171 351 2023
Fax: 0171 351 7709
Mon, Wed & Fri 9am-9pm, Tues 9.30am-9pm
Sat 9.30am-8pm, Sun 12noon-6pm
Tube: Sloane Square
There are two floors in this spacious, bustling and justifiably popular branch. The shop is well stocked and laid out with plenty of chairs for reading. An excellent shop.

39-41 Notting Hill Gate
W11 3JQ
Tel: 0171 229 9444
Fax: 0171 229 3991
Mon-Fri 9am-8pm, Sat 9am-7pm
Sun 12noon-6pm
Tube: Notting Hill Gate
An excellently-stocked branch with fiction, biography and travel taking up most of the ground floor, with other subjects upstairs. There are plenty of chairs, some tables for browsing and a pleasant, relaxed atmosphere.

99-101 Old Brompton Road
SW7 3LE
Tel: 0171 581 8522
Fax: 0171 225 2920
Mon-Fri 9.30am-9pm
Sat 10.30am-7pm, Sun 12noon-6pm
Tube: South Kensington
This three-storey branch is very welcoming with plenty of chairs for reading and the usual excellent stock. There are plenty of tables with well chosen selections and a display of the latest book review pages from the newspapers.

Trafalgar Square
WC2N 5EJ
Tel: 0171 839 4411
Fax: 0171 839 1797
Mon, Wed-Sat 9.30am-9pm
Tues 10am-9pm, Sun 12noon-6pm
Tube: Charing Cross
This large three storey branch has a massive basement and is extremely well-stocked with a particularly good children's section. There's also a Coffee Republic on the first floor.

Waterstones at Harrods
87 Brompton Road
SW1X 7XL
Tel: 0171 225 5916
Fax: 0171 225 5920
Mon, Tues & Sat 10am-6pm
Wed, Thurs & Fri 10am-7pm
Tube: Knightsbridge

On the second floor of the world famous store (reached by the hugely stylish Egyptian Escalator), this is a stunning book department in a stunning shop (NB. they have a dress code in the store, so you won't be allowed in wearing a backpack). The range of books is extensive and, catering for the well-heeled customers, there are more hardback books here than you'll find almost anywhere else in London. All subject areas (excluding children's books, which has its own department see p.40), are covered and there is a bustle about the place that is enticing. The store has plenty of chairs to relax in, and a good selection of magazines. There is something wonderful about walking through archways into rooms lined with shelves brimming over with books. In addition you'll get one of Harrods' distinctive green and gold bags if you buy a book here.

1-7 Whittington Avenue
Leadenhall Market
EC3V 1LE
Tel: 0171 220 7882
Fax: 0171 220 7870
Mon, Wed-Fri 8.30am-6pm
Tues 9.30am-6pm
Tube: Monument
The market itself has been renovated and is lovely with its high, arched roof below which are alleyways full of pricey food shops, off licences, florists, tailors and perfumeries and a great many coffee shops, wine bars and restaurants for the lunchtime trade. This is a tiny haven of character in the midst of the impersonal City and well worth a visit if you're in the area. The local Waterstones is a two storey shop with a good stock including extensive fiction, cookery, cinema, history and sports sections and some magazines on the ground floor. The basement stocks mostly the more serious subjects of management, finance and law appropriate for a branch surrounded by City institutions.

12 Wimbledon Bridge
SW19 7NW
Tel: 0181 543 9899
Fax 0181 543 5390
Mon-Fri 9.30am-7pm
Sat 9am-6pm, Sun 11am-4pm
Tube: Wimbledon
Opposite the station in the main Wimbledon shopping area, the store is not one of the largest but still carries an extensive range.

Wellspring Bookshop
5 New Oxford Street
WC1A 1BA
Tel: 0171 405 6101
Mon-Fri 10am-5.30pm, Sat 11am-5pm
Tube: Tottenham Court Road
Specialising in the texts of Rudolf Steiner and other philosophical writers.

Wesley Owen Books & Music
This is a nationwide chain specialising in Christian music, books, videos, gifts and stationery. The book selection includes Bibles and prayer Books, biblical reference titles and books about the Christian life, and fiction as well as children's literature.
Branches at:

3 Eccleston Street
SW1W 9LZ
Tel: 0171 463 1451
Mon-Fri 9.30am-6pm, Sat 9.30am-5.30pm
Tube: Victoria

82 High Street
South Woodford, E18 2NA
Tel: 0181 530 4244
Fax: 0181 518 8924
Mon-Sat 9.30am-5.30pm
Tube: South Woodford

3-9 Wigmore Street, W1H 0AD
Tel: 0171 493 1851
Fax: 0171 493 4478
Mon-Fri 9.30am-6pm, Sat 9.30am-5.30pm
Tube: Oxford Circus

West End Lane Books
277 West End Lane
NW6 1QS
Tel: 0171 431 3770
Fax: 0171 431 7655
Mon-Sat 10am-7pm
Tube: West Hampstead
A good, general bookshop with a reasonable stock and mats and beanbags for children to lounge on in a dedicated area. The shop also hosts occasional readings and signings.

Westminster Abbey Bookshop
Tel: 0171 222 5152
Mon-Sat 9.15am-4.45pm
Tube: Westminster
Alongside the Westminster Abbey souvenir keyrings, sweatshirts and mugs, there is a reasonable book selection on history, Christianity and church architecture as well as classics and children's titles.

Wholefood
24 Paddington Street
W1M 4DR
Tel: 0171 935 3924
Mon-Thurs 8.45am-6pm, Fri 8.45am-6.30pm,
Sat 8.45am-1pm
Specialising in organically grown fresh food and products, there is also a large book section in this shop, covering nutrition, vegetarian cookery, organic gardening, a variety of health issues, alternative medicine and spiritual health.

The Who Shop
4 Station Parade
High Street North
East Ham
E6 1JD
Tel: 0181 471 2356
Mon-Sat 9.30am-5.30pm
Tube: East Ham
Just across the road from the tube station, this shop specialises in books, models and general paraphernalia linked to 'Dr Who'. They also stock 'Star Wars' and other sci-fi material.

Wildy & Sons Ltd

Lincoln's Inn Archway
Carey Street
WC2A 2JD
Tel: 0171 242 5778
Fax: 0171 430 0897
E-mail: info@wildy.com
Web: www.wildy.com
Mon-Fri 8.45am-5.15pm
Tube: Chancery Lane

Hidden away at the back of the Royal
Courts of Justice in an archway that runs
through from the eastern end of Carey Street
to New Square, this is a specialist law
bookshop (established in 1830). It has a huge
stock of new and second-hand titles plus
some antiquarian rarities and a selection of
both ancient and modern prints. 'Wildy's
Book News' is published monthly,
advertising new and forthcoming titles,
current special offers and a selection of
second-hand books currently in stock.
Also at:

16 Fleet Street
EC4Y 1AX
Tel: 0171 353 3907
Fax: 0171 353 4395
Mon-Fri 9am-6pm, Sat 10am-4pm
Tube: Chancery Lane

This branch stocks only new books but has a
gallery as part of the shop with legal prints.

Willesden Bookshop

Willesden Green Library Centre
95 High Road, NW10 4QU
Tel: 0181 451 7000
Fax: 0181 830 1233
Mon-Fri 10am-6pm, Sat 9.30am-5.30pm
Tube: Willesden Green

Just a short walk from the tube next to the
library, this well-established general
bookshop has a range of titles in all areas
including Black, Irish and Asian studies, art
and design and women's and social studies. It
has a particularly good section of children's
books from simple picture books to young
adult level.

Wimbledon Books

58 Wimbledon Hill Road
SW19 7PA
Tel: 0181 879 3101
Mon-Sat 9.30am-6pm, Sun 10.30am-4pm
Tube: Wimbledon

Located a few doors further away from
Wimbledon station than Fielders, everything
in the shop is discounted (even bestsellers and
customer orders), some by up to half price.
The stock is good, as is the layout. This is a
local shop well worth a visit.

Wisdom Books

402 Hoe Street
E17 9AA
Tel: 0181 520 5588
Fax: 0181 520 0932
E-mail: 100660,2464@compuserve.com
Web: www.demon.co.uk/wisdom
Mon-Fri 9.30am-5.30pm, Sat 10am-5pm
Rail: Walthamstow Central

Ring for admission and be let upstairs into
this specialist Buddhist bookshop. It's
fabulously stocked with books from across
the globe on every school and tradition of
Buddhism, from popular general titles to
academic texts. There are also videos, tapes,
magazines, statues and artworks. Mail order is
available and they publish a catalogue.

Witherby

Book Department
Second Floor
32-36 Aylesbury Street
EC1R OET
Tel: 0171 251 5341
Fax: 0171 251 1296
Mon-Fri 9am-4.30pm
Tube: Angel

Specialising in insurance and shipping, with
an international and extensive stock, there are
up-to-the-minute catalogues available as well
as worldwide mail order.

Women and Children First
14 The Market
Greenwich
SE10 9HZ
Tel: 0181 853 1296
Mon-Fri 10am-5pm, Sat & Sun 10am-5.30pm
Rail: Greenwich
There are toys in the basement but the ground floor has an extensive selection of children's books to appeal to readers from toddlers to teenagers. The shop is welcoming with stools and a child-friendly atmosphere, there is also a small range of children's audiobooks and fiction and non-fiction of interest to women.

Word Play
1 Broadway Parade
Crouch End
N8 9TN
Tel: 0181 347 6700
Fax: 0181 347 6500
Mon-Sat 9am-5.30pm, Sun 11am-5pm
Rail: Crouch Hill
Opposite the Clock Tower, the shop is half toys and half books. The book stock is mostly fiction with a range right from early picture books to those for young adults as well as some poetry, non-fiction titles and audiobooks. The toy stock is also fun – they've plenty to choose from including some great little pocket money items for as little as 15p.

Wordsworth Books
120 Clapham High Street
SW4 7UH
Tel: 0171 627 2797
Mon-Sat 9.30-6pm
Tube: Clapham Common
Just a short walk from the tube, this store sells an excellent selection of full price and discounted new books covering all subjects and genres.

Wordsworth Bookshop
11 Butterfly Walk Shopping Centre
Denmark Hill
SE5 8RW
Tel: 0171 277 1377
Mon-Fri 9am-7.30pm, Sat 9am-6.30pm
Rail: Denmark Hill
Located in the covered shopping mall this is one branch of the South London chain which sells full price and discounted new books. The range here is excellent, the shop is spacious and there is a section with books of local interest alongside a good general stock and a range of audiobooks, cards and gift wrapping. The shop carries leaflets for Booksearch UK and TSB Booksearch, who search for difficult to find or out of print books. There's also a local noticeboard.

The Works
Unit 2, Plaza House
191 Camden High Street
NW1 7BT
Tel: 0171 284 3033
Fax: 0171 482 6680
Mon-Fri 9am-7pm
Sat 9am-8pm, Sun 10am-6pm
Tube: Camden Town
Excellent addition to the remainder and discounted book market, and located in the heart of Camden. There is a good range of general books in all subject areas including plenty of children's books, plus attractively-priced stationery, posters and cards.
Also at:
Unit 24
Lewisham Centre
SE13 7HB
Tel: 0181 318 0519
Mon-Wed 9am-5.30pm, Thurs & Fri 9am-8pm
Sat 9am-6pm, Sun 10am-4pm
Rail: Lewisham
South London branch of the popular Camden discount bookseller, with a good general subject range including children's and some excellent bargains.

NEW BOOKSHOPS

World Books

87 Newman Street
W1P 4EN
Tel: 0171 291 3321
Mon-Fri 10am-6pm, Sat 10am-4pm
Tube: Tottenham Court Road
This shop is part of Book Club Associates who run thirty or so postal book clubs, some general, some highly specialised, that you'll see advertised in the newspapers. This shop is open to the general public, but you will need to become a member before purchasing a book, for which you will need identification.

Y

YHA Adventure Shop

14 Southampton Street
WC2E 7HY
Tel: 0171 836 8541
Fax: 0171 836 8263
Mon-Wed 10am-6pm, Thurs & Fri 10am-7pm
Sat 9am-6.30pm, Sun 11am-5pm
Tube: Covent Garden
The shop specialises in good value outdoor gear but also has a book and map section with worldwide walking and trekking guides plus general guidebooks and maps. British Ordnance Survey maps are well represented and Youth Hostel Association publications are also available. In addition, the shop offers a worldwide booking system for hostels overseas.

Ying Hwa

14 Gerrard Street
W1V 7LJ
Tel: 0171 439 8825
Fax: 0171 439 1183
Mon-Sun 11am-8pm
Tube: Leicester Square
Located in the heart of Chinatown, this shop sells mainly Chinese books and magazines covering a variety of subjects. There is also a small selection of pretty specialised computer books in Chinese plus books in English on Chinese subjects.

Z

Zeno Bookseller

The Greek Bookshop
6 Denmark Street
WC2H 8LP
Tel: 0171 240 1968
Fax: 0171 836 2522
Web: www.thegreekbookshop.com
Mon-Fri 9.30am-6pm, Sat 9.30am-5pm
Tube: Tottenham Court Road
Specialising in books in Greek and in English about Greece. The stock includes dictionaries, language courses and newspapers.

Zwemmers

The Barbican Centre, Silk Street
EC2Y 8DS
Tel: 0171 382 7007
Fax: 0171 382 7097
Mon-Sat 11.30am-7.30pm,
Sun 12noon-7.30pm
Tube: Barbican
There are two small Zwemmer's shops in the Barbican Centre, one on Floor 2 (the Library Floor), stocking mostly fiction, art, biography and a few general non-fiction titles. The other is on the Mezzanine floor (close to the theatre entrance) focusing on plays, theatre, films and music and associated magazines.

Zwemmers Art

24 Litchfield Street
WC2H 9NJ
Tel: 0171 379 7886
Fax: 0171 836 7049
E-mail: zwemmer.co@BTinternet.com
Mon, Wed-Fri 10am-6.30pm
Tues 10.15am-6.30pm, Sat 10am-6pm
Tube: Leicester Square
The largest of the Zwemmer shops, this one specialises in art, design and architecture. The stock is comprehensive and well laid out and the interior is impressive with two spiral staircases down to the basement. The staff are knowledgeable and there are plenty of chairs and stools so you can browse at your leisure.

Zwemmers Design

72 Charing Cross Road
WC2H 0BE
Tel: 0171 240 1559
Fax: 0171 240 4186
E-mail: zwemmer.co@btinternet.com
Mon-Fri 10am-6.30pm, Sat 10am-6pm
Tube: Leicester Square
Titles on design in all its manifestations.

Zwemmers at the Estorick

The Estorick Collection
Northampton Lodge
39a Canonbury Square
N1 2AN
Tel: 0171 704 8282
Wed-Sat 11am-6pm, Sun 12noon-5pm
Tube: Highbury
This is a well organised little shop
concentrating on books about Italian art, but
with a good few general reference titles and
some very fine cards.

Zwemmers Media

80 Charing Cross Road
WC2H 0BN
Tel: 0171 240 4157
Mon-Fri 10am-6.30pm, Sat 10am-6pm
Tube: Leicester Square
A small two storey shop featuring mostly
new but a few out of print books and
magazines on photography, graphics and film
as well as advertising and computer graphics.
Although the shop is pretty cramped, the
range of its stock is impressive.

Zwemmers at Whitechapel Art Gallery

80 Whitechapel High Street
E1 7QX
Tel: 0171 247 6924
Fax: 0171 377 1685
Tues-Sat 11am-5pm
(longer hours during shows, ring for details)
Tube: Aldgate
Although this branch doesn't have the vast
range of the Central London Zwemmers
shops, it still has a good stock specialising in
post-1945 art, art theory and architecture.
There's a broad choice in these areas plus
special selections of titles to back up the
gallery's exhibitions; the shop also has
attractive greetings cards, postcards, posters
and magazines.

1,2,3...

30th Century Comics

18 Lower Richmond Road
SW15 1JP
Tel: 0181 788 2052
Mon-Wed 10.30am-6pm
Thurs & Fri 10.30am-7pm
Sat 10.30am-6pm, Sun 11am-5pm
Tube: Putney Bridge
Rail: Putney
Specialist comic retailer with a second-hand,
mostly paperback, book stock covering
horror, fantasy and sci-fi.

Browsing on Charing Cross Road

SECOND-HAND & ANTIQUARIAN BOOKSHOPS

A

Abbey Bookshop
Market Hall
Camden Lock
NW1 8AF
Tel: 0181 740 0713
Mon-Fri 10am-6pm
Sat & Sun:10am-6.30pm
Tube: Camden Town
Although small, this second-hand shop carries a very large stock, with extra space provided outside in the market on several open air stalls. In addition to a good general stock, a specialist range of books on art and cinema are also on offer.

Apprentice Shop
Merton Abbey Mills
Merantum Way
SW19 2RD
Tel: 0181 740 0713
Sat & Sun 9am-6pm
Tube: Colliers Wood
This weekends-only shop has a good, well-organised stock of second-hand books, rare titles, and a particularly good selection of Irish fiction. When the weather is fine there are huge tables outside the shop displaying even more books.

Alexandra Bookshop
209 Park Road
N8 8JB
Tel: 0181 889 1674
Thurs & Fri 10am-5.30pm,
Sat 10am-6pm
Rail: Hornsey
This is the sister shop of the Abbey bookshop in Camden (see opposite). It's small with a similar but smaller range of good quality second-hand books in most general subject areas, and a good selection of fiction.

Any Amount of Books
62 Charing Cross Road
WC2H OBB
Tel: 0171 240 8140
Mon-Sat 10.30am-9.30pm, Sun 11.30am-8pm
Web: www.anyamountofbooks.com/
Tube: Leicester Square
Just a couple of doors down from Charing Cross Road Bookshop (see p.94), this place also has an excellent general stock of second-hand books and a high turnover – probably encouraged by the tables of £1 books outside. It's ideal for a quick browse.

Archive Books and Music
83 Bell Street, NW1 6TB
Tel: 0171 402 8212
Mon-Sat 10.30am-6pm
Tube: Edgware Road
With plenty of bargains outside to attract the bookworm, this shop carries a good general stock (general fiction and travel are well represented). It is especially strong on sheet music and books about music. Stephen Foster's is just along the street (see p.100).

Ash Rare Books
25 Royal Exchange
Threadneedle Street
EC3V 3LP
Tel: 0171 626 2665
Fax: 0171 623 9052
Mon-Fri 10am-5pm
Tube: Bank
This shop is ideally situated to exploit the affluent City trade. The stock is mostly first editions and titles on travel and topography. The quality of books is good and it's nice that despite some pretty expensive price tags, they aren't hidden away behind glass. Catalogues of recent acquisitions are available.

B

H Baron

76 Fortune Green Road
NW6 1DS
Tel: 0171 794 4041
Fri & Sat 1pm-6pm
Tube: West Hampstead (then a bus)
Specialising in second-hand and rare books
on music and musical scores, this good-
sized shop is near the Fortune Green
Bookshop (seep.98).

Beaumont Travel Books

31 Museum Street
WC1A 1LH
Tel/Fax: 0171 637 5862
E-mail: beaumont@antiquarian.com
Web:
www.antiquarian.com/beaumont-travel-books
Tube: Holborn or Tottenham Court Road
This shop carries a large specialist stock of rare
and second-hand books on travel (covering all
areas of the globe) and on the two World
Wars, architecture and photography. Each
year they issue six catalogues.

Bell, Book and Radmall

4 Cecil Court
WC2N 4HE
Tel: 0171 240 2161
Fax: 0171 379 1062
Mon-Fri 10am-5.30pm, Sat 10.30am-4pm
Tube: Leicester Square
Packed with stock, this small shop specialises
in first editions over a wide range of subjects.

Bibliopola

The Antique Market
13-25 Church Street
Marylebone
NW8 8DT
Tel: 0171 724 7231
Tues-Fri 10am-4pm, Sat 10am-5pm
Tube: Marylebone or Edgeware Road
Specialist in children's, illustrated and private
press books, and modern first editions.

Bloomsbury Bookshop

12 Bury Place
WC1A 2JL
Tel: 0171 404 7433
Mon-Sat 11am-6pm, Sun 1pm-5pm
Tube: Holborn, Tottenham Court Road
A small shop that over two storeys carries an
extensive range of second-hand and out-of-
print books on the arts, history and social
sciences. The books are piled high sometimes
threatening to over whelm the fragile order
of the shop, but this only adds to the charm
of the place. The staff are helpful and willing
to take time to talk about books, which
explains why so many bookworms visit the
shop to browse and chat. A wonderful shop
and well worth a visit.

Book Art & Architecture

12 Woburn Walk
WC1H 0JL
0171 387 5006
Mon-Fri 11am-5.30pm
Tube: Euston
A newly established shop dealing in out of
print, rare and second-hand books
concerning art, architecture and design. They
also offer a good selection of pamphlets and
journals on the same subjects. If your looking
for a more general stock, head west to Judd
Books (see p.103 for details).

Book and Comic Exchange

14 Pembridge Road, W11 3HL
Tel: 0171 229 8420
Daily 10am-8pm
Tube: Notting Hill Gate
There is a good choice of mostly paperback
books and a wide range of comics in this small
shop. The emphasis is on fiction (both literary
and popular), music, film and art subjects.
Further along the road at No. 28, there'a a
bargain basement with all books for 10p.

Bookmongers
439 Coldharbour Lane
SW9 8LN
Tel: 0171 738 4225
Mon-Sat 10.30am-6.30pm
Tube: Brixton
A brilliant second-hand bookshop down the side of the Ritzy Cinema in Brixton. The range is wide and prices excellent with plenty of 50p bargain books. The stock is well organised with sections on professional subjects, books by Irish and Scottish writers and foreign langauage titles, as well as mainstream fiction and books concerning more academic subjects such as history and science. This is definitely one of the best second-hand bookshops south of the river.

The Book Palace
83 Church Road
SE19 2TA
Tel: 0181 768 0022
Daily 11am-6pm
Rail: Crystal Palace
A large selection of fiction, sci-fi, fantasy and horror, British and American comics (including lots of 'Marvel' comics at 50p as well as 'Eagle', 'Beezer'). The shop also has graphic novels and non-fiction books on film and television (specialising in Disney, 'Star Wars', 'The X-Files' and other things of that ilk), art and photography. This is one of a few shops in the area that are turning Crystal Palace into an area which is well worth a visit for anyone after a second-hand book bargain.

Books Bought
357 Kings Road, SW3 5ES
Tel: 0171 352 9376
Mon-Fri 1pm-6.30pm
Sat & Sun & Bank Hols 11am-6pm
(10% discount on Saturdays, 20% on Sundays)
Tube: Fulham Broadway
A small second-hand shop at the Fulham end of the Kings Road. There are bargain shelves and tables outside and inside, a wide-ranging general stock that is especially strong on art,

literary criticism, photography, film, media and psychology. The shop is well worth a visit particularly as it is opposite the excellent Chelsea Oxfam shop which always has a good range of books (see p.121).

Books and Lyrics
Apprentice Shop
Merton Abbey Mills
Merantum Way
SW19 2RD
Tel: 0181 543 0625
Tues-Sun 10am-6pm
Tube: Colliers Wood
Next to the remarkable Tlon Books (see p.110), this store is smaller and has a rather more disorganised feel – there are piles of books everywhere. Despite the clutter there is a large stock of general subjects and lots of good buys for those with the inclination to sort through. The shop also has an excellent range of sheet music covering all styles and types of music and all instruments.

The Bookshop
74 Tranquil Vale
Blackheath
SE3 0BN
Tel: 0181 852 4786
Mon-Sat 9.30am-4pm
Rail: Blackheath
Located in the heart of Blackheath near the station, this shop has a general stock of second-hand and antiquarian books. There are books for all pockets and a few new paperbacks and greetings cards.

Joanna Booth
247 Kings Road
SW3 5EL
Tel: 0171 352 8998
Fax: 0171 376 7350
Mon-Sat 10am-6pm
Tube: Sloane Square
Fabulous antique shop with top quality furniture and textiles but also a small speciality stock of early French literature.

Boutle and King

23 Arlington Way
EC1R 1UY
Tel: 0171 278 4497
Mon-Fri 10.30am-7pm, Sat 10.30am-6pm
Tube: Angel
Not far from Sadlers Wells theatre, this
second-hand shop sells an excellent range of
books with especially good selections in the
arts (both pure and applied), history, travel
and fiction. They also have plenty of
paperbacks for around £3.

Alan Brett

24 Cecil Court
WC2N 4HE
Tel: 0171 836 8222
Mon-Sat 9.30am-5.30pm
Tube: Leicester Square
Selling mostly prints and other illustrations
the shop also has a small stock of antiquarian
and rare books.

C

Camberwell Book Shop

28A Camberwell Grove
SE5 8RE
Tel: 0171 701 1839
Daily 11am-7pm
Rail: Denmark Hill
About fifteen minutes walk from
Camberwell Green, this excellent second-
hand bookshop is especially strong on
paperback fiction, art and applied art and
modern first editions. They also have good
sections on history, travel and philosophy
and large bargain trays outside as well as
prints, magazines and periodicals. The shop
is fairly small but space is extended by the
use of an upstairs balcony area. There is a
pleasant pub next door where you can
peruse your buys over a pint.

Marcus Campbell Art Books

43 Holland Street
Bankside
SE1 9JR
Tel: 0171 261 0111
Fax: 0171 261 0129
Mon-Fri 10.30am-5.30pm, Sun 12noon-5pm
Tube: Blackfriars
Located next to the new Tate Gallery of
Modern Art and close to the River
Thames, this shop specialises in modern,
second-hand art books, exhibition
catalogues and artist's books.

Cassidy's Gallery

20 College Approach
SE10 9HY.
Tel: 0181 858 7197
Sun 12noon-6pm
(Mon-Fri by appointment only)
Rail: Greenwich
Selling mostly antique maps and
watercolours, with some additional
antiquarian book stock.

Charing Cross Road Bookshop

56 Charing Cross Road
WC2H OBB
Tel: 0171 836 3697
Daily 10.30am-9.30pm
Tube: Leicester Square
Offering an excellent general stock of
second-hand books in a timeless interior
lined with packed shelves. Outside there are
shelves full of bargains – from £1 per book.

T A Cherrington

81 Grosvenor Street
W1X 9DE
Tel: 0171 493 1343
Fax: 0171 499 2983
Mon-Fri 10am-5.30pm
Tube: Bond Street or Oxford Circus
Antiquarian dealer specialising in natural
history, costume, architecture and atlases.

Church Street Bookshop

Church Street Bookshop

142 Stoke Newington Church Street
N16 0JU
Tel: 0171 241 5411
Mon-Fri 11.30am-6pm
Sat 11am-6pm, Sun 11.30am-6pm
Rail: Stoke Newington
Small but brilliantly stocked, with bargain boxes of books for £1 and an excellent choice of good quality second-hand books. The shop is especially strong on art, design, photography and fiction with a fair amount of literary biography, travel, children's books and science. A wonderful little shop.

Clarke-Hall & Kent-Nielsen

5 Bride Court, EC4Y 8DX
Mon-Fri 12noon-4pm
Tube: Blackfriars
The shop at the front (Clarke-Hall) sells antique prints and frames, the small bookshop at the back (Kent-Nielsen) sells fiction and material on Boswell and Johnson, with some superb, leatherbound antiquarian volumes. There's also a bargain shelf outside.

Coffeehouse Bookshop

139 Greenwich South Street
SE10 8NX
Tel: 0181 692 3885
Mon-Wed, Fri & Sat 10am-5.30pm
Thurs & Sun closed
Rail: Greenwich
A small shop (whose name perhaps refers to the excellent Escaped Café next door), with second-hand books on every surface. The stock is mostly fiction, but there are also some hardbacks and a variety of non-fiction titles.

Collector's Centre

98 Wood Street
Walthamstow
E17 3HX
Tel: 0181 520 4032
Mon-Wed, Fri-Sat 10.30am-5.30pm
Rail: Wood Street
The Collector's Centre is a small covered area packed with tiny shops. A couple of the units are just bookshops, with a few others mixing books into their general stock. Don't forget to visit Sporting Books which is across the road (see p.109). Units include:

House of Usher
Unit 8, 9 & 10
This shop specialises in everything from the 1950's and 1960's, including a large stock of second-hand children's annuals, and a smaller range of crime, sci-fi and spiritualist books.

Antique City Bookshop
Unit 2 & 3
Tel: 0181 520 8300
Tues & Wed, Fri & Sat 10am-5pm
An excellent selection of second-hand books on all imaginable subjects crammed into a tiny shop. The range is excellent and prices very fair with 30p bargain shelves outside.

House of Yesterdays
Unit 4, 5 & 6
Tues & Wed, Fri & Sat 9.30am-5.30pm
Specialising in music from the 1940's and
1950's, there are also plenty of books on the
music and cinema of the same era.

Memory Lane
Unit 1
Mon-Wed, Fri & Sat 9.30am-5.30pm
Stocking plenty of material on 'Star Wars',
The Beatles, 'Star Trek' and 'Dr Who', as
well as general pop music of times past, plus
a small stock of second-hand books.

Collinge and Clark

13 Leigh Street
WC1H 9EW
Tel 0171 387 7105
Fax: 0171 388 1315
Mon-Fri 11am-6.30pm, Sat 11am-3pm
Tube: Russell Square
A small, high quality second-hand,
antiquarian and rare bookshop which
specialises in volumes from private presses and
in books on history, art, literature and
typography. Much of the stock is
leatherbound and of excellent quality with
price tags to match, but there are some
leatherbound volumes for as little as £30.

Crouch End Bookshop

12 Park Road
N8 8TD
Tel: 0181 348 8966
Tues-Wed 10am-6pm, Thurs-Fri 10am-7pm,
Sat 10am-6pm, Sun 12noon-7pm
Rail: Crouch Hill
This small second-hand bookshop is just
down the road from the clock tower in
Crouch End. It is small but carries an
interesting stock in most general subject
areas, being especially strong on paperback
fiction, art, media, photography, history,
poetry, travel and biography.

D

David Drummond

11 Cecil Court
WC2N 4EZ
Tel: 0171 836 1142
Mon-Fri 11am-2.30pm and 3.30pm-5.45pm
First Sat of the month 11am-2.30pm
Tube: Leicester Square
Specialising in books and ephemera related
to the performing arts, with a large stock –
well worth a look if this is your area.

E

Earlsfield Bookshop

513 Garratt Lane
Wandsworth
SW18 4SW
Tel: 0181 946 3744
Mon-Thurs 4pm-6pm
Fri 11am-6pm, Sat 10am-5pm
Rail: Earlsfield
Right next door to Earlsfied Station, this is a
small, general second-hand book dealer.

Francis Edwards

13 Great Newport Street
WC2H 7JA
Tel: 0171 379 7669
Fax: 0171 836 5977
Mon-Sat 9.30am-6.30pm
Tube: Leicester Square
This shop specialises in second-hand naval
and military books and carries an extensive
selection.

Enigma Books

16 Church Road
SE19 2ET
Tel: 0181 653 1884
Mon-Sat 10am-6pm, Sun 11am-4pm
Rail: Crystal Palace
Excellent second-hand bookshop with a
good range of paperback fiction from
classics through popular genres to literary
stuff. There is also plenty of general non-

Bloomsbury Bookshop

fiction stock including sections on music, history and sports as well as second-hand records. Prices are good and there's plenty of titles in the £2-£3 range.

Eurobooks
2 Woodstock Street
W1R 1HD
Tel: 0171 403 2002
Mon-Fri 10am-6pm, Sat 10am-4pm
Tube: Bond Street
Just a few metres from Oxford Street, this is a popular, bustling shop with a large general stock of good quality second-hand and antiquarian books in all price brackets.

F

Faircross Books/Strand Antiques
166 Thames Road
Strand-on-the-Green
W4 3QS
Tel: 0181 994 1912
Daily 12noon-5pm
Tube: Gunnersbury or Kew Bridge
Walk along the river through Strand-on-the-Green and the shop is behind the Bull's Head pub. Located inside a general antique outlet in which the whole top floor is given over to books, Faircross offers a general second-hand stock.

Fantasy Centre
157 Holloway Road
N7 8LX
Tel: 0171 607 9433
Mon-Sat 10am-6pm
Tube: Holloway Road
This long-established specialist shop caters for readers and collectors of sci-fi, fantasy and horror with a huge second-hand, rare and out-of-print stock of both paperback and hardback titles. There is a wide range of collectable books but also some newer titles on offer from specialist publishers such as Ash Tree Press, Tartarus Press, Fedogan & Bremer and Nesfa Press. For refreshment Angel Bagel is just up the road.

Keith Fawkes
1-3 Flask Walk
NW3 1HJ
Tel: 0171 435 0614
Mon-Sat 10am-5.30pm
Sun 1pm-5.30pm
Tube: Hampstead
Everything a second-hand bookshop should be, with a massive stock ranged high on shelves and in piles that would take days rather than hours to sift through. The stock covers all general subjects and includes musical scores and is especailly strong on art, literature and first editions.

Simon Finch Rare Books

53 Maddox Street, W1R 0PN
Tel: 0171 499 0974
Fax: 0171 499 0799
E-mail: sfinchbook@aol.com
Web: www.simonfinch.com
Mon-Fri 10am-5pm, Sat 11am-6pm
Tube: Bond Street, Oxford Circus
This shop is unimposing from the outside, but inside the building has been redesigned in a simple modern style over three floors with stripped wood floors, skylights providing soft natural light and a modern staircase. The stock is equally impressive with wonderful leather bound tomes covering all subjects but with an emphasis on architecture, colour plate books, literature and travel. Catalogues are published about four times a year and prices start from around £100.

Fine Books Oriental

38 Museum Street
WC1A 1LP
Tel: 0171 242 5288
Fax: 0171 242 5344
E-mail: oriental@finebooks.demon.co.uk
Web: www.finebooks.demon.co.uk
Mon-Fri 9.15am-6pm, Sat 11am-6pm
Tube: Tottenham Court Road or Holborn
Carrying a small selection of antiquarian, rare and second-hand books on the Far and Middle East.

Jane Fior Bookseller

47 Exmouth Market, EC1R 4QL
Tel: 0171 833 4662
Mon-Sat 10am-5pm
Tube: Farringdon
Amid the trendy bars and cafés of Exmouth market, this wonderful little bookshop is certainly worth a browse. The stock is a well-organised mix of second-hand and antiquarian books as well as modern first editions and a few shelves of new discounted titles. Prices start at £1.50 for paperback fiction, going up to £550 for some of the finest antiquarian stock.

Fisher & Sperr

46 Highgate High Street
N6 5JB
Tel: 0181 340 7244
Fax: 0181 348 4293
Mon-Sat 10am-5pm
Tube: Highgate
Whilst the exterior of this fine old shop exudes an aura of expensive exclusivity, amid the stock of second-hand and rare books and prints, there is plenty here for most book lovers. The selection covers all subjects and is spread out over four floors, with lots of reasonably priced volumes (rather more hardbacks than paperbacks). Expect to see extensive shelves of Everyman and Folio Society publications.

Sam Fogg Rare Books and Manuscripts

35 St George Street
W1R 9FA
Tel: 0171 495 2333
Fax: 0171 409 3326
E-mail: samfogg@dircon.co.uk
Mon-Fri 9.30am-5.30pm
Tube: Oxfrod Circus
Right opposite the back door of Sotheby's, this exclusive shop specialises in medieval and Oriental manuscripts.

Fortune Green Bookshop

74 Fortune Green Road
NW6 1DS
Tel: 0171 435 7574
Fax: 0171 794 4937
Wed-Sat 10.30am-5.30pm
Tube: West Hampstead (then a bus)
This second-hand shop specialises in women writers and women's studies, but also has a selection of other literature, literary criticism and history. Prices are good, there is a noticeboard advertising local services and mail order catalogues are available.

Simon Finch Rare Books

Foster's
183 Chiswick High Road
W4 2DR
Tel: 0181 995 2768
Mon-Sat 10.30am-5.30pm
Tube: Turnham Green
A lovely second-hand bookshop with books in all subject areas. The range encompasses everything from bargains on the £1 table outside to rarer, antiquarian and leatherbound books. There are also prints and postcards.

Paul Foster's Bookshop
119 Sheen Lane
East Sheen
SW14 8AE
Tel/Fax: 0181 876 7424
Mon-Sat 10.30am-6pm
Rail: Mortlake
A big stock of second-hand as well as rare and antiquarian books covering a variety of subjects. They specialise in art and literature and books with fine bindings with most of the stock being hardback.

Stephen Foster's
95 Bell Street
NW1 6TL
Tel: 0171 724 0876
Mon-Sat 10.30am-6pm
Tube: Edgware Road
A well-stocked, second-hand shop with a superb art section covering all periods, nationalities and styles (and applied arts). There are also good sections on ancient and modern history, literary criticism and travel as well as a range of rare and antiquarian books. Just down the road is Archive Books & Music (see page 91 for details).

Robert Frew Ltd
106 Great Russell Street
WC1B 3NA
Tel: 0171 580 2311
Fax: 0171 631 3253
Mon-Fri 10am-6pm, Sat 10am-2pm
Tube: Tottenham Court Road

This is a shop for the serious and affluent collector, with mostly leatherbound antiquarian books (many in sets) in glass cabinets. However, staff are friendly and there are plenty of prints on offer.

G

R A Gekoski
Pied Bull Yard
15A Bloomsbury Square
WC1A 2LP
Tel: 0171 404 6676
Fax: 0171 404 6595
E-mail: gekoski@antiquarian.com
Web: www.antiquarian.com/gekoski/
Mon-Fri 10am-5.30pm
Tube: Holborn
Specialists in twentieth century literature, first editions, letters and manuscripts. The shop is conveniently located in the British Museum area with plenty of other booksellers nearby.

Martin Gladman
235 Nether Street
Finchley
N3 1NT
Tel: 0181 343 3023
Tues-Fri 11am-8pm, Sat 10am-6pm
Tube: West Finchley
This second-hand and out-of-print bookshop specialises in mostly hardback scholarly and serious books (particularly covering history, the humanities and transport), but also has a large general stock which includes some paperback fiction.

Gloucester Road Bookshop
123 Gloucester Road
SW7 4TE
Tel: 0171 370 3503
Fax: 0171 373 0610
Mon-Fri 8.30am-10.30pm
Sat & Sun & Bank Holidays 10.30am-6.30pm
Tube: Gloucester Road

This is one of the most welcoming and best value second-hand bookshops in London – especially if fiction is your interest. There is a rapid turnover of material with plenty of excellent bargains and lots of paperbacks for under £2, with £1 and 50p shelves downstairs. They are also very good on literary criticism, art and media. A small stock of antiquarian and rare books as well as irregular catalogues on various subjects are also available. Highly recommended.

Grenville Books
40a Museum Street
WC1A 1LT
Tel/Fax: 0171 404 2872
Mon-Fri 10.30am-6.30pm
Sat & Sun 11am-5pm
Tube: Tottenham Court Road or Holborn
Second-hand specialist in books on Spain, Portugal, Latin America and the social history of women. The shop is well located near the British Museum.

Griffiths and Partners
31-35 Great Ormond Street
WC1N 3HZ
Tel: 0171 430 1394
Mon-Fri 12noon-6pm
Tube: Russell Square
A small shop selling a general stock of second-hand books, especially literature, biography, poetry, history, the Middle East and the Gulf; plus Russian and classical literature. There are bargain trays outside.

H

Halcyon Books
1 Greenwich South Street
SE10 8NW
Tel: 0181 305 2675
Mon-Sat 10am-6pm,
Sun 11am-6pm
Rail: Greenwich
This shop stocks an excellent range of

second-hand and discounted new books in all general subject areas but has a particularly broad range of fiction, literary criticism, history and travel as well as discounted guidebooks. The shop is attractive and well laid out with soothing background music. Some second-hand CD's are also on sale.

Adrian Harrington
64A Kensington Church Street
W8 4DB
Tel: 0171 937 1465
Fax: 0171 368 0912
Mon-Sat 10am-6pm
E-mail: rare@harringtonbooks.co.uk
Web: harringtonbooks.co.uk/rare
Tube: High Street Kensington
Small but beautiful shop that is lined from floor to ceiling with shelves of superb quality antiquarian books – most of them gorgeously bound – covering subjects right across the board. They specialise in literature, voyages and travel, atlases, children's and illustrated books and have a good many first editions. They also stock antique maps and prints and offer a book-binding service. With modern first editions from £12 upwards, a visit here needn't break the bank. A glossy catalogue is published annually.

Peter Harrington
100 Fulham Road
SW3 6HS
Tel: 0171 591 0220
Fax: 0171 225 7054
Mon-Sat 10am-6pm
E-mail: books@peter-harrington.demon.co.uk
Web: www. peter-harrington.demon.co.uk
Tube: South Kensington
A gorgeous shop with fabulous rare and antiquarian books, displayed from floor to ceiling. All subjects are covered but the specialisms are bound sets, travel, colour plates, natural history, fore-edge paintings and fine and rare literature. This is a shop selling quality books at the top end of the market.

T A Hillyer
301 Sydenham Road
SE26 5EW
Tel: 0181 778 6361
Mon & Tues, Thurs & Fri 10.30am-4pm
Wed closed, Sat 9.30am-2pm
Rail: Sydenham, Lower Sydenham
This shop offers an unusual mix of glass and
china ware as well as a reasonable selection of
second-hand books.

P J Hilton
12 Cecil Court
WC2N 4HE
Tel: 0171 379 9825
Mon-Sat 10.30am-6.30pm
Tube: Leicester Square
Specialising in second-hand, rare and
antiquarian literature as well as volumes on
Christianity, ecclesiastical history, Bibles and
prayer books. There are plenty of gorgeous
volumes, but also a bargain shelf outside.

Holloway Book Exchange
175 Holloway Road
N7 1JE
Tel: 0171 700 2954
Fri-Sat 7.30am-4.30pm
Tube: Finchley Road
Small stock of cheap and rather scruffy
paperback fiction.

Hurlingham Books
91 Fulham High Street
SW6 3JS
Tel: 0171 736 2448
Mon-Fri 10am-6pm, Sat 10am-12noon
Tube: Putney Bridge
Rather hidden away on the north side of
Putney Bridge but well worth searching out,
this small second-hand shop is piled high
with enticing bargains. Most general subjects
are covered and there are some rare and
antiquarian titles. The selection of fiction is
especially broad in hardback and paperback
with many in the £2-£3 range.

I

Intercol London
Camden Passage
114 High Street
N1 8EG
Tel: 0181 349 2207
Wed & Sat 9am-5.30pm
Tube: Angel
Part of the Camden Passage antiques market
area, this is a specialist shop with a variety of
books covering playing cards, coins, bank
notes, gambling and maps.

J

Jarndyce
46 Great Russell Street
WC1B 3PA
Tel: 0171 631 4220
Fax: 0171 631 1882
Mon-Fri 9.30am-5pm
Tube: Holborn, Tottenham Court Road
Just across the road from the British Museum
(housed in a building where nineteenth
century artist and illustrator Randolf
Caldecott lived), this shop specialises in
nineteenth-century books covering literature
and social history, but also has some
eighteenth-century stock. Most of the books
are top quality antiquarian and rare volumes,
with lovely binding – and prices to match,
although items like a £2 paperback Sherlock
Holmes story are also on show. The shop
publishes regular catalogues on various
themes, e.g women writers, Dickens and
London. Much of the stock is very valuable
so you have to ring for admission but don't
be deterred as staff are both welcoming and
helpful. An added attraction is a chair in the
corner which W M Thackery reputedly once
occupied.

Judd Books

82 Marchmont Street
WC1N 1AG
Tel: 0171 387 5333
Mon-Sat 11am-7pm, Sun 11am-6pm
Tube: Russell Square
There is so much stock in this two storey gem
(about ten minutes from the British Library),
that step ladders are provided so customers
can climb to the upper shelves. The shop is
full of second-hand and discounted books in
all subject areas with particularly strong
sections on African studies, economics,
history, Ireland, humanities, Eastern Europe,
architecture, fiction, film, literary biography,
photography and printing and publishing.
The scope and number of volumes is vast and
the prices are competitive, with bargain tables
outside, plus a 10% student discount. One of
the best second-hand bookshops in London.

Judd Books

K

Don Kelly

Aquarius Antique Market
Stall M13
135 Kings Road
SW3 4BW
Tel: 0171 352 4690
Mon-Sat 10am-5.30
Tube: Sloane Square
Brilliant selection of second-hand illustrated
books on antiques, art, design, porcelain,
gardens, glass, jewellery and textiles.

Alison Knox Booksellers

55 Exmouth Market
EC1R 4QL
Tel:0171 833 0591
E-mail: alisonknox@bigfoot.com
Mon-Sat 10.30am-5.30pm
Tube: Farringdon
This shop has a wide range of second-hand
hardback reference books covering subjects
such as history, art and traditional pastimes
like hunting and fishing. Their selection of
contemporary art books is particularly fine.

L

Judith Lassalle

7 Pierreport Arcade
Camden Passage
N1 8EF
Tel: 0171 607 7121 and 0171 354 9344
Wed 7.30am-4pm, Sat 9.30am-4pm
Tube: Angel
Located in the Camden Passage antiques
market area, this specialist outlet has a small
stock of children's books plus children's
games, toys and ephemera.

M

Maggs Bros Ltd
50 Berkely Square
W1X 6EL
Tel: 0171 493 7160
Fax: 0171 499 2007
E-mail: jeff@maggs.com
Web: www.maggs.com
Mon-Fri 9.30am-5pm
Tube: Green Park
With a royal warrant as booksellers of rare books and manuscripts to the Queen, it's not surprising that this is one of the premier rare and antiquarian booksellers in London. Each separate department is looked after by highly knowledgeable, often multilingual staff. Specialisms are travel, early books, literature and natural history, with an enormous range of autographed letters and manuscripts. The catalogues alone are lovely books and published frequently, covering a specific subject area. Prices reflect the superb quality of material with most items over £200.

Magpie Bookshop
53 Brushfield Street
E1 6AA
Tel: 0171 247 4263
Mon-Sat 11am-4pm, Sun 10am-5pm
Tube: Liverpool Street
Located in the Spitalfields Market complex, this second-hand shop has an excellent general range including a large fiction section, 10p comics and old art magazines. Also at:
Clerks House
118 Shoreditch High Street
E1 6JN
Tel: 0171 729 5076
Daily 12noon-7pm.
A smaller branch, with the same range of books, slightly more comics and a picture gallery upstairs.

The Map House
54 Beauchamp Place
Knightsbridge
SW3 1NY
Tel: 0171 589 4325
Fax: 0171 589 1041
E-mail: maps@themaphouse.com
Web: www. themaphouse.com
Mon-Fri 9.45am-5.45pm, Sat 10.30am-5pm
Tube: Knightsbridge
Specialising in antique maps, atlases and globes, this shop is definitely worth a visit if you are interested in cartography. Don't be deterred by the affluent shopping area, prices start from just £20-£30, although they do ascend into the thousands.

Marcet Books
4A Nelson Road
SE10 9JB
Tel: 0181 853 5408
Daily 10am-5.30pm
Rail: Greenwich
In one of the alleyways leading off Greenwich Craft Market, this is a small shop but packed full with a good choice of mostly second-hand but some discounted new books in a broad range of subjects. It is particularly strong on fiction, history, art and has literary magazines in stock.

Marchmont Bookshop
39 Burton Street
WC1H 9AL
Tel/Fax: 0171 387 7989
Mon-Fri 11am-6.30pm
Tube: Green Park, Bond Street
Tucked away in what looks like a residential area but which actually has several bookshops, this second-hand outlet specialises in poetry, literary biography, and fiction. In the basement there are plenty of other books on general subjects. Paperback bargains are displayed on a table outside.

Marchpane
16 Cecil Court
WC2N 4HE
Tel: 0171 836 8661
Fax: 0171 497 0567
Mon-Sat 10.30am-6.30pm, Sun 12noon-6pm
Tube: Leicester Square
Second-hand and antiquarian children's and illustrated books, especially Lewis Carroll titles. They also have an attractive, well-priced selection of prints.

Marlborough Rare Books
144-146 New Bond Street
W1Y 9FD
Tel: 0171 493 6993
Fax: 0171 499 2479
E-mail: mrb@unico.com
Web: www.bibliocity.com/search/marlborough
Mon-Fri 9.30am-5.30pm
Tube: Bond Street
On the fourth floor, high above the Bond Street fashion windows, this shops has a small but quality stock which specialises in architecture, British topography and English literature. They also stock any books with fine bindings and colour plates. Catalogues are on the shop's web site.

Music & Video Exchange
14 Pembridge Road
W11 3HX
Tel: 0171 229 8420
Daily 10am-8pm
Tube: Notting Hill Gate
Whilst it's predominantly a second-hand video and music store, this shop also has a couple of cases of second-hand books on all aspects of stage and screen.

Music and Video Exchange
480 Fulham Road
SW6 5NH
Tel: 0171 385 5350
Web: www.demon.co.uk/mveshops
Daily 10am-7pm
Tube: Fulham Broadway

Part of the group of exchange shops, this shop specialises more in the music side of the business, but does have a good stock of general books which are especially worth a look for the 10p bargain titles.

My Back Pages
8-10 Balham Station Road
SW12 9SG
Tel: 0181 675 9346
Mon-Fri 10am-8pm
Sat 10am-7pm, Sun 11am-6pm
Rail: Balham
Part of a small second-hand chain that includes Junction Books in Putney (see p.45) and a Richmond store, this shop is just down the side of Balham Station (you can hear station announcements in the shop), and is required visiting for South London book enthusiasts. The stock of second-hand books, with a few rarer and antiquarian titles, is extensive and covers pretty much any subject (both general and more academic). There are also some new books at 10% discount and good value greetings cards. Go on a Friday or Saturday evening and The Banana Comedy club is just around the corner at The Bedford pub.

N

E C Nolan
5 Cecil Court
WC2N 4EZ
Tel: 0171 497 9228
Mon-Sat 10.30-6.30
Tube: Leicester Square
Selling mostly prints but stocks a few antiquarian books

Notting Hill Books

132 Palace Gardens Terrace
W8 4RT
Tel: 0171 727 5988
Mon-Wed, Fri & Sat 10.15am-6pm
Thurs 10.15am-1pm
Tube: Notting Hill Gate
A small shop, but packed full of discounted
and second-hand books on a variety of serious
subjects, with excellent coverage of art,
literary critiscim, architecture, design, history
and travel. The small selection of serious
fiction is offered at half the publisher's price
and there are trays of bargain books outside.

O

Ocean Books

127 Stoke Newington Church Street
N16 0UH
Tel: 0171 241 5411
Mon-Sat 11.30am-6pm, Sun 1pm-6pm
Rail: Stoke Newington
One of three second-hand bookshops within
a few metres that provide excellent range and
value. This shop is especially strong on
fiction, art and design.

Olley's Second-hand Bookshop

20 Eldon Street
EC2M 7LA
Tel: 0171 256 5347
Mon-Fri 10.30am-3.30pm
Tube: Liverpool Street
A small second-hand and discount bookshop
in the heart of the City, with low prices
(there's plenty of paperback fiction under
£2), a fast turnover and good stock of fiction
and reference titles. The shop is deservedly
popular with office workers who visit during
their lunch break, so go either early or late
for a more peaceful browse.

P

Pendlebury's

Church House
Portland Avenue
N16 6HJ
Tel/Fax: 0181 809 4922
Mon-Fri 10am-5pm, Sat 10.30-4.30pm
Rail: Stoke Newington
Created out of a disused church just behind
Stamford Hill Library, this shop specialises in
second-hand religious books, but also has a
good general stock (some of it rare and
antiquarian), including sections on politics,
literary criticism, sociology and social history,
science, travel and fiction. Don't be deterred
by having to ring for admittance as this is a
welcoming place to browse and the religious
stock includes plenty of philosophy and large
sections on Judaism, Islam and Eastern
religions.

Pickering and Chatto

36 St George Street
W1R 9FA
Tel: 0171 491 2656
Fax: 0171 491 9161
E-mail: rarebook@pandcltd.demon.co.uk
Mon-Fri 9.30am-5.30pm
Tube: Oxford Circus
One of several specialist antiquarian dealers in
the Bond Street area, this one specialises in
economics, science, health, medicine,
philosophy, history, social sciences,
technology and women's studies. The shop
publishes regular catalogues in the main
subject areas. Prices range from £100
upwards.

Plus Books

19 Abbey Parade
Merton High Street
SW19 1DG
Tel: 0181 542 1665
Mon-Sat 9.30am-6pm
Tube: Colliers Wood

This old-style second-hand bookshop is about ten minutes walk from Merton Abbey Mills. It's full of popular paperbacks: thrillers, romance, sci-fi, crime, westerns and fantasy are all covered all at reduced prices. There are also heaps of magazines concerning motoring, motorcycles, health and fitness, 'DC' comics, sport and much more. There is also a 'girlie' mag and erotic book section at the rear, but it's easily avoided. 'Out of place' stuff is also dotted about, like sheet music, literary hardbacks or a real non-fiction find.

Henry Pordes

58-60 Charing Cross Road
WC2H 0BB
Tel: 0171 836 9031
Fax: 0181 886 2201
Mon-Sat 10am-7pm
Tube: Leicester Square

This shop specialises in second-hand, rare and antiquarian books but also stocks some discounted new books. The huge selection is arranged floor-to-ceiling over two floors; the range of art books is especially good, and there are cheap paperbacks downstairs in the basement.

Jonathan Potter

125 New Bond Street
W1Y 9AF
Tel: 0171 491 3520
Fax: 0171 491 9754
E-mail: jpmaps@ibm.net
Mon-Fri 10am-6pm
Tube: Bond Street

This is a first floor showroom for a specialist seller of maps, prints and atlases. Also up here Chas S Sawyer specialises in books about nineteenth century Africana including books by and about Stanley and Burton.

Q

Bernard Quaritch

5-8 Lower John Street
Golden Square
W1R 4AU
Tel: 0171 734 2983
Fax: 0171 437 0967
E-mail: rarebooks@quaritch.com
Web: www.quaritch.com
Mon-Fri 9.30am-5.30pm
Tube: Leicester Square

One of the longest established (they set up in London in 1847) and most well respected antiquarian booksellers in London. The range of books here is impressive, as is the collection of rare manuscripts. The quality of the stock is extraordinarily high and the knowledge of the staff in each department encyclopaedic. This probably isn't a place where casual browsers will feel especially comfortable but serious collectors will find plenty to enjoy.

Quinto

48a Charing Cross Road
WC2H 0BS
Tel: 0171 379 7669
Mon-Sat 9am-9pm, Sun 12noon-8pm
Tube: Leicester Square

On the corner of Great Newport Street, this shop is everything a second-hand bookshop should be, with towering shelves, a dusty atmosphere and a labyrinthine basement. The basement houses the more academic politics, philosophy, theology and education books; whilst the upstairs selection covers general subject matter.

R

Rare Discs

18 Bloomsbury Street
WC1B 3QA
Tel: 0171 580 3516
Mon-Sat 10am-6.30pm
Tube: Tottenham Court Road

The ground floor is packed with rare vinyl discs of all ages and provenance but downstairs has plenty of books, magazines, posters, stills and memorabilia from both films and theatre.

Reg and Philip Remington

18 Cecil Court
WC2N 4HE
Tel: 0171 836 9771
Fax: 0171 497 2526
Mon-Fri 9am-5pm
Tube: Leicester Square

An excellent range of second-hand and out-of-print voyage and travel books covering pretty much the entire world from ancient to modern times. You'll find everything here from old Baedeker's to the 'Voyages of Captain Cook'.

Ripping Yarns

355 Archway Road
N6 4EJ
Tel: 0181 341 6111
Mon-Fri 10.30am-5.30pm, Sat 10am-5pm
Sun 11am-4pm
Tube: Highgate

Ignore the ghastly traffic rumbling outside (but not the bargain bins), and the interior of this shop can turn up all sorts of delights. They specialise in children's books and there are rows and rows of every type of book of every age and provenance, including some very rare and expensive old volumes, but also plenty of 'Beano' annuals to bring back childhood memories as well as second-hand books. There is also a good range of general stock to keep adults amused.

Robbie's Bookshop

118a Alexandra Park Road
Muswell Hill
N10 2AE
Tel: 0181 444 6957
Mon-Wed, Fri & Sat 9am-5.30pm, Thurs closed
Tube: Highgate (then bus)

This tiny second-hand bookshop is a real gem and well worth hiking into the wilderness of North London to visit. The stock consists largely of quality fiction of every genre from pulp to Plato. There's also a good range of children's books and the non-fiction stock covers all general subjects. Prices are fair with current paperbacks for about £3.50 as well as 50p bargains in the trays outside. The Maid of Muswell pub opposite is a reasonable place to recover from the exertions of the journey.

Roe and Moore Rare Books

29 Museum Street
WC1A 1LH
Tel: 0171 636 4787
Fax: 0171 636 6110
Mon-Sat 10.30am-6pm
Tube: Holborn or Tottenham Court Road

Catering for the serious collector, this shop specialises in modern rare books with stock from more than one dealer. Among the dealers is Carol Manheim who specialises in art reference, twenteth-century art, fashion and photography titles. There are also children's and illustrated books, French literature, posters and prints.

Rogers Turner

22 Nelson Road
SE10 9JB
Tel: 0181 853 5271
Thurs-Sun 9am-6pm
Rail: Greenwich

A small shop selling second-hand and antiquarian books of a scholarly bent, specialising in linguistics and with good selections on travel, technology, astronomy, scientific instruments and a range of German literature.

S

Bernard Shapero
32 St George Street
W1R 0EA
Tel: 0171 493 0876
Fax: 0171 229 7860
E-mail: rarebooks@shapero.com
Web: www.shapero.com
Mon-Fri 9.30am-6.30pm, Sat 11am-5.30pm
Tube: Oxford Circus
This shop is located in the area around
Sotheby's which has several rare booksellers.
Downstairs is a gallery selling photography,
art and maps while on the ground floor is a
booksellers specialising in architecture,
literature, illustrated books and natural history.
There is also a large selection of books on
voyages and travel with lots of elderly
Baedekers. The quality of the books here is
high and staff are enthusiastic yet unobtrusive.
Although there are some books under £50,
most will be significantly higher in price.

Skoob & Skoob Two
15 & 17 Sicilian Avenue, off Southampton Row
WC1A 2QH
Tel: 0171 404 3063
Fax: 0171 404 4398
E-mail: books@skoob.com
Web: www.skoob.com
Mon-Sat 10.30am-6.30pm
Tube: Holborn
Probably the best-stocked second-hand
bookshop in London, and certainly one of
the best known. It's hugely atmospheric,
with laden shelves towering to the ceiling,
and tiny aisles between them. They carry a
huge stock of academic as well as popular
titles. It's definitely worth a look here before
you splash out on new books elsewhere as
prices are usually two-thirds of the new price.
Just a couple of doors down at No.17, Skoob
Two specialises in science and technology,
religion, Oriental studies and the occult, plus
videos and CD's. Mail order is available and
subject catalogues are issued periodically.

Henry Sotheran
2-5 Sackville Street
W1X 2DP
Tel: 0171 439 6151
Fax: 0171 434 2019
Mon-Fri 9.30am-6pm, Sat 10am-4pm
Tube: Piccadilly Circus
and
80 Pimlico Road
SW1W 8PL
Tel: 0171 730 8756
Fax: 0171 823 6090
Mon-Fri 10am-6pm, Sat 10am-4pm
Tube: Victoria
A specialist seller of rare and antique prints.
The Sackville Street branch also houses an
excellent stock of rare and antiquarian books
and the Pimlico Road shop has a good
selection of discounted new titles on art,
design, architecture, crafts and style as well as
a few excellent travel titles.

Souls of Black Folks
407 Coldharbour Lane
Brixton
SW9 8LQ
Tel/Fax: 0171 738 4141
Mon-Fri 11am-8pm
Tube: Brixton
Poetry performances Fri 9pm-12midnight (or
later), £3 admission.
Live jazz bands Sun 12noon-7pm (or later).
This second-hand bookshop specialises in any
books related to Black issues, but it's also a
genial and relaxed juice bar and café during
the day, a poety venue on Fridays and a
music venue on Sundays.

South London Book Centre

18-19 Stockwell Street
SE10 9JN
Tel: 0181 853 2151
Mon-Fri 10am-6pm
Sat & Sun 9am-5.30pm
Rail: Greenwich

Large stock of hardback and paperback books (the biggest in Greenwich) in a large shop covering a broad range of general subjects with second-hand and discounted new books. At the weekends (Sunday is best) there are stalls outside selling more books. and

Upstairs at 18-19 Stockwell Street

Specialising in comics, graphic novels and books on film, there are also plenty of fiction, especially sci-fi and fantasy titles.

SPCK Second-hand, Antiquarian and Out of Print Bookshop

Holy Trinity Church
Marylebone Road
NW1 4DU
Tel: 0171 383 3097
Mon-Sat 9.30am-6pm
Tube: Great Portland Street

Located at the back of the main SPCK shop, this large and well organised shop has over ten thousand mostly second-hand and out of print books on religion and related subjects such as church architecture. If theology and the church are of interest to you this is a bookshop well worth visiting.

Sporting Bookshop

97 Wood Street
E17 3LL
Tel: 0181 521 9803
Mon-Wed, Fri 9.30am-4.30pm
Thurs & Sat 9.30am-5pm
Rail: Wood Street Walthamstow

As the name suggests this shop stocks predominantly second-hand books covering all aspects of sport with football, cricket and boxing featured very strongly, but just about all sports represented. Photographs, football

programmes and ephemera are also stocked and there is a small range of fiction and books about film for those without an interest in sport. There's a pie and mash shop just up the road for those after a genuine 'East London experience'.

Spread Eagle

8 Nevada Street
SE10 9JL
Tel: 0181 305 1666
Mon-Fri 10am-5pm (lunch for 30mins, sometime between 1pm and 2pm)
Sat & Sun 10.30am-5pm
Rail: Greenwich

A two-storey Aladin's Cave of second-hand books, records, theatrical ephemera and antiques. The book stock is well organised and especially good on theatre, film and music, but there is also a good general range of books. It's only a short walk from most of the other Greenwich bookshops.

Stage Door Prints

9 Cecil Court
WC2N 4EZ
Tel: 0171 240 1683
Fax: 0171 379 5598
Mon-Fri 11am-6pm, Sat 11.30am-6pm
Tube: Leicester Square

Whilst the stock is mainly pictures and ephemera related to the performing arts there is also a good stock of second-hand books covering the same field.

Stemmlers

53 West Ham Lane
E15 4PH
Tel: 0181 534 8455
Mon-Fri 10am-6pm, Sat 10am-5pm
Tube: Stratford

Claiming to be the largest second-hand booksellers in East London, this relaxed and congenial shop is packed with books across all subject areas. Unless otherwise marked, paperbacks are 75p and hardbacks and softback textbooks £1.50.

Tlon Books

Swan's Bookshop
5 Tooting Market
Tooting High Street
SW17 0RH
Tel: 0181 672 4980
Mon & Tue, Thurs 9am-5pm
Wed closed, Fri & Sat 9am-5.30pm
Tube: Tooting Broadway
Almost a South London institution, this market stall inside the covered market has an excellent, good value and fast-changing stock of second-hand books. Most of the stock is paperback and genre fiction but plenty of other stuff passes through as well.

T

Tlon Books
Elephant & Castle Shopping Centre
SE1 6TE
Tel: 0171 701 0360
Mon-Sat 9am-6pm
Tube: Elephant & Castle
Gem of a second-hand bookshop in the unpromising surroundings of this pink monstrosity of a shopping centre. The shop is well laid out (there's a 3-D model to help you find your way around) and has a good general and academic stock. The selection of paperback fiction of all kinds is impressive and prices are good. Subject catalogues are issued regularly. Also at:

Apprentice Shop
Merton Abbey Mills
Merantum Way
SW19 2RD
Tel: 0181 540 4371
Mon-Fri 11am-6pm
Sat 9am-6pm, Sun 10am-6pm
Tube: Colliers Wood
Brilliant academic and general second-hand bookshop packed to the rafters with great stock (there's enough to keep you browsing for hours) and great bargains. There are also vinyl records, cassettes and CD's on offer. A shop defintely worth searching out.

Travis and Emery
17 Cecil Court
WC2N 4EZ
Tel: 0171 240 2129
Fax: 0171 497 0790
Mon-Sat 10am-6pm
Tube: Leicester Square
Second-hand shop stuffed with a huge range of music scores but also stocked with a good selection of books, mostly on classical music, history and theory.

U

Ulysses

40 Museum Street
WC1A 1LT
Tel: 0171 831 1600
Fax: 0171 419 0070
E-mail: 106161.746@compuserv.com
Web: www.antiquarian.com/ulysses
Tube: Holborn or Tottenham Court Road
Neat, well-ordered shop specialising in
modern first editions and illustrated books.
They produce four catalogues each year
detailing stock.

Upper Street Bookshop

182 Upper Street
N1 1RQ
Tel: 0171 359 3785
Mon-Sat 10.30am-6.30pm, Sun 12noonn-4pm
Tube: Angel
About ten minutes walk north of Islington
Green, this second-hand bookshop has a
relaxed and welcoming atmosphere and
stocks titles in a huge range of subjects. The
shop is particularly good for art, architecture,
photography and literature. Don't miss a visit
to the basement, where even more volumes
lurk on shelves and in piles on the floor – a
great place for a rummage.

V

Vortex

139-141 Stoke Newington Church Street
N16 0UH
Tel: 0171 254 6516
Mon-Fri 11am-6.30pm
Sat 10am-6.30pm, Sun 12noon-6.30pm
Rail: Stoke Newington
Underneath the Vortex Jazz Bar, this is one
of three second-hand bookshops on this
street. The shop sells a large range of
stationery and cards but also has an impressive
selection of books on literature, all aspects of
the arts and design, history and associated
subjects, and a few modern first editions.

W

Walden Books

38 Harmood Street
NW1 8DP
Tel: 0171 267 8146
Thurs-Sun 10.30am-6.30pm
Tube: Chalk Farm, Camden Town
A bit hidden away off Chalk Farm Road,
booklovers will do well to search out this
shop jam packed with second-hand bargains –
they spill out onto shelves outside the shop.
The emphasis is on literature, art, architecture
and philosophy, but virtually every subject is
covered. Hardbacks predominate with staff
claiming to have ten thousand hardbacks and
two thousand paperbacks in stock. Ladders are
thoughtfully provided so browsers can reach
the upper shelves. A wonderful bookshop and
a welcome escape from the noise of Camden
High Street on market days.

Walrus

85 Church Road
SE19 2TA
Tel: 0181 771 7799
Mon-Sat 11am-6pm, Sun 11am-4pm
Rail: Crystal Palace
This shop specialises in records and pop
music memorabilia from the 1960's to the
present (especially the Beatles). Among the
memorabilia and records there is also a
selection of relevant books and old
magazines, including 'Melody Maker', 'Vox'
and 'Record Collector'.

Watkins Books Ltd

19-21 Cecil Court
Charing Cross Road
WC2N 4EZ
Tel: 0171 836 2182
Fax: 0171 836 6700
Mon-Wed, Fri 10am-6pm
Thurs 10am-8pm, Sat 10.30am-6pm
Tube: Leicester Square

Watkins Book

Long-established and well known mystical and occult specialist that carries a huge and varied stock of books, magazines, CD's, videos and other material on ancient and modern philosophies and religions. Staff are knowledgeable and helpful and a mail order service is also available.

Nigel Williams
22 & 25 Cecil Court
WC2N 4HE
Tel: 0171 836 7757
Fax: 0171 379 5918
E-mail: nwrarebook@tcp.co.ul
Mon-Sat 10am-6pm
Tube: Leicester Square
Two shops located in the heart of London's book trade. The shop at No.25 specialises in first editions of nineteenth and twentieth-century literarture especially P G Wodehouse and detective fiction. At No.22, children's and illustrated books are sold.

Woburn Bookshop
10 Woburn Walk
WC1H 0JL
Tel: 0171 388 7278
Mon-Fri 11am-6pm, Sat 11am-5pm
Tube: Euston
In a pleasant pedestrian street about ten minutes from the new British Library, this second-hand shop specialises in second-hand and antiquarian books on social and cultural studies. The stock also includes books on art, photography, literary criticism, psychoanalysis, Judaica, Black culture, social studies and death. There is a 10% discount offered to students with ID.

ANTIQUARIAN BOOKDEALERS

In addition to the shops listed above, a great many book dealers operate businesses from their own home. These are not shops, and business is mainly by mail order or through books fairs (see bookfairs section on page 119). In some cases dealers are willing to allow potential customers to browse their stock but in all the cases listed below, this is strictly by **appointment only**, and telephone arrangements should be made beforehand.

Robin de Beaumont
25 Park Walk
Chelsea
SW10 0AJ
Tel/Fax: 0171 352 3440
E-mail: rdebooks.@aol.com
Web: www.bibliocity.com/search/debeaumont
By appointment only
Colour printing, design, fin de siecle, Victorian illustrated.

Bertram Rota Ltd
31 Long Acre
Covent Garden
WC2E 9LT
Tel: 0171 836 0723
Fax: 0171 497 9058
E-mail: 100713.2475@compuserve.com
Contact: Anthony and Julian Rota
Mon–Fri 9.30am-5pm
Sat by appointment
Autographs, English literature, manuscripts, modern first editions, press books.

S K Biltcliffe Books
2A Eynsham Road
W12 0HA
Tel/Fax: 0181 740 5326
Contact: Susan Biltcliffe
By appointment only
Books published in the eighteenth century.

J & S L Bonham
Flat 14, 84 Westbourne Terrace
W2 6QE
Tel: 0171 402 7064
Fax: 0171 402 0955
E-mail: bonbooks@dial.pipex.com
By appointment only
Africa, Asia, Australia, mountaineering and polar.

Books & Things
PO Box 17768
W8 6ZD
Tel/Fax: 0171 370 5593
E-mail: mmsteen@aol.com
Web: www.abebooks.com/home/bookandthings
Contact: Martin Steenson
Fine and decorative art, children's books, modern first editions, photography, posters and reference.

John Boyle & Co
40 Drayton Gardens
SW10 9SA
Tel: 0171 373 8247
Fax: 0171 370 7460
By appointment only
First editions, philosophy, political economy, printing, the mind of man and science.

Fiona Campbell
158 Lambeth Road
SE1 7DF
Tel/Fax: 0171 928 1633
By appointment only
Italy.

Chelsea Rare Books
9 Elmstead Close
Totteridge
N20 8ER
Tel: 0181 445 9492
Fax: 0181 492 0470
Contact: Mr and Mrs L Bernard
By appointment only
Art and architecture, English literature, illustrated books, topography, travel.

Christopher Edwards
63 Jermyn Street
SW1Y 6LX
Tel: 0171 495 4263
Fax: 0171 495 4264
Appointment advisable
Early printed books, English literature and manuscripts.

Elton Engineering Books
27 Mayfield Avenue
W4 1PN
Tel: 0181 747 0967
Fax: 0181 995 7816
E-mail: elton_engineering_books@compuserve.com
By appointment only
Contact: Julia Elton
Fine and rare eighteenth and nineteenth-century engineering books.

Michael Graves-Johnston
PO Box 532
54 Stockwell Park Road
SW9 0DR
Tel: 0171 274 2069
Fax: 0171 738 3747
By appointment only
Africana, the Americas, ethnology and the ancient world and Oceania.

Robin Greer
434 Fulham Palace Road, SW6 6HX
Tel: 0171 381 9113
Fax: 0171 381 6499
By appointment
Children's, illustrated and original drawings and travel to the Middle and Far East.

Amanda Hall
13 Kelso Place
W8 5QD
Tel: 0171 938 4937
E-mail: amanda@ahrb.com
Web: www.ahrb.com
Seventeenth and eigtheenth-century English and Continental literature. Prices from £100 to £5,000 plus.

Robin Halwas Ltd
9 Cleveland Row
St James's
SW1A 1DH
Tel: 0171 930 2542
Fax: 0171 839 2458
By appointment only
Art, early printed books and illustrated books.

Hesketh & Ward Ltd
31 Britannia Road
SW6 2HJ
Tel: 0171 736 5705
Fax 0171 736 1089
By appointment only
Continental (especially Italian) books and those up to 1800.

Hünersdorff Rare Books
PO Box 582
SW10 9RU
Tel: 0171 373 3899
Fax: 0171 370 1244
E-mail: huner.rarebooks@dial.pipex.com
By appointment only
Continental books in rare editions, natural history, language and literature, science and medicine, and subject collections.

M E Korn
47 Tetherdown
Muswell Hill
N10 1NH
Tel/Fax: 0181 883 5251
By appointment only
Darwinism, general antiquarian, juvenile, natural history and science.

David Loman Ltd
12 Suffolk Road
SW13 9NB
Tel: 0181 748 0254
Fax: 0181 563 7806
By appointment only
Arabia, Central and East Asia, India, linguistics and Oriental manuscripts.

H D Lyon

18 Selwood Terrace
SW7 3QG
Tel: 0171 373 2709
By appointment only
Architecture, books printed on vellum, fine
binding and French and Italian books.

Barrie Marks Ltd

11 Laurier Road
Dartmouth Park
NW5 1SD
Tel: 0171 482 5684
Fax: 0171 284 3149
By appointment only
Illustrated books, private press, children's
books and colour printing.

Nicholas Morrell (Rare Books) Ltd

77 Falkland Road
Kentish Town
NW5 2XB
Tel: 0171 485 5205
Fax: 0171 485 2376
E-mail: Morbook@aol.com
By appointment only
Travel and exploration.

Hugh Pagan Ltd

PO Box 4325
SW7 1DD
Tel: 0171 589 6292
Fax: 0171 589 6303
E-mail: pagan@mistral.co.uk
By appointment only
Architecture, fine and applied arts.

Diana Parikian

3 Caithness Road
W14 0JB
Tel: 0171 603 8375
Fax: 0171 602 1178
By appointment only
Continental books 1500–1800, early printed
books, emblemata & iconology.

Nigel Phillips

5 Burleigh Place, Putney
SW15 6ES
Tel: 0181 788 2664
Fax: 0181 780 1989
E-mail: nigel.philips@dial.pipex.com
By appointment only
Medicine and science.

John Price

8 Cloudsley Square
N1 0HT
Tel: 0171 837 8008
Fax: 0171 278 4733
E-mail: johnprice@lineone.net
Web: www.antiquarian-books.co.uk/
By appointment only
Human sciences 1660–1832, philosophy, the
history of ideas, and literature.

John Randall (Books of Asia)

47 Moreton Street, SW1V 2NY
Tel: 0171 630 5331
Fax: 0171 821 6544
By appointment only
Asia (South, South-East and Central), the
Islamic world, Far East and Oriental art.

Paul Rassam

Flat 5, 18 East Heath Road
NW3 1AJ
Tel: 0171 794 9316
Fax: 0171 794 7669
By appointment only
Late nineteenth and early twentieth-century
literature, first editions and letters.

Russell Rare Books

81 Grosvenor Street
W1X 9DE
Tel: 0171 629 0532/ 493 1343
Fax: 0171 499 2983
Contact: Charles Russell
E-mail: sue@folios.co.uk
Web: www.folios.co.uk
Mon-Fri 10am-5.30pm
Plate books, natural history, atlases and travel.

Robert G Sawers Ltd
PO Box 4QA
W1A 4QA
Tel: 0171 409 0863
Fax: 0171 409 0817
By appointment only
Africana, Chinese art, Japan and Japanese
prints and paintings.

Liz Seeber
Kent Wharf, 61 Laburnum St, E2 8BD
Tel: 0171 739 3031
Fax: 0171 739 3793
By appointment only
Food, drink, cookery, herbs, mushrooms and
all related subjects, including social history.
Catalogues are produced three times
annually. Prices £5 to £2000.

Michael Silverman
PO Box 350, SE3 0LZ
Tel: 0181 319 4452
Fax: 0181 856 6006
By appointment only
Autograph letters, historical documents and
manuscripts.

Thomas Schuster
PO Box 14849, NW2 5WU
Tel: 0181 830 1311
Fax: 0181 830 1313
E-mail: tschuster@easynet.co.uk
By appointment only
Atlases and maps, Beatrix Potter, colour plate
books, fine and decorative prints, medieval
manuscripts and natural history.

A Sokol Books
PO Box 2409
W1A 2SH
Tel: 0171 499 5571
Fax: 0171 629 6536
E-mail: sokol@compuserve.com
By appointment only
Early printed books

Valentine Rare Books
Suite 12
78 Marylebone High Street
W1M YAP
Tel/Fax: 0171 636 3336
By appointment only
Contact: Gaston Chappell
Eighteenth and nineteenth-century fiction,
Dickens and modern first editions.

Graham Weiner
78 Rosebery Road
N10 2LA
Tel: 0181 883 8424
Fax: 0181 444 6505
By appointment only
Medicine, science, technology and transport.

The Provincial Booksellers Fairs Association

AUCTIONS, BOOKFAIRS, CHARITY SHOPS AND MARKETS

AUCTIONS

All of the top class London auction houses hold periodic book sales, and whilst many lots are top quality and regularly fetch tens and sometimes, hundreds of thousands of pounds (in 1994 Sotheby's sold a first edition of 'The Tale of Peter Rabbit' for over £63,000), many prices are much lower. Viewing days are a great chance for ordinary book lovers to get close to items we'd otherwise only see in our dreams and also to find out what volumes are currently in vogue with collectors. Who knows what we may discover ourselves on market stalls, in jumble sales or charity shops? The sale catalogues are often a fascinating read in their own right.

Bloomsbury Book Auctions
3 & 4 Hardwick Street
EC1R 4RY
Tel: 0171 833 2636/7
Fax: 0171 833 3954
E-mail: info@bloomsbury-book-auct.com
Web: www.bloomsbury-book-auct.com
The one specialist book auction house in town – although they also sell maps, prints, manuscripts and photographs:

Christies
8 King Street
St James
SW1 6QT
Tel: 0171 839 9060
Fax: 0171 839 1611
and
85 Old Brompton Road
SW7 3LD
Tel: 0171 581 7611
Fax: 0171 321 3321

Phillips
101 New Bond Street
W1Y 0AS
Tel: 0171 629 6602
Web: www.phillips-auctions.com

Sotheby's
34-35 New Bond Street
W1A 2AA
Tel: 0171 493 8080
Fax: 0171 293 5909
Web: www.sothebys.com

BOOKFAIRS

There are now a huge number of general and specialist book fairs in London, catering for every interest. Many booksellers who otherwise operate a mail order service from their homes (often far from London) have a stall at these fairs, so these events are an excellent opportunity to browse normally unavailable stock and to make contact with booksellers who share your specialist interest. In addition to contacting the major fair organisers listed below, it's worth looking out for flyers in specialist bookshops, advertisements in the weekly London listings magazines 'Time Out' and 'What's On', and in magazines such as 'Book and Magazine Collector', 'Antiquarian Book Monthly', and 'Comics International'.

The Antiquarian Bookseller's Association
Sackville House
40 Piccadilly
W1V 9PA.
Tel: 0171 439 3118
Fax: 0171 439 3119
E-mail: ABA@antiquarian.com
Web: www.antiquarian.com/aba
They organise a large and illustrious international book fair each June at Olympia and a national autumn fair at Chelsea Town Hall, as well as biannual fairs in Bath and Edinburgh.

Artists' Books Fair/ Marcus Campbell Art Books

43 Holland Street
Bankside
SE1 9JR
Tel: 0171 261 0111
Fax: 0171 261 0129
In the last few years there has been growing interest in artists' books and an annual fair – most recently at the Barbican Centre – brings together both national and international exhibitors.

The National Small Press Fair

Enquiries by post to:
308c Camberwell New Road
SE5 0RW
A free programme is produced in February
(send an SAE).
This is an annual event that takes place in the Royal Festival Hall foyer in March as part of the London Literature Festival. There are a multitude of stalls displaying the wares of small independent publishers from across the country, who produce all manner of material from poetry and literature through to comics, local history and artists' books. The fair also includes a series of free workshops which cover all aspects of independent publishing with expert advice available.

The Provincial Booksellers Fairs Association

The Old Coach House
16 Melbourn Street
Royston, Herts
SG8 7BZ.
Tel: 01763 2448400
Fax: 01763 248921
Web: www.antiquarian.com/pbfa
They publish an annual pamphlet, 'Calendar of Book Fairs', which lists general and specialist fairs throughout the country. There are general London fairs every month at the Hotel Russell, Russell Square WC1, as well as specialist fairs which take place at various locations.

CHARITY SHOPS

Books For Amnesty

139 King Street
Hammersmith
W6 9JG
Tel: 0181 746 3172
Mon-Fri 8am-6pm, Sat 8am-4pm
Tube: Hammersmith
This well-stocked second-hand shop is dependent on book donations from Amnesty supporters but has a large, good value range in every subject area. There is an Amnesty 'Resource Area' at the back of the shop where visitors can browse Amnesty information, learn more about the organisation and write letters in support of the prisoners of conscience that Amnesty support. The local Amnesty Group meet here at 7.30pm (for 8pm) on the second Monday of each month.

Crusaid Charity Shop

17-19 Upper Tachbrook Street
SW1P 1JU
Tel: 0171 233 8736
Mon-Sat 10.30am-5.15pm
Tube: Victoria
A general charity shop with an excellent selection of books covering both fiction and non-fiction in hardback and paperback. The shop is always busy with locals rummaging for a bargain and with lots of discount bins they are usually not disappointed.

Nettlefold Hall

Upstairs in West Norwood Library
Thurs 10am-2pm
Rail: West Norwood
A mixed batch of stalls, including some selling second-hand books.

South Bank Book Market

LIBRARIES
SPECIALIST LIBRARIES

In addition to public and academic libraries, there are a vast number of other specialist libraries located in the capital. These libraries are run by numerous and varied private bodies and their policy toward public access is equally varied. The more serious academic libraries often house important collections and restrict access to academics that can demonstrate the necessity of their visit for research purposes. Many other specialist libraries (such as those catering for members of a certain society or group of professionals) see the provision of information and library facilities for members of the public as very much part of their work. Nonetheless, in almost all of the libraries listed below, space and staff time is limited, so potential users should telephone in advance to find out the policy on access. It is also a good idea to phone to see whether the library holds the relevant material, and if required, to make an appointment. Many of the libraries have quite restricted opening times and sometimes charge access fees.

Actionaid
Hamlyn House
MacDonald Road
N19 5PG
Tel: 0171 281 4101
Tube: Archway
Material on developing countries in Asia, Africa and Latin America and on development issues such as agriculture, aid, debt, the environment, gender, health, poverty and water.

Action For Sick Children
300 Kingston Road
SW20 8LX
Tel: 0181 542 4848
Rail: Wimbledon Chase
The only library in Britian dedicated specifically to material on the psychological and social needs of children undergoing medical treatment.

Africa Centre Library
38 King Street
WC2E 8JJ
Tel: 0171 836 1973
Tube: Covent Garden
Newspapers, journals and books covering all African countries and relevant issues.

Age Concern
Astral House
1268 London Road
SW16 4ER
Tel: 0181 679 8000
Rail: Norbury
Ageing and all related issues, including health and healthcare, community care and welfare benefits.

Alcohol Concern
Waterbridge House
32-36 Loman Street
SE1 0EE
Tel: 0171 928 7377
Tube: Borough or Waterloo
All aspects of alcohol use are covered including treatment, government policy, and the effects on health, family and society.

Alpine Club Library
55 Charlotte Street
EC2A 3QT
Tel: 0171 613 0755
Tube: Old Street
One of the largest collections of mountaineering literature in the world, including newspaper cuttings from the nineteenth century, books from the sixteenth century onwards, journals, pamphlets, expedition reports. They also hold the 'Himalayan Index', a computerised record of major expeditions to Karakoram and Himalaya.

Alzheimers Disease Society
Ann Brown Memorial Library
Gordon House, 10 Greencoat Place
SW1P 1PH
Tel: 0171 306 0606
Tube: St James's Park
Everything about different types of dementia: research, treatment, social aspects and care.

Amateur Rowing Association
6 Lower Mall
W6 9DJ
Tel: 0181 741 5314
Tube: Hammersmith
Both historical and current material about the sport of rowing.

Anti-Slavery International
Thomas Clarkson House
The Stable Yard
Broomgrove Road
SW9 9TL
Tel: 0171 924 9555
Tube: Stockwell
Resources concerning human rights, a historical collection of eighteenth and nineteenth-century anti-slavery material, and modern collections on related issues including child labour and prostitution.

Arab British Centre
21 Collingham Road
SW5 0NU
Tel: 0171 373 8414
Tube: Gloucester Road or Earls Court
The history and politics of Arab countries and the Arab-Israeli conflict.

Architectural Association Library
34-36 Bedford Square
WC1B 3ES
Tel: 0171 887 4036
Tube: Tottenham Court Road
Architecture, design, construction, art and landscape gardening.

Bank of England Information Centre
Bank of England
Threadneedle Street
EC2R 8AH
Tel: 0171 601 4846
Fax: 0171 601 4356
Tube: Bank
Essentially a resource for Bank staff, the material covers banking, finance, economics and central bank reports from the UK and overseas. Researchers may be granted access if information is uavailable elsewhere; applications should be made in writing detailing what stock you wish to consult.

Birth Control Trust
Pamela Sheridan Resources Centre
16 Mortimer Street
W1N 7RS
Tel: 0171 580 9360
Tube: Oxford Circus or Goodge St
Legal, medical and sociological information and statistics relating to pregnancy, contraception and abortion.

Bishopsgate Institute
230 Bishopsgate
EC2M 4QH
Tel: 0171 247 6198
Tube: Liverpool Street
Reference library specialising in London history, trade unions and the Co-operative Movement.

Body Positive
14 Greek Street
W1V 5LE
Tel: 0171 287 8010
Tube: Leicester Square
An information room with material covering all aspects of HIV and AIDS including treatment, research, counselling, legal and financial issues, welfare benefits, health and statistics.

Brewers and Licensed Retailers Association

42 Portman Square
W1H 0BB
Tel: 0171 486 4831
More than ten thousand publications on brewing (including the relevant science and technology), pubs and the history of British brewing.

British College of Naturopathy and Osteopathy

6 Netherhall Gardens
NW3 5RR
Tel: 0171 431 2436
Tube: Finchley Road
Historical and modern collections on naturopathy, osteopathy and related disciplines.

British Film Institute

21 Stephen Street
W1P 1PL
Tel: 0171 255 1444
Tube: Tottenham Court Road

The national library for cinema, TV, video and related fields; there are a huge number of books, pamphlets, journals and over one and a half million newspaper cuttings.

The British Library

96 Euston Road
NW1 2DB
Reader admissions: 0171 412 7677
This is the library for the nation. Access to the galleries is free, whereas access to what is often regarded as the world's finest collection of books, journals, manuscripts, maps, printed music and sound recordings is much more restricted. The material sweeps across all subject areas and covers all known languages – there are more than one hundred and fifty million individual reference items. As a research library, admission to the reading rooms on this site (where all the humanities material is housed) is only allowed when you can demonstrate no other institution can supply all the information you need. The collections of material on science, technology and industry, and the Newspaper Library, are housed elsewhere and have different admissions criteria.

British Library of Political and Economic Science

10 Portugal Street
WC2A 2HD
Tel: 0171 955 7229
For admission information: 0171 955 6733
Tube: Holborn, Aldwych or Temple
Largest collection in the world of material covering the social sciences.

British Medical Association

BMA House
Tavistock Square
WC1H 9JB
Tel: 0171 383 6625
Tube: Russell Square or Euston
Medicine and related subjects.

British Museum Ethnography Library
Museum of Mankind
6 Burlington Gardens
W1X 2EX
Tel: 0171 323 8031
Tube: Piccadilly Circus
All aspects of anthropology plus traditional art, linguistics and archaeology.

British Music Information Centre
10 Stratford Place
W1N 9AE
Tel: 0171 499 8567
Tube: Bond Street
Reference collection of scores and recordings (there are listening facilities in the library), as well as information on twentieth-century classical British music.

British Refugee Council
3 Bondway
SW8 1SJ
Tel: 0171 820 3018
Tube: Vauxhall
Books, reports, journals and cuttings on refugees in both Britain and worldwide.

Catholic Central Library
Lancing Street
NW1 1NB
Tel: 0171 383 4333
Tube: Euston
Over fifty thousand books and one hundred and fifty journals on all aspects of Catholic theology, history and life.

Catholic Fund for Overseas Development (CAFOD)
Romero Close
162 Stockwell Road
SW9 9TY
Tel: 0171 733 7900
Tube: Stockwell or Brixton
Material on developing countries, development and development education.

Centre of Medical Law and Ethics Library
Old Library
King's College
The Strand
WC2R 2LS
Tel: 0171 873 2382
Tube: Holborn
Books and journals related to medical law and ethics in Britain, America and the Commonwealth. Material is housed in the main library and several branch libraries.

Change International: Women and Society
106 Hatton Square
EC1M 7RJ
Tel: 0171 430 0692
Tube: Farringdon or Chancery Lane
Change International's own publications plus information on all issues relating to the women. Areas covered include health, migration, education and work.

CIBA Foundation for the Promotion of International Co-operation in Medical and Chemical Research
41 Portland Place
W1N 4BN
Tel: 0171 636 9456
Tube: Oxford Circus or Regent's Park
Specialist scientific library.

Commonwealth Institute
Kensington High Street
W8 6NQ
Tel: 0171 603 4535
Tube: High Street Kensington
Information on all apsects of the Commonwealth countries.

Confraternity of St James

1 Talbot Yard
Borough High Street
SE1 1YP
Tel: 0171 403 4500
Tube: Borough
Reference material on medieval pilgrimage
routes to St James of Compostela in North-
West Spain, as well as general information
about pilgrimage.

Congregational Library

14 Gordon Square
WC1H 0AG
Tel: 0171 387 3727
Tube: Euston
Sharing premises with the Dr Williams
Library, this site has been established since
1831 as the main library for the
Congregational denomination.

Council for the Care of Churches

Fielden House
13 Little College Street
SW1 3SH
Tel: 0171 222 3793
Tube: Westminster
Books, survey files, journals, guidebooks
and slides relating to church art and
architecture, building and restoration,
conservation, history and ecclesiastical
heraldry as well as details of over fifteen
thousand churches.

Crafts Council

44a Pentonville Road
N1 9BY
Tel: 0171 806 2501
Tube: Angel
Books, exhibition catalogues and journals
on crafts, related careers and training, as well
as on business, export and marketing.

Department of the Environment

Eland House
Bressenden Place
SW1E 5DU
Tel: 0171 890 3199
Tube: Victoria
and
Great Minster House
(ex-Department of Transport library)
Tel: 0171 676 2002
and
Ashdown House
Tel: 0171 890 3039
(which includes the map library).
All publications relevant to the work of the
Department of the Environment.

The Dicken's House Museum

48 Doughty Street
WC1N 2LF.
Tel: 0171 405 2127
Tube: Russell Square
Located in, but separate from the museum,
the library houses books by and about
Dickens and his contemporaries plus
photographs and autographed letters.

Egypt Exploration Society

3 Doughty Mews
WC1N 2PG
Tel: 0171 242 2266
Tube: Russell Square
Ancient Egypt and the ancient Near East.

English Folk Dance And Song Society

Vaughan Williams Memorial Library
Cecil Sharp House
2 Regents Park Road
NW1 7AY
Tel: 0171 284 0523
Tube: Camden
Multimedia archive of films, videos,
recordings and photographs, in addition to
printed material dating from the seventeenth
century on British folk arts. The library
includes material on overseas cultures.

SPECIALIST LIBRARIES

The Evangelical Library

78A Chiltern Street
W1M 2HB
Tel: 0171 935 6997
Tube: Baker Street
Evangelical literature covering all aspects of the movement from the Puritans through to contemporary times.

Family Planning Association

2/12 Pentonville Road
N1 9FP
Tel: 0171 837 5432
Tube: Angel
All aspects of reproductive health.

Family Policy Studies Centre

9 Tavistock Place
WC1H 9SN
Tel: 0171 388 5900
Tube: Euston Square or Euston
Information on family-related matters, including employment, poverty and the Child Support Agency plus a huge body of statistics.

Fan Museum

12 Crooms Hill
SE10 8ER
Tel: 0181 858 7879
Rail: Greenwich
An archive covering anything related to the history and collecting of fans.

Fawcett Library

London Guildhall University
Old Castle Street
E1 7NT
Tel: 0171 320 1189
Tube: Aldgate East
Consisting of material that charts the position of women in society since the sixteenth century, there are sixty thousand books plus other archives and artefacts. The library has just received a grant of over four million pounds from the National Lottery towards building the National Library of

Women, due to open in October 2000. Plans include an exhibition hall, conference facilities and education area.

Feminist Library and Information Centre

5a Westminster Bridge Road
SE1 7XW
Tel: 0171 928 7789
Tube: Waterloo or Lambeth North
Books and journals on contemporary feminism worldwide, including sections on working class women, women of colour, Jewish and Irish women and women with disabilities.

Educational Advisory Service for the Fulbright Commission

Fulbright House
62 Doughty Street
WC1N 2LS
Tel: 0171 404 6994
Web: www.fulbright.co.uk
Tube: Chancery Lane or Russell Square
Information and advice about the education system in America for people interested in studying in America.

Geffrye Museum

Kingsland Road
E2 8EA
Tel: 0171 739 9893
Tube: Liverpool Street
English decorative arts, furniture and interiors. Also information on the furniture trade in London' East End.

Geological Society

Burlington House
Piccadilly
W1V 0JU
Tel: 0171 734 5673
Tube: Green Park or Piccadilly
Hundreds of thousands of books, maps and journals, including rare books and manuscripts about geology and allied subjects.

Geothe-Institut Library
50 Princes Gate
Exhibition Road
SW7 2PH
Tel: 0171 411 3452
Tube: South Kensington
German and English material about
Germany and German culture, including
literature, language, history, the arts and
social studies.

German Historical Institute Library
17 Bloomsbury Square
WC1A 2LP
Tel: 0171 404 5486
Tube: Tottenham Court Road
History of Britain and Germany, the
Commonwealth and Anglo-German
relations.

Great Britain-China Centre
15 Belgrave Square
SW1X 8PS
Tel: 0171 235 6696
Tube: Hyde Park Corner
English language collection of material about
China (especially contemporary subjects),
which includes tapes, videos and slides.

Health Education Authority
Trevelyan House
30 Great Peter Street
SW1P 2HY
Tel: 0171 413 1995
Tube: St James's Park
All aspects of health education in the form
of books, journals and audiovisual materials.

**Highgate Literary and
Scientific Institution**
11 South Grove
N6 6BS
Tel: 0181 340 3343
Tube: Archway or Highgate
A general library with an emphasis on
fiction, history and biography, local writers
and volumes about London with particular
emphasis on Highgate, Islington and
Hampstead.

Hispanic and Luso-Brazilian Council
Canning House Library
2 Belgrave Square
SW1X 8PJ
Tel: 0171 235 2303
Tube: Hyde Park Corner
Books in English, Spanish, Portuguese,
Catalan, Basque and Amer-Indian languages
on the art, politics, literature, history,
culture and economics of Spain, Portugal,
the Caribbean, Latin America and Britain.

Horniman Library
Horniman Museum
100 London Road
SE23 3PQ
Tel: 0181 699 1872 ext.108
Rail: Forest Hill
Specialist reference library for ethnography,
natural history and musical instruments.

Imperial War Museum

Lambeth Road
SE1 6HZ
Tel: 0171 416 5000
Tube: Lambeth North
The museum specialises in all aspects of twentieth-century warfare in which British and Commonwealth forces have been involved. It has a great deal of material on the First and Second World war and considerable post-1945 holdings which cover both social and technological issues.

Institut Francais

17 Queensberry Place
SW7 2DT
Tel: 0171 838 2144
Tube: South Kensington
General and a children's French language library and video library of French films.

Institute of Indian Culture

The Bhavan Centre
4a Castletown Road
W14 9HQ
Tel: 0171 381 3045
Tube: West Kensington
Small library on Indian philosophy, religion, literature, art and history.

Institute of Psychoanalysis

63 New Cavendish Street
W1M 7RD
Tel: 0171 580 4952
Tube: Oxford Circus or Regent's Park
Psychoanalysis and related subjects.

Institute of Public Relations

The Old Trading House
15 Northburgh Street
EC1V 0PR
Tel: 0171 253 5151
Tube: Barbican or Farringdon
Specialist library on the practice of public relations.

International Coffee Organization

22 Berners Street
W1P 4DD
Tel: 0171 580 8591
Tube: Oxford Circus or Goodge Street
Material on coffee, the commodities trade and development published by the International Coffee Organization and other bodies.

International Institute for Strategic Studies

23 Tavistock Street
WC2E 7NQ
Tel: 0171 379 7676
Tube: Covent Garden or Charing Cross
Security, arms control and international relations over the last forty years.

International Labour Office

Millbank Tower
21-24 Millbank
SW1P 4QP
Tel: 0171 828 6401
Tube: Pimlico
All International Labour Office papers since its inception in 1919. The ILO is a specialist agency of the United Nations.

International Planned Parenthood Federation

Regents College, Inner Circle
Regents Park
NW1 4NS
Tel: 0171 487 7900
Tube: Baker Street or Regents Park
Family planning, sex education, reproductive rights and the status of women.

Japanese Information and Cultural Centre

Embassy of Japan
101-104 Piccadilly
W1V 9FN
Tel: 0171 465 6500
Tube: Piccadilly or Green Park
Japanese literature, education, history and culture, in both Japanese and English.

Dr Johnson's House

17 Gough Square
EC4 3DE
Tel: 0171 353 3745
Tube: Blackfriar's or Chancery Lane
Located in the house where Dr Johnson
compiled his famous dictionary, the library
contains volumes of his work and of
Boswell's 'Life of Johnson'. The library also
holds more modern material on Johnson
and his era.

King's Fund Centre Library

11-13 Cavendish Square
W1M 0AN
Tel: 0171 307 2400
Tube: Oxford Circus
The management and delivery of health and
social care services – mainly in the UK.

Laban Centre for Movement and Dance

Laurie Grove
E14 6NH
Tel: 0181 692 4070
Tube: New Cross Gate
Dance, movement and related subjects –
books, dance scores and theatre programmes.

Lambeth Palace

SE1 7JU
Tel: 0171 928 6222
Tube: Westminster or Lambeth North
Lambeth Palace Library is the main library
and record office for the Church of England.
There is a vast range of archives, books and
manuscripts covering church and English
history, art, architecture and geneology.

Liberty

21 Tabard Street
SE1 4LA
Tel: 0171 403 3888
Tube: Borough
Reference material and resources regarding
civil liberties and human rights – mostly
concerning Britain.

London's Buddhist Vihara

The Avenue
W4 1UD
Tel: 0181 995 9493
Tube: Turnham Green
Books on all schools of Buddhism especially
the courses of Vihara.

London Contemporary Dance School

The Place, 17 Dukes Road
WC1H 9AB
Tel: 0171 387 0152 ext 245
Tube: Euston Square or King's Cross
Contemporary modern dance.

The London Library

14 St James's Square
SW1Y 4LG
Tel: 0171 930 7705
Tube: Piccadilly Circus
Founded in 1841 as a subscription library, it
now has over one million volumes and is
the largest independent lending library in
the world. Its emphasis is on the humanities
(particularly literature and history) with
good coverage on art, architecture,
bibliography, philosophy, religion and
travel. Applications for membership are
considered by the committee, for which
you will need a reference. The annual
membership fee is currently £130.

London Society

4th Floor, Senate House
Malet Street
WC1E 7HU
Tel: 0171 580 5537
Tube: Goodge Street or Russell Square
The history and development of London.

Marx Memorial Library

37a Clerkenwell Green
EC1R 0DU
Tel: 0171 253 1485
Tube: Farringdon
Marxism and the history of socialism and
the working class movement.

Marylebone Cricket Club Library

Lords Ground
NW8 8QN
Tel: 0171 289 1611
Tube: St John's Wood
Specialist cricket reference library.

Museum and Library of the Order of St John

St John's Gate, St John's Lane
EC1M 4DA
Tel: 0171 253 6644
Tube: Farringdon
All subjects relating to the Order of St John, which dates from the twelfth century.

Museum of Childhood (Renier Collection)

Cambridge Heath Road
E2 9PA
Tel: 0181 983 5200
Tube: Bethnal Green
Collection of children's books, toys and games from the sixteenth century onwards.

National Art Library

Victoria & Albert Museum
SW7 2RL
Tel: 0171 938 8315
Tube: South Kensington
The largest library of fine and applied art and design in Britain.

National Children's Bureau

8 Wakley Street
EC1V 7QE
Tel: 0171 843 6008
Tube: Angel
All issues relating to children and young people, including health and disability, rights, residential care, sex education, solvent and drug abuse and HIV and AIDS.

National Portrait Gallery

Heinz Archive and Library
St Martin's Place
WC2H 0HE
Tel: 0171 306 0055 ext.257
Tube: Charing Cross or Leicester Square
The prime centre for all research into British portraiture, dating back to the gallery's foundation in 1856. Holds thirty five thousand books, files of engravings, reproductions and photographs of portraits, and over one hundred and fifty thousand prints and negatives which make up the gallery's portrait photograph collection.

Natural History Museum

Cromwell Road
SW7 5BD
Tube: South Kensington
Over a million books and periodicals on all branches of natural history and related subject areas, divided into several libraries:
General and Zoology Tel: 0171 938 9191
Botany Tel: 0171 938 9421
Entomology Tel: 0171 938 9491
Palaentology and Mineralogy
   Tel: 0171 938 9207

NSPCC

42 Curtain Road
EC2A 3NH
Tel: 0171 825 2706
Tube: Liverpool Street
Books, articles, journals and NSPCC archives relating to child abuse, child protection, therapies and social welfare.

Oxfam

4th floor, *4 Bridge Place*
SW1V 1XY
Tel: 0171 931 7660
Tube: Victoria
Information and teaching materials on all aspects of development and aid relief. It includes Oxfam materials and catalogues as well as those from other publishers.

135

The Poetry Library

Level 5, Royal Festival Hall
SE1 8XX
Tel: 0171 921 0943 / 0664
Tube: Waterloo
The most comprehensive collection of twentieth-century poetry in Britain, with free membership to all. Founded in 1953 to support modern British poetry, the library now has about sixty thousand volumes, including almost all the poetry published in Britain in this century. There is a wide range of international work and children's poetry, as well as an audiovisual collection of poetry on video, tape, CD and record. 'The Voice Box', a literature performance space, is next to the library.

Religious Society of Friends (Quakers)

Friend's House
Euston Road
NW1 2BJ
Tel: 0171 663 1135
Tube: Euston or Euston Square
Quaker philosophy and history as well as issues of special interest to the Friend's, including peace-promotion and anti-slavery.

Royal Geographical Society

1 Kensington Gore
SW7 2AR
Tel: 0171 591 3040
Tube: South Kensington, High Street Kensington
Material on geography, travel and exploration. There is a map room (Tel: 0171 591 3050) housing the largest private collection of maps in the world, plus atlases and expedition reports. The society also operates an Expedition Advisory Service (Tel: 0171 591 3030) to help plan that trip of a lifetime.

Royal Horticultural Society

Lindley Library
80 Vincent Square
SW1P 2PE
Tel: 0171 821 3050
Tube: Victoria, St James's Park or Pimlico
Books, journals, drawings and catalogues relating to all things horticultural, dating from the sixteenth century onwards.

Royal National Institute for the Blind

224 Great Portland Street
W1N 6AA
Tel: 0171 388 1266
Tube: Great Portland Street
Material covering all aspects of partial sight and blindness.

Save the Children

Mary Datchelor House
17 Grove Lane
SE5 8RD
Tel: 0171 703 5400
Rail: Denmark Hill
Tube: Oval or Elephant & Castle (then a bus)
Overseas development and childcare issues, plus SCF publications.

Science Museum Library

Imperial College Road
SW7 5NH
Tel: 0171 938 8234
Tube: South Kensington
Sharing a building with the Imperial College library, this is a major British library for science and technology, which includes reference material on the history of science.

SCOPE for People with Cerebral Palsy

6 Market Road
N7 9PW
Tel: 0171 619 7100
Tube: Caledonian Road
Cerebral palsy, related disabilities and related areas, including education and care and information on the work of SCOPE.

Society for Co-operation in Russian and Soviet Studies

320 Brixton Road
SW9 6AB
Tel: 0171 274 2282
Tube: Brixton
Around thirty thousand books, mostly in Russian (although some are in English), on all subjects related to Russia.

Rudolf Steiner House Library

Rudolf Steiner House
35 Park Road
NW1 6XT
Tel: 0171 723 4400
Tube: Baker Street
All aspects of the work of Rudolf Steiner and anthroposophical material.

Halley Stewart Library

St Chrisopher's Hospice
51-59 Lawrie Park Road
Sydenham
SE26 6DZ
Tel: 0181 778 9252
Rail: Sydenham or Penge East
Books, journals, pamphlets and articles on hospices, bereavement, death and dying.

Tate Gallery Library

Millbank
SW1P 4RG
Tel: 0171 887 8838
Material on the areas of art covered by the gallery collections: historical British painting, modern international art from 1870 and (a particular specialism), contemporary art since World War Two.

The Terence Higgins Trust

52-54 Gray's Inn Road
WC1X 8JU
Tel: 0171 831 0330
Tube: Chancery Lane
Information concerning HIV and AIDS in books, journals, newspapers and videos.

Theatre Museum Library & Study Room

The National Museum of the Performing Arts
Main entrance: Russell Street, WC2E 7PA.
Study room: 1e Tavistock Street, WC2E 7PA.
Tel: 0171 836 7891
Tube: Covent Garden
Books, programmes, cuttings, pictures and designs on all the performing arts.

Theosophical Society

50 Gloucester Place
W1H 4EA
Tel: 0171 935 9261
Tube: Baker Street
Theosophy, world religions, philosophy, psychology, myth, parapsychology, astrology and related fields.

Thomas Cook Travel Archive

45 Berkeley Street
W1A 1EB
Tel: 0171 408 4175
Tube: Green Park or Piccadilly Circus
Reference collection including guidebooks, material on the history of travel and the archives of the Thomas Cook company.

Wallace Collection Library

Hertford House
Manchester Square
W1M 6BN
Tel: 0171 935 0687
Tube: Bond Street
Material on all areas of the collection (one of the best of its kind in London) encompassing European art up to the late nineteenth century.

Wellcome Institute for the History of Medicine

183 Euston Road, NW1 2BE
Tel: 0171 611 8582
Tube: Euston or Euston Square
The history of medicine.

Westminster Abbey Library

The Cloisters, Westminster Abbey
SW1P 3PA
Tel: 0171 222 5152 ext.228
Tube: St James's Park
Ecclesiastical library including theology, the
scriptures and history, a collection of
sixteenth and seventeenth-century
manuscripts, special collections and early
printed music.

Whitechapel Art Gallery

Whitechapel High Street
E1 7QX
Tel: 0171 522 7879
Tube: Aldgate East
Twentieth-century art plus the archives of the
gallery, amassed since its opening in 1901.

Wiener Library

4 Devonshire Street
W1N 2BH
Tel: 0171 636 7247
Tube: Great Portland Street or Regents Park
I discovered this library through a mention
in the acknowledgements to Gitta Sereny's
book 'Into that Darkness' in which she
states, "I don't think any serious book on
National Socialism could be undertaken
without the help of this unique institution".
The library also covers contemporary Jewish
and post-war Middle Eastern history, the
Holocaust and the Cold War.

Dr Williams' Library

14 Gordon Square
WC2H 0AG
Tel: 0171 387 3727
Tube: Euston

General theological library, sharing premises
with the Congregational Library.

Kenneth Ritchie Wimbledon Library

Wimbledon Lawn Tennis Museum
Church Road, SW19 5AE
Tel: 0181 946 6131
Tube: Southfields or Wimbledon
Worldwide material about lawn tennis.

Women's Art Library

Fulham Palace
Bishops Avenue
SW6 6EA
Tel: 0171 731 7618
Tube: Putney Bridge
Books, slides, photographs, catalogues,
monographs, videos and press cuttings on
women artists – both contemporary and
historical.

Women's Health

52 Featherstone Street
EC1Y 8RT
Tel: 0171 251 6580
Tube: Old Street
Information on women's health.

Worshipful Company of Goldsmiths

Goldsmiths' Hall
Foster Lane
EC2V 6BN
Tel: 0171 606 7010
Tube: St Pauls
Reference library of material related to gold,
silver and the goldsmith's trade; including
books, designs, slides and photographs.

Zoological Society of London

Regent's Park
NW1 4RY
Tel: 0171 449 6293
Tube: Baker Street or Regent's Park
All aspects of zoology.

ACADEMIC LIBRARIES

Each of the universities in London maintains its own libraries, all of which are serious academic resources maintained primarily for their own students. Regulations on access for individual researchers vary enormously; in some cases there is leniency towards students at other London or British universities, but in many others access is allowed only for reference rather than borrowing and fees are often charged. Anyone interested in using one of these libraries is advised to telephone first to find out the exact entrance criteria. It's also worth remembering that university libraries tend to have different opening hours outside term time.

South Bank University

There are several libraries within the university:

Faculty of the Built Environment
Wandsworth Road
SW8 2JZ
Tel: 0171 815 8320
Architecture, civil engineering, construction and town planning.

Harold Wood Education Centre
Harold Wood Hospital
Gubbins Lane
Romford
RN3 0BE
Tel: 0171 815 5959
Medical library.

Learning Resources Centre
105-108 Borough Road
SE1 0AA
Tel: 0171 815 6670
Computers, databases, audiovisual collection and a language learning centre.

Perry Library
250 Southwark Bridge Road, SE1 6NJ
Tel: 0171 815 6627
The main university library, which covers all academic fields.

Whipps Cross Education Centre
Whipps Cross Hospital
Leytonstone
E11 1NR
Tel: 0171 815 4747
Medical library.

University of East London

The university has libraries at:

Barking Tel: 0181 590 7722 ext.2614
Duncan House Tel: 0181 590 7722 ext.3346
Business.
Greengate Tel: 0181 590 7722 ext.3434
Art, design, film and photography.
Holbrook Annexe Tel: 0181 590 7722 ext.3251
Architecture.
Maryland House, Stratford
Tel: 0181 590 7722 ext 4224
Biological, environmental, life and social sciences, health, maths and technology.

University of Greenwich

The university has libraries at:

Avery Hill Campus Tel: 0181 331 8484
Education, sociology, psychology, law and economics.
Dartford Campus Tel: 0181 331 8585
Architecture and construction.
Elizabeth Raybould Centre, Dartford
Tel: 0181 331 8599.
Nursing and midwifery.
Medway Campus, Chatham
Tel: 0181 331 9617
Geology, geography, environmental science and engineering.
Woolwich campus Tel: 0181 331 8160
Science, computing, maths, history, politics, geography, philosophy, theology, the media, literature, business.

University College London Library
Gower Street
WC1E 6BT
Tel: 0171 387 7050
Tube: Warren Street or Euston
General academic library including many special collections (notably, the George Orwell Archive and James Joyce Collection) and the libraries of several specialist societies (including the London Mathematical Society and the Folklore Society). There are also several branch libraries including:

The University of London
The University of London is made up of a huge number of colleges and specialist schools and institutes, each with its own specialised library. Admission regulations are set by each individual establishment and vary enormously between libraries. The university has libraries at:

University of London Library
Senate House
Malet Street
WC1E 7HU
Tel: 0171 862 8461/2
Tube: Russell Square or Goodge Street
Huge academic library with over one million books and five thousand current journals. Specialisms are humanities and social sciences but the library's material also covers medicine and science, and encompasses many special collections.

Birkbeck College Library
Malet Street
WC1E 7HX
Tel: 0171 631 6239
Tube: Goodge Street
and
7-15 Gresse Street
W1P 1PA
Tel: 0171 631 6492
Tube: Tottenham Court Road
General academic library, but excluding medicine, music or engineering. The

economics and geography stocks are at the Gresse Street Library, with the remainder at Malet Street.

Goldsmiths College
Lewisham Way
SE14 6NW
Tel: 0171 919 7189
Tube: New Cross or New Cross Gate
General academic library covering arts, humanities, social science, maths, education and ethnomusicology.

Heythrop College Library
Kensington Square
W8 5HQ
Tel: 0171 795 6600
Tube: High Street Kensington
Theology and philosophy (especially continental and medieval) and a large collection of Roman Catholic material.

Imperial College of Science,
Technology and Medicine
SW7 2AZ
Tel: 0171 594 8820
Tube: South Kensington
All aspects of science, technology and medicine. The library shares its site and services with the Science Museum Library.

Institute of Advanced Legal Studies
17 Russell Square
WC1B 5DR
Tel: 0171 637 1731
Tube: Russell Square
One of Britain's major legal research libraries.

Institute of Child Health
30 Guilford Street
WC1N 1EH
Tel: 0171 242 9789 ext.2424
Tube: Russell Square
Specialist medical library on child health.

Institute of Classical Studies
5th floor, 31-34 Gordon Square
WC1H 0PY
Tel: 0171 387 7697
Tube: Russell Square, Goodge Street or Euston
Everything related to the classical world.

Institute of Commonwealth Studies
28 Russell Square
WC1B 5DS
Tel: 0171 862 8844
The modern history, politics and economics
of the Commonwealth and its member
countries.

Institute of Education
20 Bedford Way
WC1H 0AL
Tel: 0171 580 1122
One of the country's major libraries
specialising in education. There is also a
collection of school resource material.

Institute of Germanic Studies
29 Russell Square
WC1B 5DP
Tel: 0171 580 3480
Tube: Russell Square
German language and literature from the
mid-nineteenth century to modern times.

Institute of Latin American Studies
35 Tavistock Square
WC1H 9HA
Tel: 0171 387 4055
Tube: Russell Square
Everything related to Latin America.

Institute of Neurology
Queen Street
WC1N 3BG
Tel: 0171 837 3611
Tube: Russell Square
Neurology and related subjects. The library
also holds some historical collections.

Institute of Ophthalmology
11 Bath Sreet
EC1V 9EL
Tel: 0171 608 6814/5
Tube: Old Street
Reserach library for ophthalmology,
including historical material and book stock
in several languages.

Institute of Psychiatry
De Crespigny Park
SE5 8AF
Tel: 0171 703 5411
Rail: Denmark Hill
Britain's largest library for psychiatry and
clinical psychology.

Kings College
The Strand
WC2R 2LS
Academic library for all subjects taught at
the college. There are four separate libraries:
The Strand Campus (Tel: 0171 873 2424),
Chelsea (Tel: 0171 873 4851)
Cornwall House (Tel: 0171 873 3000)
Kensington (Tel: 0171 873 4378).

Kings College School of Medicine and Dentistry
Bessemer Road
SE5 9PJ
Tel: 0171 312 5542
Rail: Denmark Hill
Medicine, dentistry, science and health
services, plus a small antiquarian collection
of medical books.

London Business School
Sussex Place
Regent's Park
NW1 4SA
Tel: 0171 262 5050
Tube: Baker Street
All aspects of business studies.

Queen Mary and Westfield College
Mile End Road
E1 4NS

Tel: 0171 975 5555
Tube: Mile End
General academic library.

Royal Academy of Music
Marylebone Road
NW1 5HT
Tel: 0171 873 7323
Tube: Baker Street
A vast stock of books, recordings, sheet
music, manuscripts and sound recordings.

School of Oriental and African Studies
Thornhaugh Street
Russell Square
WC1H 0XG
Tel: 0171 323 6109
Tiube: Russell Square
Everything related to the study of Asia and
Africa. The huge and scholarly collection
includes material on languages, literature,
maps, photographs and prints, as well as a
vast number of books and journals.

School of Pharmacy
29-39 Brunswick Square
WC1N 1AX
Tel: 0171 753 5833
Tube: Russell Square

School of Slavonic and East European Studies
Senate House
Malet Street
WC1E 7HU
Tel: 0171 636 8000
Tube: Goodge Street

Trinity College of Music
11-13 Mandeville Place
W1M 6AQ
Tel: 0171 935 5773
Tube: Bond Street
Music: books, scores and audio materials.

The Institute of Archaeology
31-34 Gordon Square
WC1H 0PY
Tel: 0171 387 7050

Environmental Studies Library
Faculty of Environmental Studies
22 Gordon Street
WC1H 0QB
Tel: 0171 387 7050

Warburg Institute
Woburn Square
WC1H 0AB
Tel: 0171 580 9663
Tube: Russell Square
European cultural history and the history of
art, science and religion.

University of North London
The university has two libraries:
Ladbroke House
62-66 Highbury Grove
N5 2AD
Tel: 0171 753 5149
Tube: Highbury & Islington
Geography, social science and law.

The Learning Centre
236-250 Holloway Road
N7 6NA
Tel: 0171 753 5170
Tube: Holloway Road
Architecture, business, computing,
engineering, environmental and social
studies and humanities.

Thames Valley University
St Mary's Road
W5 5RF
Tel: 0181 231 2248
Tube: Ealing Broadway
General academic library. There is also a
library on the Slough campus (Tel: 01753
697819).

University of Westminster
There are several libraries:

Euston Centre
9-18 Euston Centre
NW1 3ET
Tel: 0171 911 5000 ext.4347
Tube: Warren Street
Language and linguistics.

Harrow Campus
Watford Road
Northwick Park
Harrow
HA1 3TP
Tel: 0171 911 5000 ext 5885
Tube: Northwick Park
Art, design, computing, engineering,
humanities and social sciences.

35 Marylebone Road
NW1 5LS
Tel: 0171 911 5000 ext.4903
Tube: Baker Street
The built environment.

115 New Cavendish Street
W1M 8JS
Tel: 0171 911 5000 ext.3616
Tube: Goodge Street
Computing, engineering, maths and health
sciences.

4-7 Little Titchfield Street
W1P 7FW
Tel: 0171 911 5000 ext.2537
Law and criminology.

Riding House Street
Tel: 0171 911 5000 ext.3887
Social sciences and business studies.

PUBLIC LIBRARIES

A ll of the London boroughs provide free public libraries for the use of the whole community. Each borough usually has a main lending and reference library and then a spread of smaller, local libraries which frequently have more restricted stock, fewer facilities and shorter opening hours. The range of facilities available in the reference libraries is increasing greatly as technology develops, and many now have public internet access and material on CD-Rom. Below are details for each of the main libraries, followed by telephone numbers for branch libraries. Opening hours vary enormously so do give the smaller libraries a call before making a special journey.

Barnet

Hendon Library
The Burroughs
NW4 4BQ
Tel: 0181 202 5625

Also at:
Burnt Oak 0181 959 3112
Childs Hill 0181 455 5390
Chipping Barnet 0181 449 0321
Church End 0181 346 5711
East Barnet 0181 440 4376
East Finchley 0181 883 2664
Edgeware 0181 958 5550
Friern Barnet 0181 368 2680
Golders Green 0181 458 2168
Grahame Park 0181 200 0470
Hampstead Garden Suburb 0181 455 1235
Mill Hill 0181 959 5066
North Finchley 0181 445 4081
Osidge 0181 368 0532
South Friern 0181 883 6513
Totteridge 0181 445 5288

Brent

Willesden Green Library
95 High Street
NW10 2ST
Tel: 0181 937 3400

Also at:
Barham Park 0181 937 3550
Brent Town Hall 0181 937 3500
Cricklewood (includes the local history library and archives) 0181 937 3540
Ealing Road 0181 937 3560
Harlesden 0181 965 7132
Kensal Rise 0181 969 0942
Kilburn 0181 9937 3530
Kingsbury 0181 937 3520
Neasden 0181 937 3580
Preston Road 0181 937 3510
Tokyngton 0181 937 3590

Bromley

Central Library
High Street
Bromley
BR1 1EX
Tel: 0181 460 9955

Also at:
Anerley 0181 778 7457
Beckenham 0181 650 7292
Biggin Hill 01959 574468
Burnt Ash 181 460 3405
Chislehurst 0181 467 1318
Hayes 0181 462 2445
Mottingham 0181 857 5406
Orpington 01689 831 551
Penge 0181 778 8772
Petts Wood 01689 821607
Shortlands 0181 460 9692
Southborough 0181 467 0355
St Paul's Cray 0181 300 5454
West Wickham 0181 777 4139

ACADEMIC LIBRARIES

Camden

Swiss Cottage Library
88 Avenue Road
NW3 3HA
Central reference 0171 413 6533/4
Lending 0171 413 6523

Also at:
Belsize 0171 722 1186
Belsize Park 0171 413 6578
Camden Town 0171 911 1563
Chalk Farm 0171 722 5571
Heath (Hampstead) 0171 435 8002
Highgate 0171 272 3112
Holborn 0171 413 6346, local studies and
archives 0171 413 6342
Keats Grove 0171 413 6520
Kentish Town 0171 485 1121
Kilburn 0171 413 6524
Queens Crescent 0171 485 1312
Regents Park 0171 387 8544
St Pancreas 0171 860 5833
West Hampstead 0171 413 6539

Corporation of London

Guildhall Library
Aldermanbury
EC2P 2EJ
Tel: 0171 606 3030

Also at:
The Barbican 0171 638 0569
Camomile Street 0171 247 8895
City Business Library
(reference) 0171 638 8215
St Bride Printing Library
(reference) 0171 353 4660
Shoe Lane 0171 583 7178

Ealing

Central Library
103 Ealing Broadway Centre
W5 5JY
Lending 0181 567 3670
Reference 0181 567 3656

Also at:
Acton 0181 752 0999
Greenford 0181 578 1466
Hanwell 0181 567 5041
Jubilee Gardens, Southall 0181 578 1067
Northfields 0181 567 5700
Northolt 0181 845 3380
Perivale 0181 997 2830
Pitshanger 0181 997 0230
Southall 0181 574 3412
West Ealing 0181 567 2812
Wood End 0181 422 3965

Enfield

Central Library
Cecil Road
Enfield
Middlesex
EN2 6TW
Tel: 0181 366 2244

Also at:
Bowes Road 0181 368 2085
Bullsmoor 01992 788779
Bush Hill Park 0181 367 4917
Edmonton Green 0181 807 3618
Enfield Highway 0181 443 2300
Merryhills 0181 367 5250
Ordnance Road 01992 710588
Palmers Green 0181 886 3728
Ponders End 0181 443 2313
Ridge Avenue 0181 360 9662
Southgate Circus 0181 882 8849
Weir Hall 0181 884 2420
Winchmore Hill 0181 360 8344

Greenwich

Woolwich Library
Calderwood Street
SE18 6QZ
Lending 0181 312 5750
Reference 0181 316 6663

Also at:
Abbey Wood 0181 310 4185
Blackheath 0181 858 1131
Charlton 0181 319 2525

Coldharbour 0181 857 7346
Eltham 0181 850 2268
Ferrier 0181 856 5149
Greenwich 0181 858 6656,
        local history 0181 858 4631
New Eltham 0181 850 2322
Plumstead 0181 854 1728
The Slade 0181 854 7900
West Greenwich 0181 858 4289

Hackney
Central Library
219 Mare Street
E8 3QE
Tel: 0181 356 2542

Also at:
Clapton 0181 356 2570
C L R James Library,
        Dalston Lane 0181 356 2571
Homerton 0181 356 2572
Rose Lipman Reference Library,
        De Beauvoir Road 0181 356 2576
Shoreditch 0181 356 4351
Business Information Library,
        Shoreditch 0181 356 4358/9
Stamford Hill 0181 356 2573
Stoke Newington 0181 356 5230/1

Hammersmith and Fulham
Hammersmith Library
Shepherd's Bush Road, W6 7AT
Lending 0181 576 5050
Reference 0181 576 5053

Also at:
Askew Road 0181 576 5064
Barons Court 0181 576 5258
Fulham   0181 576 5254 (reference),
        0181 576 5252 (lending)
Sands End 0181 576 5257
Shepherds Bush 0181 576 5060

Haringey
Central Library
High Street, N22
0181 888 1292

Also at:
Alexandra Park 0181 883 8553
Castle Bruce Museum
(archive and local history) 0181 808 8772
Coombes Croft 0181 808 0022
Highgate 0181 348 3443
Hornsey 0181 348 3351
Muswell Hill 0181 883 6734
St Ann's 0181 800 4390
Stroud Green 0181 348 4363
Tottenham 0181 365 1155

Islington
Central Library
2 Fieldway Crescent, N5 1PF
Tel: 0171 619 6900
Local history 0171 619 6932

Also at:
Archway 0171 619 7820
John Barnes Library,
        Camden Road 0171 619 7900
Lewis Carroll Children's Library,
Copenhagen Street 0171 619 7996
Finsbury 0171 619 7960
Mildmay 0171 619 7880
North Library,
        Manor Gardens 0171 619 7840
Arthur Simpson Library,
        Hanley Road 0171 619 7800
St Luke's, Lever Street 0171 619 7940
South Library, Essex Rd 0171 619 7860
West Library,
        Bridgeman Road 0171 619 7920

Kensington and Chelsea
Central Library
Phillimore Walk, W8 7RX
Tel: 0171 937 2542

Also at:
Brompton 0171 373 3111
Chelsea 0171 352 6052,
        local studies 0171 361 3038
Kensal 0181 969 7736
Norh Kensington 0171 727 6583
Notting Hill Gate 0171 229 8574

Lambeth
Tate Library
Brixton Oval
SW2 1JQ
Reference 0171 926 1067
Lending 0171 926 1056

Also at:
Archives 0171 926 6076
Carnegie, Herne Hill Road 0171 926 6050
Clapham 0171 926 0717
Clapham Park 0171 926 0108
Durning, Kennington Lane 0171 926 8682
Minet, Knatchbull Road 0171 926 6073
North Lambeth, Lower Marsh 0171 926 8690
South Lambeth Road 0171 926 0705
Streatham 0171 926 6768
Streatham Vale 0171 926 6591
West Norwood 0171 926 8092

Lewisham
Lewisham Library
199-210 Lewisham High Street
SE13 6LG
Lending 0181 297 9677
Reference 0181 297 9430
Local studies 0181 297 0682

Also at:
Blackheath Village 0181 852 5309
Catford 0181 314 6399
Crofton Park 0181 692 1683
Downham 0181 698 1475
Forest Hill 0181 699 2065
Grove Park 0181 857 5794
Manor House 0181 852 0357
New Cross 0181 694 2534
Sydenham 0181 778 7563
Torridon Road 0181 698 1590
Wavelengths, Deptford 0181 694 2535

Merton
Wimbledon Library
35 Wimbledon Hill Road
SW19 7NB 0181 946 7432
Reference 0181 946 1136

Also at:
Donald Hope Library,
     Colliers Wood 0181 542 1975
Mitcham 0181 648 4070
Morden 0181 545 4040
Morden Park 0181 337 3405
Pollards Hill 0181 764 5877
Raynes Park 0181 542 1893
West Barnes 0181 942 2635
Wimbledon Park 0181 946 3999

Newham
East Ham Library
High Street South, E6 4EL
Reference 0181 552 7852
Lending 0181 557 8882
and
Stratford Library
Water Lane
E15 4NJ
Reference 0181 519 6346
Lending 0181 557 8968

Also at:
Canning Town 0171 476 2696
Custom House 0171 476 1565
Forest Gate 0181 534 6952
Green Street 0181 472 4101
Manor Park 0181 478 1177
North Woolwich 0171 511 2387
Plaistow 0181 472 0420

Southwark
Newington Library
155-157 Walworth Road
SE17 1RS
Lending 0171 703 3324
Reference 0171 708 0516

Also:
Blue Anchor 0171 231 0475
Brandon 0171 735 3430
Camberwell 0171 703 3763
Dulwich 0181 693 5171, reference 0181 693 8312
East Street 0171 703 0395
Grove Vale 0181 693 5734

John Harvard, Borough High Street 0171 407
0807, local studies 0171 403 3507
Kingswood 0181 670 4803
North Peckham 0171 639 1255
Nunhead 0171 639 0264
Peckham 0171 639 1624
Rotherhithe 0171 237 2010

Tower Hamlets
Bethnal Green Library
Cambridge Heath Road
E2 0HL
Lending 0181 980 3902
Reference 0181 980 6274

Also at:
Bancroft Library and
        Local History 0181 980 4366
Bow Community Hall 0181 980 2282
Cubbitt Town 0171 987 3152
Dorset 0171 739 9489
Fairfoot 0171 987 3338
Lansbury, Chrisp Street Market 0171 987 3573
Limehouse 0171 987 3183
Stepney 0171 790 5616
Wapping 0171 488 3535
Watney Market 0171 790 4039
Whitechapel 0171 247 5272

Waltham Forest
Central Library
High Street, Walthamstow
E17 7JT
Tel: 0181 520 3031

Also at:
Friday Hill 0181 529 6660
Hale End 0181 531 6423
Harrow Green 0181 539 5997
Higham Hill 0181 531 6424
Lea Bridge 0181 539 5652
Leyton 0181 539 1223
Leytonstone 0181 539 2730
North Chingford 0181 529 2993
St James 0181 520 1292
South Chingford 0181 529 2332
Wood Street 0181 521 1070

Wandsworth
Battersea Library
265 Lavender Hill
SW11 1JB
Lending 0181 871 7466
Reference 0181 871 7467

Also at:
Alvering 0181 871 6398
Balham 0181 871 7195
Battersea Park 0181 871 7468
Earlsfield 0181 871 6389
Northcote 0181 871 7469
Putney 0181 871 7090
Roehampton 0181 871 7091
Southfields 0181 871 6388
Tooting 0181 871 7175
West Hill 0181 871 6386,
        reference 0181 871 6387
York 0181 871 7471

Westminster
Westminster Library
35 St Martin's Street
WC2H 7HP
Lending 0171 641 4636
Reference 0171 641 2036
Music library 0171 641 2192
City archives 0171 641 2180

Also at:
Charing Cross 0171 641 2058
Church Street 0171 641 1479
Maida Vale 0171 641 3659
Marylebone 0171 641 1037,
        reference 0171 641 1039
Mayfair 0171 641 1391
Paddington 0171 641 3705
Pimlico 0171 641 2983
Queen's Park 0171 641 3575
St James's 0171 641 2989
St John's Wood 0171 641 1487

MUSEUMS, GALLERIES & HISTORIC HOUSES OF LITERARY INTEREST

The places listed below are a good way for book lovers to get a more intimate knowledge of their literary hero's. Those who don't see the point in such things and prefer to read the works should read Julian Barnes', 'Flaubert's Parrot', a wonderful account of walking in the footsteps of a great writer.

The British Library

96 Euston Road
NW1 2DB
Tel: 0171 412 7332
Mon, Tues 9.30am-8pm,
Wed-Fri 9.30am-6pm, Sat 9.30am-5pm
Sun 11am-5pm
Admission: Free
Tube: Euston, King's Cross or St Pancras
This is the undoubted highlight for any book lover in London – a place to savour and visit to again and again. As well as holding the twelve million books (on three hundred and fifty kilometres of shelving!) which make up the national library of Britain (see p.128 for details about reading rights), there are three exhibition galleries for visitors. The real delight is the John Ritblat Gallery's 'Treasures of the British Museum', which displays some incredible texts, manuscripts, maps and musical scores. Here you can view the likes of the Lindisfarne Gospels, the Gutenberg Bible, a First Folio of Shakespeare, the Magna Carta and Leonardo da Vinci's notebooks.
The Pearson Gallery of Living Words uses items from the collection and multimedia and interactive displays to look at themes such as 'The Story of Writing', 'The Art of The Book', 'Images of Britain' and 'The Scientific Record'. There is also an extensive display of children's books through the ages and a reading area. 'The Workshop of Words, Sounds and Images'

looks at book production from the earliest written material to modern digital methods. A visit to the café is a grand experience, located as it is beside the stunning King's Library, the collection of around sixty five thousand books collected by King George III and given to the nation in 1823 by his son, King George IV. The stack of fabulous leatherbound volumes stretches upwards, housed in a six storey, seventeen-metre high glass tower situated at the centre of the library.

There are guided tours (£3) of the building on Mon, Wed, Fri and Sun (at 3pm) and twice on Sat (at 10.30am or 3pm). Booking is advisable, either at the Information Desk or by ringing the number above..

Carlyle's House

24 Cheyne Row
SW3 5HL
Tel: 0171 352 7087
29 March-2 Nov: Wed-Sun and Bank Holidays Mondays 11am-5pm
Admission: £3 (adult), £1.50 (children).
Tube: Sloane Square
Although he is no longer a well known figure, the Victorian historian, Thomas Carlyle (1795-1881) was hugely influential and famous in his own lifetime. He lived at this house from 1834 until his death. Most famous for works such as 'The French Revolution' and 'Frederick the Great', Carlyle was also a founder of The London Library (see p.134).
He was visited at this house by many of the great names of the day including Dickens, Tennyson, Chopin, Browning, Darwin, Thackeray, John Stuart Mill and John Ruskin. The house still contains the original furniture as well as Carlyle's books and belongings. However, don't get too carried away imagining domestic tranquility – the Carlyles had a famously volatile relationship. Such was Carlyle's fame that a statue in nearby Cheyne Walk was erected only a year after his death.

The Dicken's House Museum,

48 Doughty Street, WC1
Tel: 0171 405 2127
Admission: £3.50 (adults), £2.50 (concessions),
£1.50 (children), £7 (family ticket).
Tube: Russell Square

Charles Dickens (1812-1870) lived in this late-Georgian terrace between 1837 and 1839. During his time here he wrote parts of 'The Pickwick Papers' and 'Barnaby Rudge' and all of 'Nicholas Nickleby' and 'Oliver Twist'. Dickens lived at around fifteen London addresses but this is the only house which remains intact. Some of the rooms are laid out as they would have been in his time while others hold displays including letters, papers, pictures (it includes the earliest known portrait of the author, painted by his aunt in 1830), furniture and first editions of his books. The history video in the library is a useful introduction to the man and his work.

The Freud Museum

20 Maresfield Gardens, NW3 5SX
Tel: 0171 435 2002 / 5167
Wed-Fri 12noon-5pm
Admission: £3 (adults), £1.50 (concessions),
children under 12 years free.
Tube: Finchley Road

In 1938 Sigmund Freud fled from the Nazis in Vienna with enough belongings to recreate a replica of his Austrian home in London, including his famous couch. When Freud arrived in London he was already sick with cancer and he died here in 1939. Anna, Freud's daughter (herself a psychoanalyst), lived here until her death in 1982. The house remains as it was in Freud's time, with many of the ancient antiquities that he collected, and the portrait painted by Salvador Dali. Video footage from the Freud family home movies is also on show.

The Freud Museum

Dr Johnson's House

17 Gough Square
EC4A 3DE
Tel: 0171 353 3745
Mon-Sat 11am-5.30pm (Oct-April 11am-5pm)
Admission: £3 (adults),
£2 (concessions), £1 (children)
Tube: Blackfriars or Chancery lane
Dr Samuel Johnson (1709-1784) is famous as the compiler of the first dictionary of the English Language and for his many sayings – carefully recorded by his biographer, James Boswell. He moved to this house, built around 1700, with the advance that he got for his dictionary and it was during his time here (1748-1759) that he and his six scribes, standing at high desks in the attic, compiled the enormous work (containing over forty thousand definitions and over one hundred thousand quotations), which was published in 1755. The house has been restored to something like its original condition and furnished with eighteenth-century pieces, including Johnson memorabilia such as his coffee cup, portraits of him and his circle and a first edition of the dictionary. There is an interesting video show and there are free information sheets in each room. If the museum ignites an interest in Dr Johnson, there are two portraits of him, as well as one of James Boswell, in the National Portrait Gallery (see p.154).

Keat's House

Keats Grove
NW3 3RR
Tel: 0171 435 2062
April-Oct: Mon-Fri 10am-1pm and 2-6pm,
Sat 10am-1pm and 2-5pm, Sun 2-5pm
Nov-Mar: Mon-Fri 1-5pm,
Sat 10am-1pm and 2-5pm, Sun 2-5pm
Admission: free
NB: Currently closed for building repairs –
telephone for information.
Tube: Belsize Park or Hampstead
The Romantic poet (1795-1821) John Keats lived in this Regency house from 1818 to 1820 and is said to have written his famous 'Ode to a Nightingale' in the garden. The Brawne family lived next door and Keats fell in love with and became engaged to Fanny Brawne, the daughter of the house. Sadly, they never got married as Keats died from TB at the age of just twenty five. The house contains many momentos of their love, including one of his love letters, her garnet engagement ring and a lock of hair. Other items include Keats' manuscripts, a letter from Wordsworth and a poem by Thomas Hardy. The museum offers a 45 minute audio tour for a small charge. There is a portrait of Keats in the National Portrait Gallery (see p.154).

National Portrait Gallery

St Martin's Place
WC2H 0HE
Tel: 0171 306 0055
Mon-Sat 10am-6pm
Sun 12noon-6pm
Admission free.
Tube: Leicester Square or Charing Cross
The National Portrait Gallery is a wonderful institution and a very good way for book lovers to discover what their literary heros actually looked like. It's fascinating to see images of favourite writers for perhaps the first time and to try to square their picture with what may be in your mind's eye. 'The Gallery' is a room of national portraits so, don't expect to see any writers from outside Britain. The oldest portraits are on the second floor and so for a chronological visit, start from the top and work your way down: *Room 1: Mary I and Elizabeth I.* The highlight here is the portrait of William Shakespeare (1610) attributed to John Taylor (his identity has never been fully established). It is an extremely well known picture and especially important as it is the only portrait of Shakespeare to have a valid claim to being painted from life. Sir Walter Ralegh (1552-1618), a writer and poet as well as explorer, is also here.

Room 2: Early Stuarts James I and Charles I.
John Donne (1572-1631), poet and
clergyman, and Ben Johnson (1573-1637),
dramatist and poet.
Room 3: Seventeenth-century Arts and Sciences.
Poet Andrew Marvell, philosopher and poet
Thomas Hobbes and poet John Milton
(1608-74), painted by an unknown artist in
1629 when he was a Cambridge scholar.
Room 4: The Restoration. Features John
Dryden, poet, dramatist and literary critic,
philosopher John Locke and famous diarist
Samuel Pepys.
*Room 6: Early Eighteenth-century Arts and
Science.* Writer, Jonathan Swift and the poet,
Alexander Pope.
Room 9: Eighteenth-century Arts. Laurence
Sterne, Samuel Johnson, Oliver Goldsmith,
James Boswell and Fanny Burney.
Room 13: The Romantics – Poets and Painters.
This room has a huge number of interesting
literary portraits, including those of John
Clare, John Keats, Samuel Taylor
Coleridge, Mary Shelley, William
Wordsworth, Percy Bysshe Shelley, Robert
Southey, William Blake, Charles Lamb and
Robert Burns. There are also life masks of
William Wordsworth and John Keats. One
of the most famous pictures here is of
George Gordon, Lord Byron (1788-1824)
painted by Thomas Phillips in 1835 with
Byron wearing a suitably flamboyant
Albanian costume.
Room 15: The Regency. A room dominated
by the huge canvas of 'The Reformed
House of Commons 1833' by Sir George
Hayter. However, in a small cabinet to the
right of the door (covered by a protective
cloth), is the small pencil and watercolour
portrait of Jane Austen drawn in around
1810 by her sister Cassandra. It is believed
to be the only portrait of the author that
was almost certainly drawn from life.
Room 20: Early Victorian Arts. This room
contains some of the best known Victorian
portraits held by the gallery. There are the
oil paintings of Anne, Emily and Charlotte

Bronte and the single portrait of Anne
Bronte painted by Patrick Branwell Bronte
in 1834. Other paintings include Charles
Dickens (painted in 1839 by his friend
Daniel Maclise), Lord Tennyson, Charles
Kingsley, Robert Browning, Elizabeth
Barrett Browning, George Eliot, William
Wilkie Collins, and William Makepeace
Thackeray. This is the era in which
photography first appeared as a medium of
portraiture – there are several photographs
here of Lord Tennyson.
Room 23: Portraits by G F Watts. Swinburn,
John Stuart Mill, Thomas Carlyle, William
Morris and Matthew Arnold.
Room 24: Late Victorian Arts. Contains
Robert Louis Stevenson (both a painting
and a bronze head), and Jerome K Jerome.
Room 26: The First World War. Somewhat
dominated by soldiers, but the photographs
of Wilfred Owen, Siegfried Sassoon,
William Gibson and Isaac Rosenberg are
very evocative, as is a painting of Rupert
Brooke by Clara Ewald, painted in 1911.
*Room 27: The Armistice to the New
Elizabethans.* This room contains a mixture
of paintings, sculptures and photographs,
including likenesses of E M Forster,
D H Lawrence, George Bernard Shaw,
Vanessa Bell, James Joyce, H G Wells,
Laurie Lee, T S Eliot, Dylan Thomas,
Dorothy Sayers and Mervyn Peake.
Ground Floor: Britain Since the 1960s. There
are plenty of writers among the displays,
including Alan Bennett, A S Byatt, Alan
Ayckbourn, Harold Pinter, Derek Walcott,
John Mortimer, Iris Murdoch, Graham
Greene, Kazuo Ishiguro, Seamus Heaney,
L P Hartley, Philip Larkin and P D James.
Visitors should note that displays do change
and especially fragile older images (the chalk
drawing of Charlotte Bronte done by
George Richmond in 1850 is one famous
example) may not be on regular display.
Telephone in advance if you are hoping to
see a particular portrait on your visit.

Shakespeare's Globe Theatre

New Globe Walk
SE1 9DT
Tel: 0171 902 1500
(Exhibition and tours)
May-September: 9am-12noon;
October to April: 10am-5pm.
Admission: £5 (adults), £4 (concessions),
£3 (children), £14 (family)

This remarkable project has, as both its centre-piece and raison d'etre, a reconstruction of The Globe Theatre in which Shakspeare was an actor and shareholder, and in which many of his greatest plays were first performed (including 'Hamlet', 'Othello', 'King Lear' and 'Macbeth'). The Globe opened in 1599, and was one of four theatres on Bankside – known in those days as an area of rough and bawdy entertainment. It is thought that at that time, London had a population of around one hundred thousand and that a estimated forty thousand people went each week to one of the Bankside theatres. The original site of The Globe was in fact in what is now Park Street (about three hundred metres away), but this was the closest piece of land available for the project, right on the river with fine views across to St Paul's Cathedral. The original Globe was burned down on 29th June 1613 when a stray spark from a cannon fired in a performance of 'Henry VIII' totally destroyed it. By that time Shakespeare had retired to Stratford-upon-Avon a rich man. The theatre was rebuilt the next year but eventually shut when under the regime of the Puritans, all entertainment was deemed unacceptable.

Although even now the reconstruction project is far from complete, the theatre and attached buildings are well worth a visit. Constructed of green (unseasoned) oak, held together with nine thousand five hundred tapered oak pegs (rather than nuts and bolts), and topped by a thatch roof (the first in London since 1666), the theatre can hold one and a half thousand people. With its centre open to the elements, the theatre only stages performances from May to September (twice daily Tuesday-Saturday and once on Sunday: tickets £5-£20). However, a visit to the exhibition and a tour of the theatre is worthwhile at any time of the year, as it shows the history of the original Globe, information about the reconstruction project, future plans and costumes from the plays. If you need refreshment, the café offers good food and has windows that look out across the river.

The Sherlock Holmes Museum

221b Baker Street
NW1 6XE
Tel: 0171 935 8866
Daily 9.30am-6pm
Admission £5 (adults), £3 (children).
Tube: Baker Street

This is a reconstruction in a building with no known connection to Holmes or to his inventor, Sir Arthur Conan Doyle. It is intended to show how Holmes and Watson could have lived in the nineteenth century had they not been creations of Conan Doyle's over active imagination. It's an interesting idea for fans of the Sherlock Holmes, but of no historic merit.

William Morris Gallery

Lloyd Park
Forest Road
E17 4PP
Tel: 0181 527 3782
Tues-Sat and the first Sun of each month
10am-1pm and 2-5pm
Admission: free
Tube: Walthamstow Central

Designer, craftsman, writer and Socialist, William Morris (1834-1896), lived in this house as a young man, from 1848-1856. It is now a celebration of his life and work and that of his contemporaries such as Edward Burne-Jones, Philip Webb, Rossetti and Ford Madox Ford, and features paintings, drawings, fabrics, rugs, carpets, wallpaper, stained glass and tiles. As well as an involvement in the Arts and Crafts Movement and with the Pre-Raphaelites, Morris was also involved in the Socialist League and published several political works. For book lovers, the items of most interest relate to the Kelmscott Press – the very beautiful Kelmscott edition of Chaucer (published in 1896), is on display here.

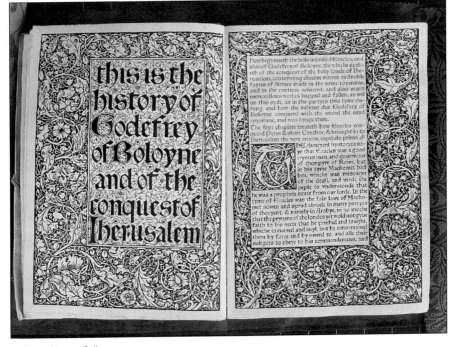

William Morris Gallery

PLACES OF LITERARY INTEREST

The literary heritage of London is indisputably rich: Chaucer's pilgrims departed from the Tabard Inn in Southwark, Shakespeare's plays were first performed in the theatres of Bankside, Dickens' novels were steeped in both the author's love of and contempt for the Victorian capital he lived in, and more recently, the Bloomsbury area (around the British Museum) became inextricably linked to the eponymous literary group.

However, in addition to the illustrious writers most closely associated with the city, London has played host to numerous other literary notables. They include Dostoevsky, James Joyce, Emile Zola, T.S Eliot (who became naturalised in 1927), Voltaire, Tolstoy, Henry James (who became naturalised in 1915), Rudyard Kipling, Ezra Pound, Jane Austen, A E Houseman and George Eliot.

Whilst the historic connections are strong, many modern and contemporary writers, including Angela Carter, Martin Amis, Peter Ackroyd, Penelope Lively, Anita Brookner, Iain Sinclair and Michael Moorcock have chosen London as the backdrop to their work.

In addition to the actual literary works, the landmarks of literary London take several forms: graves, memorials, statues and blue plaques are the most common.

Graves and Memorials:

Brompton Cemetery

Not as illustrious as the other big London cemeteries, but this site nevertheless contains Fanny Brawne (Keat's fiancee) and Emmeline Pankhurst, the Suffragette.

Golders Green Crematorium and Jewish Cemetery

Many famous figures have been cremated here and commemorated with plaques – although finding any particular one isn't easy. The literary figures include T S Eliot, Enid Blyton, Rudyard Kipling, George Bernard Shaw, Bram Stoker and Sigmund Freud is another name to seek out.

Highgate Cemetery

East Cemetery
April to September: Daily 10am-5pm
October to March: Daily 10am-4pm
Admission: £1
West Cemetery
Guided tours Mon-Fri 12noon, 2pm & 3pm;
Sun hourly from 10am-4pm
Admission: £3

In the nineteenth century, as a means of coping with the terribly overcrowded city churchyards, a number of cemeteries were opened in what were in those days the green areas outside London. Highgate Cemetery was established in 1839 and with its attractive layout, stone carvings, catacombs and Egyptian obelisks soon became an extremely popular place to be buried. As a result, the western half of the cemetery was soon full and the newer, eastern section opened in 1857.

The most famous grave in this part of the cemetery is that of Karl Marx (1818-1883), while nearby is the grave of George Eliot (1819-1880), who lived openly with her lover, George Lewes for many years (a state of affairs that outraged the society of the time) – he is buried nearby.

It is only possible to visit the western section of the cemetery on a guided tour. Christina Rossetti, the poet (1830-1894) is buried in the family tomb, Radclyffe Hall and her lover Mabel Batten is also here, as is the Charles Dickens' family tomb containing the author's wife and daughter. Dickens had also wanted to be buried here but his request was vetoed by Queen Victoria, who insisted he be buried in Westminster Abbey.

PLACES OF LITERARY INTEREST

Kensal Green Cemetery

Opened in 1832, this was the first of the large Victorian cemeteries and it soon gained in popularity: Thackeray (1811-1863), Leigh Hunt (1784-1859), Anthony Trollope (1815-1882) and Wilkie Collins (1824-1889) are all buried here.

St Paul's Cathedral

Tel: 0171 236 4128
Mon-Sat 8.30am-4pm
Admission: £3.50
(or £6 for a combination ticket which includes the galleries in the dome, open 9.30am-4pm).
Tube: St Paul's

There are far fewer memorials to literary figures here than in Westminster Abbey, but John Donne (1572-1631), Dean of St Paul's and preacher and poet is here, as is the philosopher Francis Bacon and Dr Johnson. There is also a commemorative bust to the writer and adventurer T E Lawrence in the crypt.

Westminster Abbey

Tel: 0171 222 5152
Mon-Fri 9.15am-3.45pm
Wed 6pm-7.45pm (tickets half price and photography is permitted)
Sat 9am-1.45pm
Admission: £5
(with a range of concessions and family tickets).
Tube: Westminster

Poets' Corner in the South Transept contains a huge number of memorials to literary figures. The first two poets to be buried there were Geoffrey Chaucer (1400) and Edmund Spencer (1599). Other memorials include those for John Dryden, Samuel Johnson, Robert Browning, Tennyson, Thomas Hardy (apart from his heart, which was buried in Dorset) and Dickens. Other statues are simply memorials to major figures who were buried or cremated elsewhere, for example, Shakespeare, Milton, Keats, Rudyard Kipling and Oscar Wilde. This part of the abbey also contains graves of other artistic figures, including the composer Handel, and David Garrick, the eighteenth-century actor. Apparently the overcrowding is now so bad that no further burials will be possible – the actor Laurence Olivier (who died in 1989) was supposedly the last to get a plot.

Particular areas of London are renowned for their literary associations:

Bloomsbury

Built in the seventeenth century by the Earl of Southampton, this area of graceful squares, tree-lined streets and attractive houses expanded considerably in the following century as its popularity and fashionable status grew. Over time it has acquired an unmistakable cultural and intellectual atmosphere by virtue of its proximity to the British Museum and the University of London. Many famous people have lived in the area, including the artists Constable and Rossetti, and the writers Dickens and Shaw. However, the name Bloomsbury will be forever associated with the group of writers, artists and thinkers who lived, worked and entertained here in the early twentieth century. The Stephen sisters who were to become Vanessa Bell and Virginia Woolf moved to 46 Gordon Square when their father died (this caused outrage as the girls were young, unmarried, and unchaperoned), and gradually a group of young, upper-middle class, like-minded friends established a network around them. The Bloomsbury Group's guiding principle was a rejection of the established ideas and morals of the time; members included Woolf and her husband Leonard, Bell, Virginia and Vanessa's brothers Thoby and Adrian, Lytton Strachey, artist Duncan Grant, John Maynard Keynes, Clive Bell and Roger Fry. Virginia and Leonard Woolf founded the Hogarth Press in 1917 to champion new literature, and published T S Eliot's poem, 'The Waste Land' in 1922, and the works of Katherine Mansfield, although they refused to publish James Joyces' 'Ulysses'.

Blue plaques mark the houses associated with the group: Lytton Strachey (critic and biographer), 51 Gordon Square; John Maynard Keynes (economist), 46 Gordon Square and Virginia Woolf, 29 Fitzroy Square. She lived at this address between 1907 and 1911 with her brother Adrian, in a house previously occupied by George Bernard Shaw. Other significant buildings not marked by plaques include 24 Russell Square, where T S Eliot worked at the publishers Faber and Faber.

Chelsea

Initially a fishing village on the north bank of the River Thames. In the sixteenth-century it became the home of royal courtiers such as Sir Thomas More. By the early nineteenth century Chelsea had become fashionable among artistic and literary figures. Shelley and Turner were early residents and later the writers George Eliot, Swinburne, Henry James, Oscar Wilde and the historian Thomas Carlyle (see p.150) lived here.

In the 1950's the focus of interest was The Royal Court Theatre on Sloane Square, where the dramatists who became known as the 'Angry Young Men' (a group which included John Osborne and Arnold Wesker) had their plays staged. The theatre (currently undergoing major rebuilding work) has retained its reputation for showcasing new and exciting high-quality writing. In the 1960's Chelsea became famous for the fashions available in the Kings Road and music and media stars moved in.

Cheyne Walk is probably the most illustrious street with an impressive list of famous past residents: George Eliot lived at No.4, Dante Gabriel Rossetti at No.16, Hilaire Belloc at No.104, Henry James at Carlyle Mansions, and Mrs Gaskell was born at No.93. Elsewhere in Chelsea, Leigh Hunt

lived at 22 Upper Cheyne Row, Tobias Smollett at 16 Lawrence Street, Mark Twain at 23 Tedworth Square and Bram Stoker at 18 St Leonard's Terrace. In the same area, Oscar Wilde lived first at 3 Tite Street and then in 1885 at 34 Tite Street, until he was sent to Reading jail in 1895. He wrote 'The Picture of Dorian Gray' in the house and also first met Lord Alfred Douglas here – it was their relationship which ultimately led to Wilde's downfall. He was arrested at the Cadogan Hotel in 1895, in which Jane Austen had stayed around a hundred years before.

Thomas Carlyle wrote in a letter in 1834 that "Chelsea is a single heterogenous kind of spot, very dirty and confused in some places, quite beautiful in others, abounding in antiquities and the traces of great men..." It's a description which still rings true over one hundred and sixty years later.

Hampstead

At one time Hampstead used to be covered in forest, but a lot of the trees were cut down to rebuild London after The Great Fire in 1666. Then in the eighteenth century, many country houses were constructed here as Londoners gravitated towards the open space, fresh air and spring water of Hampstead Heath. Hampstead still has something of a village feel even though it is now very much part of London. Keats' House (see p.152) is open to the public as a museum celebrating one of the area's most famous inhabitants. Other literary figures associated with Hampstead include William Blake, Dirk Bogarde, John le Carré, Agatha Christie, Ian Fleming, Sigmund Freud (see p.151), Gerald Manley Hopkins, A A Milne, George Orwell Robert Louis Stevenson and John Galsworthy. Today the association of Hampstead with London's writing community is so strong it is almost a cliché and the local supermarket is often awash with well known literary figures stocking up the Volvo – so much for the artists garret.

HERE AND IN NEIGHBOURING HOUSES DURING THE FIRST HALF OF THE 20th CENTURY THERE LIVED SEVERAL MEMBERS OF THE BLOOMSBURY GROUP INCLUDING VIRGINIA WOOLF CLIVE BELL AND THE STRACHEYS

ERECTED BY CAMDEN LONDON BOROUGH COUNCIL

Literary Pubs

Fitzroy Tavern
16 Charlotte Street, W1
Between the wars this area was named
Fitzrovia by the group of artists and writers
who met in the pub. Patrons included
Dylan Thomas (he first met his wife, Caitlin
here) and George Orwell.

Museum Tavern
49 Great Russell Street, WC1
Opposite the entrance to the British
Museum – Karl Marx was a regular.

Spaniards Inn, *Spaniard's Road, NW3*
A four hundred year-old pub, located
between Kenwood House and Hampstead
Heath. Writers Dickens, Shelley, Keats and
Byron were all patrons, and it is said that the
highwayman Dick Turpin drank here.

Trafalgar Tavern, *5 Park Row, SE10*
Beside the river at Greenwich and
mentioned in 'Our Mutual Friend', this pub
was supposedly a favourite drinking spot of
Charles Dickens.

Ye Olde Cheshire Cheese,
Wine Office Court, 145 Fleet Street, EC4
The oldest parts of the building date from
the mid-seventeenth century, when the pub
was rebuilt after the Great Fire. Dr Johnson
was supposedly a regular customer which
made it a place of pilgrimage for later
writers, including Thackeray, Dickens and
Mark Twain.

Ye Olde Cock Tavern,
22 Fleet Street, EC4
T S Eliot was a regular here in the 1920's.

APPENDIX

LITERARY VENUES

R eading and enjoying books is considered by many a rather solitary pastime, and yet the capital is host to public readings, signings and book events virtually every day of the week. Book events vary in scale and character tremendously, from local poetry meetings where you might be expected to read your own verse; to a major book reading by a literary star where you will be lucky to get a seat.

For regular information about what is on offer, 'Time Out', 'What's On in London' and 'Poetry London Newsletter' all have sections devoted to literary events. Independent bookshops host occasional readings, but the famous literary names tend to limit their appearances to large branches of the major chains. Generally these events are free, but tickets may need to be reserved. Look out particularly for events in Books etc, Borders, Dillons and Waterstones – they all advertise in the magazines mentioned above and Waterstones also publishes 'Reading London', a monthly leaflet which advertises events in each of its branches across the city. Waterstones also publish details about book events on their website (see the Internet section for details). As well as the major bookshops there are many alternative venues for literary events some of which are listed below:

British Library
96 Euston Road
NW1 2DB
Tel: 0171 412 7760,
events 0171 412 7222
There are regular lunch-time talks by British Library staff, usually on non-specialist, general interest themes. There is also a programme of evening talks and lectures, many by very prominent literary figures.

Café and Jazz Bar
407 Coldharbour Lane
SW9 8LQ
Tel: 0171 738 4141
Tube: Brixton.
Regular poetry readings.

Centerprise Community Bookshop and Café
136 Kingsland High Street
E8 2NS.
Tel: 0171 254 9632
Programme of readings.

Enterprise
2 Haverstock Hill
NW3 2BL
Tel: 0171 485 2659
Tube: Chalk Farm.
Weekly poetry readings.

Filthy MacNasty's
68 Amwell Street, EC1
Tel: 0171 837 6067
This bar is a regular venue for literary readings and performances. They produce a monthly listing of events.

Foundry Gallery
84-86 Great Eastern Street, EC2
Tel: 0171 739 6900
Tube: Old Street.
Weekly poetry evening.

Hammersmith Irish Centre
Blacks Road, W6
Tel: 0181 741 3211
Monthly storytelling club.

The Klinker
The Sussex Pub
107a Culford Road, N1
Tel 0181 806 8216
Regular poetry.

Poetry Society

22 Betterton Street
WC2H 9BU
Events: 0171 420 9890,
enquiries 0171 420 9880
E-mail: poetrysoc@dial.pipex.com
Web: www.poetrysoc.com
Tube: Covent Garden
The Poetry Society is engaged in a huge
range of activities aimed at promoting
poetry throughout Britain. It publishes
'Poetry News' and 'Poetry Review' and the
Poetry Café (Mon-Fri 11am-11pm, Sat
6.30-11pm) is a great place for members to
meet, eat and relax. Full membership costs
£32 (£25 concessions).

Royal Festival Hall

South Bank
SE1 8XX
Tel: 0171 960 4242
Tube: Waterloo
There are plenty of events (including visits
by internationally renowned writers) and a
wide range of poetry at the 'Voice Box', a
dedicated poetry space. The 'Literature
Bulletin' is published quarterly listing the
future programme. The Royal Festival Hall
also hosts 'Poetry International', a biennial
event which is the biggest poetry festival in
Britain, involving a huge number of poets
from here and abroad.

T2 at Turnmills Nightclub

63a Clerkenwell Road
EC1M 5NP
Tel: 0171 250 3409
The first Tuesday of each month features a
night of readings with audiovisual backing.

FESTIVALS

L ondon plays host to a number of annual
arts festivals, both big and small, many of
which feature literary events. For a
countrywide 'Festivals List' contact:

The Literature Department

The British Council
11 Portland Place,
W1N 4EJ.
Tel: 0171 389 3170
The list is also available on the Council's
website: *www.britcoun.org/literature/litfest.htm*
Some of London's bigger annual festivals
include:

The Clerkenwell Literary Festival

Staged every July, with the programme
published about three months before. A
number of venues in the Clerkenwell area
put on events mixing literature with other
media and focusing particularly on linking
established and underground writers.
Information is available from Clerkenwell
Arts on Tel: 0171 689 0322, or their web
site: *www.clerkenwell-arts.com*

Dulwich Festival

Annual community arts festival held in May,
which includes the work of both amateur
and professional locals. It encompasses
literary events and The Dulwich Festival
Poetry Competition. Tel: 0181 299 1011.

Greenwich and Docklands International Festival

An annual general arts festival in July,
featuring a wide range of events including
literary ones. Tel: 0181 305 1818.

Haringey Literature Festival

An annual literary festival with both an
autumn and summer season of talks,
readings, workshops and activities for
children. Contact Haringey Arts Council on
Tel: 0181 365 7500.

APPENDIX

161

Islington International Festival

An annual summer arts festival which includes some literary events.
Tel: 0171 833 3131 or 0171 354 2535 or try their web site:
www.islington-festival.co.uk

London Festival of Literature

'The Word' is a ten day festival packed with events spread right across the capital which feature local, national and international writers. Some of the venues are a little unorthodox, with places such as the Royal Courts of Justice, the Royal Geographical Society and the London Dungeon opening their doors. Tel: 0171 837 2555 for more information.

Stoke Newington Midsummer Festival

An annual, general arts festival in June, which includes poetry, workshops and readings with both national and local authors. Tel/Fax: 0171 923 1599.

COURSES

London offers many full and part-time courses of interest to anyone who loves books. The spectrum stretches from craft courses like bookbinding right through to the more esoteric pursuit of creative writing. Classes run during academic terms: the autumn term runs from September to December, the spring term from January to March and the summer term from April to June. Contact the college enrollment office for detailed information about course content, cost, enrollment dates and location. There are also three useful publications for those looking for a course. 'Floodlight' is published in two versions: one details day and evening classes throughout the Greater London area and is published twice a year (in the summer, and in the spring). 'Full-time Floodlight' is a smaller format, annual publication which lists all available full-time

courses. 'On Course' is an alternative to 'Floodlight'. All three publications are available in bookshops and larger newsagents.

All courses listed below are part-time, *except* those marked with a star★ which are full-time only, or those marked with a double star★★, which indicates that both part-time and full-time courses are offered in the relevant subject area.

Please note that only the address of the central building for each institution is given below. Many colleges operate classes at several different sites.

Bookbinding

Camberwell College of Art; Central Saint Martins College of Art and Design; The City Lit; Greenwich Community; Hampstead Institute; Kensington and Chelsea College; London College of Printing★★; Morley College; Roehampton Institute★

Bookselling

University College★

Literature

Those who want to increase their knowledge or appreciation of literature are well served by courses in London.
Courses that cover a wide subject area include:
Indian Literature (Kensington and Chelsea College), Irish Poetry (Morley College), Literature and Women (Hammersmith and Fulham), Modern Fiction (City Lit) or Caribbean Texts (Goldsmiths College)
Courses that concentrate on just one author, or even one work include:
Dante's 'Divine Comedy' (Morley College), Gerald Manley Hopkins (City Lit), Jane Austen (Morley College) and Thomas Hardy (South Thames College).

In addition to general courses (locations are listed below), a great many colleges offer part-time and full-time examination classes at all levels. These are too numerous to list here (see 'Floodlight' or 'On Course').

General courses

Birkbeck College; The City Lit; Community Education Lewisham; Goldsmith's College; Greenwich Community College; Hammersmith & Fulham Community Learning and Leisure Service; Hampstead Garden Suburb Institute; Kensington and Chelsea College; Lambeth Community Education; Mary Ward Centre; Merton Adult College; Morley College; South Thames College; Tower Hamlets Adult Education; Westminster Adult Education

Papermaking

The City Lit; Greenwich Community College; Kensington and Chelsea College; Mary Ward Centre; Morley College; South Thames College

Publishing

London College of Printing

Writing and Scriptwriting

Some of the courses under this heading are general creative writing courses while others specialise in a specific form of writing such as poetry, sitcoms or short stories.

Birkbeck College; Brent Adult and Community Education Service; Central Saint Martins College of Art and Design; City and islington College; The City Lit; City University; Community Education Lewisham; Goldsmiths College★★; Greenwich Community College; Hackney Community College; Hammersmith and Fulham Community Learning and Leisure Service; Hampstead Garden Suburb Institute; Hendon College; Kensington and Chelsea College; Kingsway College; Lambeth Community Education; London College of Printing; Mary Ward Centre; Merton Adult College; Middlesex University★★; Morley College; South Thames College; Thames Valley University; Tower Hamlets Adult Education; Westminster Adult Education

Addresses

Birkbeck College
26 Russell Square, WC1B 5DQ
Tel: 0171 631 6633 / 6650 / 6675

Brent Adult and Community Education Service
1 Morland Gardens, NW10 8DY
Tel: 0181 838 0808

Camberwell College of Arts
Peckham Road, SE5 8UF
Tel: 0171 514 6311

Central Saint Martins College of Art and Design
Southampton Row, WC1B 4AP
Tel: 0171 514 7015

City and Islington College
383 Holloway Road, N7 0RN
Tel: 0171 700 9200

The City Lit
16 Stukeley Street, WC2B 5LJ
Tel: 0171 831 9631

City University
Northampton Square, EC1V 0HB
Tel: 0171 477 8268

Community Education Lewisham
Stanley Street, SE8 4BL
Tel: 0181 691 5959

Goldsmiths College
New Cross, SE14 6NW
Tel: 0171 919 7200

Greenwich Community College
Kidbrooke School
Corelli Road, SE3 8EP
Tel: 0181 319 8088

Hackney Community College
Falkirk Street, N1 6HQ
Tel: 0171 613 9123

Hammersmith and Fulham Community Learning and Leisure Service
Cambridge House
Cambridge Grove, W6
Tel: 0181 576 55335

Hampstead Garden Suburb Institute
Central Square, NW11 7BN
Tel: 0181 455 9951

Hendon College
Park Way, NW9 5RA
Tel: 0181 200 8300/0181 266 4046

APPENDIX

Kensington and Chelsea College
Hortensia Road, SW10 0QS
Tel: 0171 573 5333

Kingsway College
Gray's Inn Centre
Sidmouth Street, WC1H 8JB
Tel: 0171 306 5721(has moved(susi)

Lambeth Community Education
Strand Centre
Elm Park, SW2 2EH
Tel: 0171 926 6020 / 7293 / 0730

London College of Printing
Elephant & Castle, SE1 6SB
Tel: 0171 514 6514

Mary Ward Centre
42 Queen Square, WC1N 3AQ
Tel: 0171 831 7711

Merton Adult College
Whatley Avenue, SW20 9NS
Tel: 0181 543 9292

Middlesex University
White Hart Lane, N17 8HR
Tel: 0181 362 5000

Morley College
61 Westminster Bridge Road, SE1 7HT
Tel: 0171 928 8501

Roehampton Institute
Senate House
Roehampton Lane, SW15 5PU
Tel: 0181 392 3000

South Thames College
Wandsworth High Street, SW18 2PP
Tel: 0181 918 7777 / 7555

Thames Valley University
St Mary's Road, W5 5RF
Tel: 0181 579 5000

Tower Hamlets Adult Education
Tredegar Centre
Stafford Road, E3 2EW
Tel: 0181 983 1047

University College
Gower Street, WC1E 6BT
Tel: 0171 380 7365

Westminster Adult Education
Amberley Road, W9 2JJ
Tel: 0171 289 2183

LITERARY WALKS

A guided walk is a great way for Londoners as well as visitors to learn some unusual and less well-known facts about the city. Walks are on offer from a number of companies, covering a variety of subjects and many have a literary theme. Both the listings magazines 'Time Out' (in the 'Around Town' section) and 'What's On in London' (in the 'Diary' section) list the walks available in London each week (there are generally over a hundred). You turn up at the time and location (usually a tube station) listed, pay the guide and then begin the walk. It's advisable to ring beforehand to check it's actually going ahead. Below are listed some of the walks which have literary associations:

Dickens' London *Tel: 0181 980 5565*
Sunday afternoon
This touches just the tip of a large iceberg of associations between London and the works of Dickens. It both considers his career and links characters to buildings, taking in Covent Garden, The Strand, Doughty Street, Lincoln's Inn and Chancery Lane.

Guided Walks In London
Tel 0171 243 1097 or 0181 455 7833
Web: www.guided-walks-in-london.net
Although not especially aimed at those with literary interests, their programme includes 'Beautiful Belgravia' (Oscar Wilde), 'Saucy Southwark' (The Canterbury pilgrims and Shakespeare), and 'Heavenly Highgate and Happy Hampstead'.

Historical Walks of London
Tel/Fax: 0181 668 4019
Walks include 'Literary London', 'The London of Dickens and Shakespeare', 'Charles Dickens' London' and 'A Walk in the Footsteps of Sherlock Holmes'.

Original London Walks

Tel: 0171 624 3978
Fax: 0171 625 1932
Web: www.walks.com
Their huge programme (their leaflet is available in many central London bookshops) includes several walks involving Dickens, Shakespeare, Sherlock Holmes, Bloomsbury, the British Library; and 'Dracula - The Walk', 'The London of Oscar Wilde' (the guide dresses as the man himself), 'Old Literary London', 'Samuel Pepys' London', 'George Bernard Shaw's London' and 'The London of Jane Austen.'

Shakespeare's Bankside

Tel: 0171 274 9170. Weekday mornings.

Sherlock Holmes and Conan Doyle – A Walk through Fact and Fiction

Tel: 0181 674 5458. Alternate Sundays.
The walk considers how Doyle's life is reflected in his fiction (ring for dates and meeting place).

Stepping Out

Tel: 0181 881 2933
Web: www.walklon.ndirect.co.uk
Tours include 'Charles Dickens', 'Chelsea', 'Historic Fleet Street', 'Oscar Wilde's London', 'Highgate' and 'Bohemians and Bluestockings – Literary London', a walk through Bloomsbury and Fitzrovia.

Original London Walks

BOOKBINDERS

Bookbinders are a very diverse group and those included below range from individuals making one-off handmade books at a very high price to industrial binders who will take on individual projects alongside more mundane work.

Alinea Bindery
46 Porchester Road
London
W2 6ET
Tel: 0171 727 6659
This is a new and imaginative bookbindery that will undertake all kinds of projects and offers a design service. The bindery also works with small publishers to produce small print runs of books with fine bindings.

Susan J Allix
19 Almorah Road
N1 3ER
Tel: 0171 359 2949
Susan Allix sells handmade books in very small print runs and also makes fine bindings to commission (prices start from around £250); she doesn't do restoration work.

Natalie D'Arbeloff
Tel: 0171 267 1719
Natalie is not a bookbinder, but makes wonderful books containing her illustrations.

Bardel Bookbinding Ltd
Unit D2, Aladdin Work Space
426 Long Drive
Greenford
UB6 8UH
Tel/Fax: 0181 575 2583
A small bookbinders who specialise in binding theses and wedding albums and repairs. They don't do restoration work.

Bartlett Books
The Basement
28 Chaucer Road
SE24 0NU
Tel/Fax: 0171 274 0647
This bookbinders is one of the few that do both book and paper restoration as well as undertaking basic repairs, original designs and handmade boxes.

Bookbinders of London
11 Ronalds Road
N5 1XJ
Tel: 0171 607 3361
This small family business largely bind small print runs, but will also undertake commissions for leather presentation books, ring binders, boxes, theses and wedding albums.

Bookends Bindery Ltd
1b Orieston Road
N7 8LJ
Tel: 0171 609 2613
Fax: 0171 700 5593
Bookends are a long established bookbinders who will undertake both restoration and repair as well as bespoke re-binding.

Tracey Bush
Flat 9, 657-663 Commercial Road
E14 7LW
Tel: 0171 791 3396
Tracey makes fine bindings of her own art work.

Paul Anthony Collet
36 Marlborough Road
N19 4NB
Tel/Fax: 0171 272 1437
Mr Collet is a fine binder with twenty years experience who will undertake restoration, repair and original bindings.

Collis Bird & Whithey
1 Drayton Park
N5 1NU
Tel/Fax: 0171 607 1116
This well organised bookbinding company undertake restoration, repair and original binding work.

Sue Doggett
11 Hollingbourne Road
SE24 9NB
Tel: 0171 274 0429
Sue Doggett is a well known teacher and bookbinder, specialising in fine art bindings. Her work of the highest quality, but comes at a price: few commissions are cost under £500. Sue doesn't undertake restoration work.

Ex-Libris
24c Hereford Road
W2 4AA
Tel: 0171 229 4134
This small company has been offering a bespoke bookbinding service for over forty years and will undertake most commissions, from detailed restoration to simple cloth re-binding.

Flora Ginn
25 Ferndale Road
SW4 7RJ
Tel: 0171 737 3295
Flora designs and makes original bindings, but most of her effort is involved in restoration work.

Grays (Bookbinders) Ltd
Unit 5, 24 Willow Lane
Mitcham, CR4
Tel: 0181 640 1449
Fax: 0181 687 0937
Grays are a long-established bookbinders with a staff of twelve who will undertake most bookbinding tasks and who can usually give an accurate quote over the phone. They also make presentation boxes to order.

B J Heard Bindery
41 Pickford Road
DA7 4AG
Tel: 0181 304 1229
Mr Heard will undertake all kinds of bookbinding including one-off commissions, repairs and restoration. He can also make book and folio boxes.

Homerton Bookbinders
166a Glyn Road
E5 0JE
Tel: 0181 986 4424
A small team of binders that mainly specialise in theses, but will undertake all commissions from restoration to original bindings.

Keypoint Bookbinders Ltd
Unit 8, Balmoral Grove
N7 9NQ
Tel: 0171 609 1050
Fax: 0171 609 1020
Keypoint largely deal in short-run case bindings and thesis binding, but also work on individual commissions.

Marba Bookbinding
63 Jeddo Road
W12 9EE
Tel: 0181 743 4715
Fax: 0181 742 9235
Marba bookbinding do all kinds of repair and rebinding and can also make bespoke boxes. They don't do restoration work.

J Muir & Co. (Bookbinders) Ltd
64 Blackheath Road
SE10 8DA
Tel 0181 692 7565
Fax 0181 692 2072
J Muir are a very well known bookbinders, established in 1900. Although a lot of their work is for the book trade they also maintain a craft bindery which undertakes commissions and restoration work.

Kathy Robert
Studio 409
31 Clerkenwell Close
EC1R 0AT
Tel: 0171 250 1803
Fax: 0171 490 3231
Kathy will undertake most tasks from original bookbindings to restoration and repair. She also makes fine boxes and folios to order.

Rook's Books
9 Coopers Yard
SW19 1TN
Tel: 0181 766 6398
Fax: 0181 761 0933
Web: www.rooksbooks.com
Gavin Rookledge has acquired a reputation as one of the country's most skilled and imaginative bookbinders. The emphasis here is on one-off, handcrafted books, in some cases incorporating the use of precious metals in collaboration with silversmith Gabriella Lane. Rook's Books are always busy, so it's essential to commission work well in advance to avoid disappointment.

Tracey Rowledge
Standpoint Studios
45 Coronet Street
N1 6HD
Tel/Fax: 0171 739 7633
Artists books and one-off commissions, as well as fine boxes.

Sally Lou Smith
6 Leighton Grove
NW5 2RA
Tel: 0171 267 7516
Modern fine bookbinding designs in leather, costing at least £1,000.

Shepherds Bookbinders
76 Rochester Row
SW1P 1JU
Tel: 0171 630 1184
Fax: 0171 931 0541
This shop specialises in bookbinding, restoration and paper conservation and framing, as well as supplying binding materials (including some fabulous papers). In addition to their specialist services, this is an excellent shop to visit for unusual gifts - they sell wonderful notebooks, address and visitors books.

Toms & Grantham Bookbinders Ltd
86 Camberwell Road
SE5 0EG
Tel/Fax: 0171 701 5833
This small company will undertake restoration, repairs and commissions.

The Wyvern Bindery
56-58 Clerkenwell Road
EC1M 5PX
Tel: 0171 490 7899
Fax: 0171 490 1391
E-mail: wyvernbindery@cyncronet.com
Web: www.cyncronet.com/wyvernbindery.htm
Wyvern Bindery has a small, enthusiastic team of bookbinders who will undertake any task. One of their most popular services is the construction of drop-back boxes and portfolios, with prices starting from £70.

THE INTERNET

Although this book is concerned with the bookshops of London, it is almost impossible to ignore the web, particularly as so many of London's bookshops are now on-line. Below are listed some of the best sites on which to buy new, second-hand, antiquarian and digital books, as well as a summary of London's on-line bookshops and other useful addresses – happy surfing! (Please note that for the sake of space the standard prefix http:// is not written before each web address; sites can be found without using it).

Internet Bookshops

Alphabet Street Books UK
www.alphabetstreet.com
A well designed London-based internet bookshop, with lots of information about the stock and discounts of up to 50% on promoted titles.

Amazon
www.amazon.co.uk
The first, largest and best-known internet bookshop with millions of titles available, a good search and browse system and competitive discounts on certain titles.

Barnes and Noble
www.barnesandnoble.com
This is the on-line bookshop of the massive American book chain. It has the advantage of stocking many titles not normally available in Britain, although prices are all stated in dollars, which often makes the true cost of the books difficult to calculate.

Bibliofind
www.bibliofind.com
If you are looking for an old, used or rare book this internet bookseller has over nine million titles available through a network of thousands of book dealers. I put the service to the test by searching for one of the more obscure books on my shelf and Bibliofind came up with sixteen different copies, ranging from a tatty edition for $5 to a very fine first edition for $50. All the books listed were from America and priced in dollars, but it's still a useful resource if you are prepared to pay the postage fee for delivery.

Blackwells
www.bookshop.blackwell.co.uk
This site has a nice clear design and a good search and browse system, but not much information about the books available and very few discounts. However, it's a good site for those interested in academic titles.

BOL
www.bol.com
Bertelsmann is one of the world's largest publishing companies; having failed in their attempt to buy Amazon they now have plans to launch their own on-line bookshop at the above address.

Book Browse
www.bookbrowse.com
This site publishes extracts from some of the most popular fiction and non-fiction titles and also offers a web-wide comparison of prices, delivery times and postal charges. Book Browse also has a book-buying facility through its affiliation with a good value internet bookshop, Al books (www.albooks.com).

The Book Pl@ce
www.thebookplace.com
This British-based internet bookshop has the advantage of quick and cheap delivery, but has fewer titles and discounts than some of the larger internet bookshops.

British Magazines
www.britishmagazines.com
This site allows you to order from a range of over three thousand five hundred magazine titles, ranging from the mainstream to obscurities rarely found in even the largest newsagents.

APPENDIX

The Internet Bookshop

www.bookshop.co.uk

This internet bookshop is owned by W H Smiths and has their full book list on-line with some good discounts - as well as videos, games and CD's.

OK UK Books

www.okukbooks.com

This site specialises in children's books and has a colourful design, detailed reviews and a browse system that allows you to specify the age group you're seeking books for.

On-line Originals

www.onlineoriginals.com

This is an entirely digital publishing company which publishes around forty titles (both fiction and non-fiction) from its website. Visitors can browse, read extracts and order the books for only £4 a title; the book is then sent via e-mail to be read either on screen or printed out. A clever idea and perhaps the shape of things to come...

Waterstones

www.waterstones.co.uk

The search and browse system on this site is a little frustrating, with tables of books and not much detail, making intelligent on-line purchasing quite difficult. On the plus side, it is a quick and easy way to buy books if you know the title you want, as well as a good way to find out about forthcoming Waterstones book events.

London Bookshops with Websites

New Books

Blue Silver Comics	www.bluesilver.com
Books For Cooks	www.booksforcooks.com
British Museum Bookshop	
	www.british-museum.ac.uk
Building Bookshop	
	www.buildingbookshop.co.uk
Chess & Bridge	www.chess.co.uk
	www.bridgemagazine.co.uk
Church House Bookshop	
www.herald.co.uk/clients/c/Church-House/chb.html	
CIB Bookshop	www.cib.org,uk
Classic Collection	www.classiccollection.com
The Dover Bookshop	
	www.thedoverbookshop.com
Dress Circle	www.dresscircle/co.uk
The Economist Shop	www.economist.com
Esperanto Bookshop	www.esperanto.demon.co.uk
French's Theatre Bookshop	
	www.samuelfrench-london.co.uk
George Godber Bookshop	
	www.kingsfund.org.uk
Grant and Cutler	www.grant-c.demon.co.uk
The ICA Bookshop	www.ica.org.uk
Intermediate Technology Bookshop	
	www.oneworld.org/itdg/publications.html
Karnac Books	www.karnacbooks.com
The Marine Society	www.marinesociety.org.uk
Mega-Byte Computer Bookshop	
	www.megabytebooks.co.uk
PC Bookshop	www.pcbooks.co.uk
Politico's	www.politicos.co.uk
RICS Bookshop	www.rics.org.uk
St Paul's Multimedia	
www.ukbusiness.com/stpaulsbywestminstercathedral	
Bernard Shapero	www.shapero.com
The Sherlock Holmes Memorabilia Company	
	www.sh-memorabilia.co.uk
SothebyÒs Bookshop	www.sothebys.com
The Travel Bookshop	www.thetravelbookshop.co.uk
Wildy & Sons Ltd	www.wildy.com
Wisdom Books	www.demon.co.uk/wisdom
Zeno Bookseller	www.thegreekbookshop.com

Second-hand & Antiquarian Books

Any Amount of Books	www.anyamountofbooks.com/
Robin de Beaumont	
	www.bibliocity.com/search/debeaumont
Beaumont Travel Books	
	www.antiquarian.com/beaumont-travel-books
Books & Things	
	www.abebooks.com/home/bookandthings
T A Cherrington Rare Books	www.folios.co.uk
Simon Finch Rare Books	www.simonfinch.com
Fine Books Oriental	www.finebooks.demon.co.uk
R.A.Gekoski	www.antiquarian.com/gekoski/
Amanda Hall	www.ahrb.com

Adrian Harrington
　　　　　www.harringtonbooks.co.uk/rare
Peter Harrington
　　　　　www. peter-harrington.demon.co.uk
Maggs Bros Ltd　　　www.maggs.com
The Map House　　　www. themaphouse.com
Marlborough Rare Books
　　　www.bibliocity.com/search/marlborough
Music and Video Exchange
　　　　　　www.demon.co.uk/mveshops
John Price　　www.antiquarian-books.co.uk/
Bernard Quaritch　　www.quaritch.com
Russell Rare Books　　www.folios.co.uk
Skoob & Skoob Two　　　www.skoob.com
Ulysses　　　www.antiquarian.com/ulysses

Reference Sites on the Net

The Internet Public Library

www.ipl.org/ref/

This site is an excellent way to find information on the net about any academic subject. Simply choose an area on the libraries home page and then scroll down the list of website reviews until you find something of interest.

The On-line Books Page

www.cs.cmu.edu/books.html

It's surprising how many entire book texts are now available on the net. This site can search for any title, although because of copyright law many recent books are not available.

The Mining Company

englishlit.mining.co.com/msub-authors1.htm

If you have a favourite author and want to find out more about them this is a great place to start, with brief biographies of hundreds of authors and links to relevant home pages.

On-line Literary Magazines

The Atlantic Unbound

www.theatlantic.com

An on-line version of 'The Atlantic Monthly' with all the literary criticism, poetry and essays of the original – but this virtual offspring is better designed than the magazine itself.

The Barcelona Review

www.BarcelonaReview.com

An international on-line literary magazine featuring the best in new fiction (frequently in a number of different languages), and many useful literary links.

The Richmond Review

www.demon.co.uk/review

This literary magazine offers some excellent fiction and poetry by such luminaries as Salman Rushdie, on a site which keeps the design element to a minimum.

Salon Magazine

www.salonmagazine.com

This cultural magazine has all the latest literary news, reviews and interviews and a searchable archive of previously featured articles.

On-line Services for Writers

trAce

trace.ntu.ace.uk

Established by Nottingham Trent University, this site operates as an international forum for writers with a chat room, information about conferences and events and links with other sites of literary interest.

Web del Sol

www.webdelsol.com

This site is a bit of a mixed bag with extracts, articles, literary news, literary chat groups and links to other literary sites.

INDEX

SUBJECT INDEX

This subject index is not comprehensive but will help you to locate bookshops specialising in a particular field. There are of course large book stores that will cover all subjects comprehensively, the best of these are:

Africa / Orient

Anarchism / Alternative

Antiques and collectibles

Arabic / Middle Eastern / Muslim Studies

Archaeology

Architecture / Building

Art

Astrology

Audio Books

Australia

BBC Publications

Order Form

Bargain Hunters' London
by Andrew Kershman
0-9522914-2-8   £5.99

A comprehensive guide to finding bargains in the capital including the best charity shops, auctions, designer sales and much more. The book contains 11 area maps and 50 photos.

Museums & Galleries of London by Abigail Willis
0-9522914-3-6   £8.99

A guide combining reviews of all the museums and galleries of London with listings of the commercial galleries, archives and details of London's many art degree shows. The guide contains 50 black and white and 16 colour photos.

Gay London
by Graham Parker
0-9522914-6-0   £6.99

A guide to London's gay scene which doesn't just concentrate on gay clubs (although they are reviewed), but takes a broader look at what's on offer for gay Londoners and visitors to the capital.

Taste of London
by Jenny Linford
9522914-7-9   £6.99

A Taste of London contains over 80 cosmopolitan recipes, many of them recommended by Londoners of diverse ethnic origin and using all the ingredients to be found in the Capital.

The Guide to Cookery Courses by Eric Treuille
0-9522914-9-5   £4.99

This is the only detailed guide to the UK's cookery courses and includes a section on cooking holidays abroad as well as cookware shops, cookbook shops and useful reference information for cooks.

The London Market Guide (2nd Edition)
by Andrew Kershman
1-902910-001   £5.99

The second edition of The London Market Guide containing all the essential information to explore London's street markets with maps, photos, travel information and consumer tips.

Food Lovers London (2nd Edition)
by Jenny Linford
0-9522914-8-7   £6.99

The second edition of this very popular guide to international cuisine in London. The book lists all the best food outlets as well as providing a glossary for each cuisine.

To order any of the above titles send a cheque (including £1 p&p) to:

Metro Publications
PO Box 6336
London N1 6PY
e-mail: metro@dircon.co.uk

Make your cheque payable to **Metro Publications**
Please allow 14 days for delivery.